Take My Spouse, Please

Take My Spouse, Please

How to Keep Your Marriage Happy,
Healthy, and Thriving by Following
the Rules of Comedy

Dani Klein Modisett

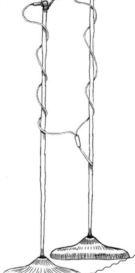

TRUMPETER · *Boston & London* · 2015

TRUMPETER BOOKS
An imprint of Shambhala Publications, Inc.
Horticultural Hall
300 Massachusetts Avenue
Boston, Massachusetts 02115
www.shambhala.com

9 8 7 6 5 4 3 2 1

First Edition
Printed in the United States of America

♾ This edition is printed on acid-free paper that meets
the American National Standards Institute Z39.48 Standard.
♻ This book is printed on 30% postconsumer recycled paper.
For more information please visit www.shambhala.com.

Distributed in the United States by Penguin Random House LLC
and in Canada by Random House of Canada Ltd

Designed by James D. Skatges

Library of Congress Cataloging-in-Publication Data

Modisett, Dani Klein.
Take my spouse, please: how to keep your marriage happy, healthy, and thriving
by following the rules of comedy / Dani Klein Modisett.—First edition.
pages cm
ISBN 978-1-61180-147-7 (pbk.: alk. paper)
1. Marriage—Humor. 2. Married people—Humor.
3. Husband and wife—Humor. I. Title.
PN6231.M3M83 2015
818'.602—dc23
2014039443

Contents

Acknowledgments

This book would not have been possible without my husband, Tod. This one is simple: no marriage, no book. Without a husband equally committed to getting in the ring and duking out life together, willing to show up consistently and collaborate on a shared life, I would have nothing to say on the subject of marriage. Thank you, Tod, for letting me expose bits of our life with the sole caveat that I make it entertaining.

As far as the actual production of this book, not to mention insight, good taste, and a constant push for me to go deeper than my instincts would have led me, I must thank my dear editor, Rochelle Bourgault. I must also thank Caroline Grant and Lisa Catherine Harper for including me in their book, *The Cassoulet Saved Our Marriage*, which is how I was introduced to Ms. Bourgault.

I also want to thank the generous and talented people who helped beyond measure in reading earlier drafts, particularly the discerning Claudette Sutherland, who taught me everything I know about writing with clarity and from the heart and gut. No one has busted my chops more than Ms. Sutherland sitting around her workshop table, and for this—and her friendship—I am most grateful.

Others who gave me their time and insight include but are not limited to: Karly Gilbert, Marcy Etlinger, Lisa and Pete Cook, Heidi Levitt, Johanna Stein, Lisa Brody, and Sherri Hirsch. Also, thank you to Dan Bucatinsky for essential cheerleading lunches, and Donna Emmanuelle for sharing her knowledge of transcription software and then making sure I had it.

A heartfelt thank-you to my sister, Toni Klein, for sharing her experiences from a nearly twenty-year marriage, particularly in a not-so-easy year to do so. My cousin, Laura Peck, used her finely honed coaching skills on me when I got tripped up by fear.

Thank you to Karen Bergreen, Tom Pappa, Steve Skrovan, Lew Schneider, and all the comedians who not only weighed in on the subject of marriage and laughter, but led me to others who would.

A big thank-you to the long-term married couples who opened up their hearts, their histories, and often their homes to me and shared the minutiae of enduring love with a sense of humor. Additional thanks to the experts who answered all my questions and then some. If you don't see your name on these pages, please know that our conversations mattered, and all of your stories informed these pages and, selfishly, my own marriage.

Last but not least, I would like to thank my parents, Muriel and Victor Klein. Their marriage was not one long joyride, but they showed up for each other for forty years until my father passed away. My most vivid memories are of them laughing with each other until they cried, wiping tears from their eyes, and then laughing some more.

Introduction

"Guess what? It's not working for me, either!" I said, slamming the bedroom door behind me. I threw myself on our bed like a silent film star and curled up in the fetal position. I'd love to tell you this was the first time in our ten-year marriage I had engaged in such theatrics, but I'd be lying. It was, however, the last. Because on this particular evening, my husband, Tod, retreated to the darkened living room lit only by the blue light of *The Colbert Report*, and I finally had to admit that although effective in other areas of my life, I simply wasn't very good at being happily married.

I'd already figured out from observing my parents' forty years of questionable marital bliss, and the other long-term couples around me, and even from my own relatively novice experience, that marriage can feel as fragile as a soap bubble or as enduring as Mount Rushmore, sometimes flip-flopping within minutes. What I couldn't seem to get, though, was how to tame the marriage beast, how to keep the home fires burning with consistent warmth and grace, and, for the love of God, how to have some laughs along the way.

I've spent most of my professional life, more than twenty years, either writing or producing live comedy shows or actually performing stand-up comedy myself. I'd challenged myself to make people laugh just about everywhere: from appearing in bowling alleys (yes, they do hold comedy shows in them, and the crash of a strike will upstage you 100 percent of the time) to assisting a Tony Award–winning theater director doing everything from fetching coffee to running replacement rehearsals to teaching stand-up at UCLA. I could tell you why something was funny or why it wasn't, and most of the time, how to make it funnier. But what I couldn't tell you—or, more important, me—was how to bring some much-needed levity to my marriage. Where was the funny in my own home?

True, we had two children under five, but is that a reason to grow so full of resentment you can barely look at each other? Frankly, from most couples I know, yes. But regardless, we both felt we couldn't keep going like that. We also knew we'd be brutal competitors in any kind of child-custody battle, so no one had called any lawyers yet. Nevertheless, I felt exhausted and defeated.

After my Sarah Bernhardt moment on our bed, I pulled my tear-stained face out of the pillow to breathe and thought of something people say to me whenever I tell them I do stand-up: "You do stand-up comedy?" they ask, their eyes wide with amazement. "I could never do that. That's the hardest thing to do in the world!"

Really? The hardest thing? Even the worst set is over in thirty minutes—two hours if you're a superstar. This marriage gig is, like . . . endless.

Clearly for me, maintaining a happy relationship had turned out to be the hardest thing in the world to do. Remembering these comments, besides making me smile, highlighted what had been missing from our marriage in the last year or three. Laughter. We had laughed a lot in the past, so I knew it was possible. But I needed help, so I went looking for a book about marriage that focused specifically on how we as a couple could laugh more.

I did not find this book.

A few days later I was cleaning out the hall closet, disorganization being one of the aspects of my "highly creative" nature that we fight about. I had decided that the most effective way to streamline our stuff was to clear out all of Tod's old coats and set fire to them. Perhaps a cleansing bonfire of his accumulated outerwear would make more room for some laughter—or, at least, my shoes. That's when it hit me. Literally—a three-ring binder fell off the top shelf and hit me on the head. Its cover read "Performing Stand-Up Comedy, UCLA 1999"; it was the course book for a class I had taught in the university's extension program. I opened the binder and scanned the syllabus.

There were all the tools and tricks of the comedy trade: showing up, listening to the audience, being present, timing, the element of surprise, and about ten other tools. The more I turned the pages of the syllabus, the more I thought, "Huh, I know somewhere else where these could be helpful!"

Forget about making audiences of strangers laugh. What long-term relationship wouldn't benefit from better listening, being more present, and doing something unexpected once in a while?

I stuffed the giftwrapping scraps, lightbulbs, assorted batteries, and a broken Dustbuster back into the closet and quickly shut the door. The bonfire could wait. I wasn't sure how I would do it, but I decided that if I couldn't find a book on laughter and marriage, I would write one. Let other wives organize closets. My life had a higher purpose!

Knowing the effectiveness of learning how something works from people who are good at it, the first thing I did was set up interviews. I focused on long-term couples I'd met through *Afterbirth*, a storytelling show I had produced for ten years where writers perform true, raw stories about the trials of parenting. I contacted the couples who had been married for decades and still laughed together. Then, trying not to sound too desperate, I grilled them on how they had kept their sense of humor. They introduced me to their friends, and just like in that eighties Fabergé shampoo commercial, they told their friends, and their friends told *their* friends, and pretty soon I had a wealth of long-term couples to interview. Some of them famous, some not, all of them still genuinely enjoying each other.

Because I live and work mostly in Los Angeles, I had access to many people who make their living being funny. But that didn't mean they knew how to be happy in marriage. I specifically sought out husbands and wives who, after decades together, were at ease with each other and had figured out how to use what they know about comedy in their homes. All of the people I had the good fortune to interview—from Jerry Stiller to Patricia Heaton to Emmy-winning comedy writers to a mother of three in Denver, a cinematographer in Berkeley, and some schoolteachers in Los Angeles—believe that when it comes to their marriage, it is better to laugh than to leave.

I also wanted the therapeutic perspective on the value of humor and laughter for couples, so I consulted with several marriage counselors who had logged many years in the trenches, or on the couches, if you will. I wanted to find out if my suspicion that couples who laugh together stay together rang true for them.

I also read and listened to anything I could get my eyes and ears on about shared laughter and long-term relationships. This is how I found an interview that Terry Gross did on *Fresh Air* with the comedy legend Henny Youngman, then eighty-five, whose signature joke I pay homage to in the title of this book. When asked where the punch line "'Take my wife, please" came from, Henny let out a quick chuckle that suggested how many times he'd been asked this question. "I was in a show," he said, "and my wife came backstage half an hour before showtime and said, 'Henny, I need eight tickets.' Luckily the ushers had the seats. I gave them two dollars a week to take care of me, so they saved the tickets for me. So I got the tickets for Sadie and then I said, 'Take my wife, please'—like, get her outta here, I want her in the audience. And that joke stuck all these years."

What I love most about this anecdote is what it reveals about their sixty-year marriage. Sadie obviously had a sense of humor, otherwise hearing this joke and all other "my annoying wife" type jokes that were Henny's stock-in-trade surely would have trashed their marriage. Not all women would find their husband's jokes about her terrible cooking or his efforts to lose her in a crowd (just to name a few) entertaining. But by all accounts Sadie did, and there she was that night, clamoring for tickets to see Henny perform. They loved, they laughed, they stayed—that's exactly what I wanted for my marriage.

With the interviews under way, I started dissecting each of the tools from my class syllabus and seeing where and how they could help couples. If it worked for me, I would take the venture public.

Before we dig in, I have two more minor epiphanies to tell you about. I didn't fully anticipate the effect writing this book would have on me personally. I was willing to look at my marriage; I just didn't realize that in the process I would also have to look at myself. I was not Jane Goodall studying apes from the safe psychological perch of being a human. I was one of the apes, and in a very short time it was clear there had already been some shit tossing in our marriage I was not proud of. In talking to all these happy couples and assessing the effectiveness of each of these tools of comedy, it quickly dawned on me that if what I wanted was a successful marriage, I would have to take a close look at my own behavior and make some changes there as well.

The last point I want to make is probably obvious to you by now. What you are about to read is not a scientific study featuring double-blind statistics, graphs, placebos, and grant funding. I've been called a lot of things in my life, but "scientist" is not one of them. Don't get me wrong: The experts I spoke with and the studies I consulted are legitimate. Still, the value of what you are about to read comes from the power of these comedy tools to help you make your relationship more honest and more connected and then, when you have created all that warm, fuzzy trust, to make you able to laugh together again, or laugh more. There is also a lot to be learned from the couples who opened up to me. I feel so lucky to have spoken with them so that I could bring their stories of perseverance and laughter to you.

Now before I start blushing from all this heartfelt sincerity, let's get the show on the road.

Take My Spouse,
Please

1

Show Up

EVEN WHEN YOU DON'T
WANT TO, EVEN WHEN
IT'S REALLY HARD

Before I got married, I dated a nice guy who had potential,
until he told me his parents were dead. I broke up with him
because that meant we'd have to spend the holidays with my
family.

— MARLA SCHULTZ, comedian

It was 7:30 A.M., the morning of yet another relentlessly sunny day in
Los Angeles, where I'd been living full-time for less than a year. I was
wearing running shorts, a T-shirt from the 17th Street Café, the restaurant where I worked, a very snug bra, and sneakers previously used only
for walking to get coffee. In this moment, however, I was standing in a
parking lot the size of a football field scanning a crowd of thousands of
scantily clad (even by LA standards) serious runners.

I was getting anxious looking for a familiar face, anyone with an
Island of Misfit Toys quality about them weaving through this mass of
eager, fit people. We were meeting there as part of a class of aspiring

comics, tasked with meeting at the LA Marathon by our teacher, Shel-ley Bonis. Bonis is a former comic, go-go dancer, wife of Richard Pryor, and—most important at the time—an inspiring comedy guide. We didn't have to run the marathon itself—good thing, since wannabe comics weren't the most athletic bunch twenty-five years ago—but we were expected to finish, by whatever means necessary, the 5K that was also being held that day.

Bonis wasn't concerned with what shape her students were in. For her, turning out for this race had as much to do with running as men buying the *Sports Illustrated* swimsuit issue has to do with a love of sports.

No, coming out this morning was part of Bonis's curriculum, a sweaty metaphor for what she believed was the most essential ingredi-ent of a successful stand-up career: showing up. Fat, thin, tired, hung-over, bad-hair day, cramps—no matter what, you show up at your gig and you give it your best. There's plenty of time to sleep after you've killed. Or bombed, or anything in between.

"You made it!" I yelled to the cop in the class whose name I can't remember today but who I have a faint recollection of seeing with his shirt off on the last night of class. Then a few more of our group ar-rived: the tall lanky dentist, lover of puns; the corpulent tech dude, an original beardo who struggled with eye contact; the forty-something woman who had taken the class three times, and yet making anyone laugh remained elusive; and the petite, blonde housewife inspired by Roseanne (who else?). Otherwise disconnected, learning together to show up whether you felt like it or not, for this brief moment in time we became a motley crew of comedy comrades.

After finishing the class, I started working on the road almost im-mediately. Coffee houses, bowling alleys, mall openings, wherever a mic could be plugged in I showed up and told jokes. Ms. Bonis's 5K challenge had stuck with me. Then, almost ten years later, on one of my extended layovers in Los Angeles, I met a guy at a bar who asked me what I thought about Jerry Lewis's comment that women aren't funny. I thought the guy was a wise-ass and a provocateur. I also thought he was cute.

Despite my reluctance to date a man nine years younger, I would go on to marry that wise-ass. But I didn't know that the night I was at his apartment when his friend called. He was visibly upset after he hung up.

"Who was that?" I asked. We hadn't been together that long, so I was in recon mode, gathering information about who he was, who his friends were, what pissed him off, important details like that. Seeing him so unhappy, this seemed like an opportunity to get a valuable new piece of the Tod puzzle.

"Steve's wife isn't going to Thanksgiving dinner at his family's house with him. She doesn't like his father and apparently she has some gig later that night she has to prep for," he said.

I'd met Steve a few times. He was one of Tod's best friends, a warm, funny guy and the only one of his cohort who was married. Steve's wife was a musician-slash-Wiccan. She had purple hair, black eyeliner, and distracting nipples. I wasn't looking for them, but they were tough to miss through her see-through tank top.

"The show must be important to her," I said. "And isn't she a Wiccan? Do they even believe in Thanksgiving?"

"She probably doesn't, but that's not the point," Tod snapped. "They're married. When you're married you go to stuff you don't want to go to. You show up. *That's* being married."

My head cocked like a dog hearing a strange noise. I don't mean to sound naïve, or imply that I was raised by wolves, but hearing Tod's passionate stance on what it means to show up for each other in marriage was, in a word, surprising. One might say terrifying. Particularly if that "one" was used to doing whatever the heck she wanted whenever she wanted to in whatever city she happened to be in.

Obviously, I knew about showing up as a comedian. In fact, like my mentor Ms. Bonis, it's something I emphasize on day one of any stand-up class I teach, or even in any conversations I have with comedians. You show up and do your work, no matter what, including getting to the club on time—early, in fact—and prepared. Yet despite knowing in my bones about showing up for work, and even in friendship for that matter, somehow I hadn't ever made the connection to my romantic relationships. Which may explain why the longest one I'd been in before Tod was nine months.

Woody Allen said, "Eighty percent of success is showing up." Although I'm pretty sure Allen wasn't talking about marriage when he said it. Clearly, if you want 100 percent success in marriage you have to adopt your wife first. I kid, but I understand better now, that showing up in marriage is everything. And it's a bit more complicated than showing up for one holiday dinner.

If you don't show up for your spouse—if you disappear, either literally by walking away, or by being preoccupied with work, your children, a bottle of Chardonnay, with slice-and-bake cookie dough or with someone who has better abs than your current mate—you have no chance of connecting. If you don't connect, you're sunk. If you stop showing up in all the ways that mean something for a couple—listening, talking, touching, even being in the same room—ultimately there is no marriage.

One of my favorite comics, Janeane Garofalo, used to do a bit about how much she preferred dating to any more consistent interaction with men. She referred to dating as a "greatest hits" album. I loved this joke and completely related to it. In my twenties and thirties, I found it very satisfying to try attempting to dazzle someone who didn't know me for a few hours and then going home, locking the door of my studio apartment behind me, and retreating to my urban womb.

Marriage, however, is not a "greatest hits" situation. Long-term marriage is the whole album plus the outtakes. It includes the experimental cuts, maybe some sad, atonal songs, and a few crazy hopped-up whiny passages where you're sure the CD is damaged and wonder why you bought it. You start thinking you want to return it, but you're not sure, you want a little time to think about it. But for now just hearing the album makes your ears hurt, like you want to forget about music altogether for a while. Sometimes, as Greta Garbo famously said in *Grand Hotel*, you "vant to be alone." But you can't always have vat you vant. We're not Swedish movie stars living in black-and-white films that end in 112 minutes. We live in full-blown Technicolor, where we rarely know the end of the story. Long-term marriage means being present and staying with your spouse. And then staying some more.

I was excited to talk to couples who had been showing up for each other for years, in some cases decades. I posed the question directly, "What has it meant to show up in your marriage?" No one responded with "holding hands and taking long walks on the beach at sunset." *Showing up* immediately brought to mind the stuff spouses didn't want to do, the not-fun parts. One of the most frequent responses to how couples show up for each other involved difficult in-laws. I found out that, just like for any comedian who has ever shown up and bombed, even with the best intentions, not all "showing up" ends well. Fortunately for comics, the worse the gig, the better the story it makes later. If you manage to stay together, the same is true in marriage. Joanne and Ralph Humphrey learned this fact early on in their thirty-five-year marriage.

JOANNE AND RALPH HUMPHREY
It Could have Been the Last Supper

Joanne is a painter and sculptor, and Ralph is a professional drummer who also teaches at a music academy. When they met each had already been married once, but their situations were very different. Ralph had married his high school sweetheart, and they were still together. Joanne's first marriage, on the other hand, had been a means to an end, the end being a trip to the New Orleans Jazz Festival. Her mother wouldn't let her go with her boyfriend unless they got married in a church first. So they did. When they got back, her father had the union annulled.

Joanne is an attractive woman with blue-green eyes and a breezy, Southern sexuality, a quality that did not go unnoticed by Ralph's father, who was there the night she and Ralph met. Ralph's mother was also there and she didn't appreciate the men in her life falling all over themselves to please this mysterious temptress. Joanne was wearing an alluring hand-painted skirt that night, which prompted Ralph's mother to give her the nickname Skirt.

"When I asked people what that meant, why she called me that," Joanne told to me, "I was told it was a word she used for prostitutes and whores. My biggest sacrifice of myself to Ralph is to keep showing up for my mother-in-law, who has mellowed with age and, frankly, dementia."

Fourteen years after they tied the knot, Joanne and Ralph were invited to Ralph's parents' thirty-fifth wedding anniversary dinner. By this point, Joanne knew she had to do some serious mental prepping to deal with her mother-in-law. She put her animosity aside for the occasion and created a huge oil painting as a gift to them. Ralph appreciated her efforts and told her so. The dinner was held in a restaurant. When Joanne, Ralph, and their two children walked in; all of his mother's friends were standing around a long table. Ralph's mother made a fuss about introducing Ralph and his family. "I look over at Ralph and notice, even all these years later, it's hard for him to stay still, his foot seems to be tapping a beat," Joanne told me. Once all the guests were seated, Ralph's mother stood up to show everyone a beautiful ring her husband had given her. She went around the table and stood in front of each person to show it off.

Joanne stretched out her hand for me, imitating the grand gesture.

"Then she came to me and walked by," Joanne said. "I thought, 'No, no, no.' And Ralph's brother, Glenn, who is basically a mute, says, 'Mom, you didn't show Joanne the ring. Why didn't you show Joanne the ring?' Ralph's foot stopped tapping. He looked up and took a breath that said, 'OK, here it comes.'

"And then, with everyone looking at me, she announces to the whole table, 'Well, you never know, she might steal it.' I couldn't speak, and Glenn says, 'She's not going to steal your ring.' This is going on in front of [everyone]. I'm sitting with my head in my hands, thinking, talking to myself. *Fuck* comes to mind, and then *you*. As in 'Fuck you!'" Instead of blurting out obscenities, Joanne drank a glass of water.

She finished the story: "Then Glenn repeated, 'She's not going to steal your ring!'

"'With her you never know,' my mother-in-law says, looking right at me, and keeps walking down the table. Then Cally, our daughter, the cutest little thing you've ever seen with her ringlets and her little party dress on, she goes to my mother-in-law with her hands cupped and says, 'I won't drop it. Can I see your ring?' And I thought, this is pathetic, my mother-in-law just painted me as a thief in front of my daughter." Being reminded that Joanne and Ralph's daughter was in the room during all of this, I started to feel a little queasy. Had I been in her position, I would have fled the scene faster than you can say "August Osage County." Where was her darling husband?

"Ralph didn't say anything because he becomes nine years old again around his parents, which I totally understand," Joanne said.

She *totally* understands this? Even when his mother was being petty and spiteful? No wonder they had stayed married thirty-five years.

"I did this for my husband," Joanne told me, referring to attending the dinner. "And he totally understood why I would never do this again and he probably loved me even more for just sitting there and not flipping the table over. I didn't, because this was something he asked me to do for him. It wasn't about me."

There it was. Joanne was showing up for her spouse. *It wasn't about her.*

After her daughter asked to see the ring, Joanne stood up, told her two children to follow her, and called out to Ralph, "We're going to be in the lobby and I'm going to get the car and we're going home, if you want a ride." About twenty minutes later Ralph came out. They got into the car and didn't speak for about an hour. "After the children fell asleep, we talked it through."

"What happened to the painting you made?" I asked.

"That painting is still hanging in their house," Joanne said, taking a sip of water. "Yep," she said, looking at Ralph.

"Yep," he said, reaching over to touch her arm. "The good ol' days."

Rather than acting out, Joanne knew that the wiser action was to preserve her dignity and protect her children and her marriage. This story is such a great illustration of what it means to show up. To stay present and keep focused on the bigger picture, your long-term commitment to each other, and, when that seems impossible, to excuse yourself and depart for the bathroom.

There's one other lesson I learned from this. Joanne's reaction impressed me as much for what she *didn't* say as for what she did. I'm often looking for the "right" response, the quick barb, the dig, or the brilliant finish. But in a charged situation with your spouse, this is not a good move. Most of the time a better choice is to say nothing in the moment, but allow the drama to settle before you talk.

In terms of frequent responses to the question of what you show up for in your marriage, next in line after "difficult in-laws" is children from previous marriages. Most people go into second or third marriages fully aware of already existing offspring. But not always.

For Bonnie and Russ Tamblyn, a child appeared in their marriage who was a surprise to both of them. Although admittedly (and thankfully) not that common a scenario, the way they handled this news, particularly Bonnie, struck me as a great example of what is possible for a couple with compassion, an open mind, and a lot of love to share between them.

BONNIE AND RUSS TAMBLYN
What to Expect When Your Spouse Is Not Expecting

When I met them, Bonnie and Russ Tamblyn had been married for thirty-six years and lived in a charming apartment near the beach. The front steps were brightened with potted plants, and when I walked into the house there was such a shag-rug, well-worn-couch vibe, I could have sworn it was 1972 and Katherine Ross was about to come out of the bedroom in a maxi dress and beads. Bonnie and Russ married in 1981 and have lived in the same apartment for over thirty years. They have one daughter together, the actress Amber Tamblyn. Russ, who is now in his early eighties, is a former dancer whose name you might recognize from the films *West Side Story*, where he played Riff, the leader of the Jets, or *Seven Brides for Seven Brothers*. He also appeared in Quentin Tarantino's *Django Unchained*. Bonnie, in her sixties, still sings with a band. Free spirits when they met, they knew each other for a few years before they wed.

One afternoon soon after they had married, when he was at the height of his fame, Russ got a call from his agent, who told him that a man was looking for him. "'Yeah, Russ, this guy is trying to get in touch with you about this girl you knew in Topanga, but it won't be today because he's in court all day,'" Russ told me his agent said. (The bottom of the Topanga Canyon intersects with the Pacific Coast Highway. In the 1960s and '70s it was the quintessential hippie free-love beach community.) "And I thought, 'Oh my God, what's this about? I'm going to get sued or something.' I thought the guy trying to get in touch with me was a lawyer."

Bonnie interrupted: "Like it was a paternity suit or something."

Later that afternoon while Russ was playing tennis a man approached him.

It was the guy who had called his agent looking for him, but he wasn't a lawyer, he was a tennis player. He had been *on* the court, not in court. The mysterious man was a good friend of a former girlfriend of Russ's who had moved up to Northern California.

The visitor revealed that when Russ and this woman had been lovers, nearly sixteen years before, the woman had gotten pregnant. So Russ had a fifteen-year-old daughter who wanted to connect with him now. Russ's initial reaction was, no way. "'If it's true, I was just a seed source,' I told the guy. 'I had no involvement with the woman—she ran off.'"

Bonnie elaborated. "It was the sixties, you know, free love and all that. The woman never told Russ she was pregnant. He didn't know. She wanted to do the right thing and Russ was married to someone else at the time. She didn't want to cause a scandal. So she left town. I guess everyone was very free in those days and so Russ assumed 'It wasn't my baby because she didn't say anything to me about it.' All of a sudden fifteen years later, there we were."

This very devoted friend to Russ's former girlfriend and her daughter was about to walk away, but before giving up he made one last effort. He told Russ, "The girl made a scrapbook about herself for you. Would you be willing to look at it?" Russ agreed, so the man brought it over that night. His daughter's name was China. According to Bonnie, "With each page he turned, the tears started rolling down Russ's face."

"It's true," Russ confirmed. They laughed at this life-altering memory. Russ changed his mind and wanted to meet his daughter, so he called her right away. He was worried about how Bonnie would feel about meeting her, but she wasn't concerned about this at all. She thought it was a blessing. "I don't think Russ had a happy time in To-panga," she told me. "For China to come out of a dark period of his life was so wonderful. And now we have grandchildren." Russ's eyes grew misty. "How about that? Grandchildren!"

Bonnie added, "Two of them. And Dylan and Vivian are going to be in *West Side Story*. So it comes full circle."

Russ beamed when he talked about both of his daughters. He is forever grateful to Bonnie for welcoming his entire family with no shame or apologies. To her credit, she intuitively knew that responding with a generous heart was the way to keep Russ, and their marriage, happy. Hearing how Bonnie's mind worked through this was such a fascinating example to me about what is possible in relationships when you trust there's enough love to go around for everyone.

Hearing these couples, I couldn't help reflecting back on my be-havior when I was single, a perpetual wanderer, a young woman who thought showing up was something you only *had* to do if someone had spent a lot of money on tickets. Even though I'd figured out how to stay in a relationship long enough to marry, I hadn't given a lot of thought to what it meant to show up consistently for one person. The more I spoke with these long-term couples, the more embarrassed I started to feel about my cluelessness. These people just seemed to know instinc-tively how to show up in marriage.

I met with one couple, Lori and David Rousso, who had been married over fifty years. They understood so well about how important showing up is that they started teaching their children about it practi-cally from birth.

When I asked David what showing up had meant in their marriage, he answered, "You mean Hineni!" He and Lori must have seen the blank look on my face because they quickly elaborated.

"In the ancient texts, when God calls a Jew, a Jew says, 'Hineni,'" David said. Lori interrupted. "It means, 'Here I am.'"

"Right," David said, "'Here I am.' Our kids joke about it all the time since we drilled it into them—Hineni, it means . . . you just don't duck. The full meaning of it is 'I am here. What do you want of me?'"

Make fun of your parents all you want, kids, but it seems to me David and Lori gave you a great primer for marriage.[1]

Comics don't tend to be joiners. Before having children I didn't spend a lot of time—OK, make that no time—learning about organized religion. Talking to David and Lori made me curious: Was there a Christian point of view on showing up? A friend of mine who is passionate about her faith introduced me to Kathy Keller, the wife of a well-known New York City pastor, Tim Keller. The Kellers are coauthors of the New York Times best seller The Meaning of Marriage: Facing the Complexities of Commitment with the Wisdom of God. The Kellers have been married for thirty-eight years.

"The vow of marriage is all about promising to show up," Kathy told me. "You are making a promise to your future self and your spouse's future self not to walk away when circumstances get tough. These are not TV vows—like on Rhoda, remember that show?"

"Yes," I said, surprised by the question. Living in Los Angeles I'd have to go to a retirement village to find someone to talk with about the genius of Rhoda.

"Do you remember Rhoda's wedding vows?" Kathy asked.

Since I was eleven when it aired and was more focused on flavored lip gloss than on weddings, I had to admit I didn't.

"'As long as we both shall love,'" Keller said. "That's what she vowed. What a bunch of malarkey! Please. Showing up when you're feeling warm and fuzzy is kids' stuff. Don't bother to take a vow if you're not going to show up whether you're feeling romantic or not. Serving one another is the heart of a marriage. Your spouse is not a fashion accessory."

Fortunately, I have never confused Tod with an Hermès bag. I could, however, learn a thing or two about being less selfish in my marriage. This Christian idea of serving each other being at the heart of showing up for your marriage seems like a good one to keep in mind. Tough to remember when you want to strangle your spouse, but nevertheless a good reset button when you're hot and bothered and not in a sexy way. And you certainly don't have to be a devout Christian to incorporate it into your marriage.

The character actor Paul Dooley and his wife of over thirty years, the writer Winnie Holzman, were very clear that being of service to each other absolutely informs how they show up for each other in their marriage.

PAUL DOOLEY AND WINNIE HOLZMAN
The Yellow Brick Road Less Traveled

Winnie Holzman created the television show *My So-Called Life* and wrote the book for the musical *Wicked*. She's a small woman, with sensitive eyes and a lilting voice that can distract from how smart she is. Paul Dooley is a well-respected writer, actor, and comedian. In his long career he has done everything from stand-up, including an appearance on *The Tonight Show,* to being a head writer for the PBS kids' show *The Electric Company* to acting in the indie hit *Breaking Away.* When Paul and Winnie met, he was fifty-four and she was twenty-six. Or, as Winnie was quick to tell me, "We have a sick fucking age difference. And when I was twenty-three I looked like I was sixteen."

Paul added, "I too looked like I was sixteen."

"Well . . . yes," Winnie said. "He looked amazingly young."

If showing up in a marriage sometimes means putting your own fears aside to make the other person happy, then credit Paul Dooley with doing this even before he and Winnie walked down the aisle. Although it was Winnie's first marriage, Paul had been married twice before and it hadn't ended well either time. Paul and Winnie shared with me a little of their prewedding deliberation.

Winnie wanted a child, but "I already had three kids," Paul said. "And I had been through a not very good divorce. I was obviously gun-shy. I was wary but I was very much in love with her. I didn't think it would be fair for me to have another child when I was fifty-seven."

Winnie added, "He was the age I am now. When I picture somebody asking me, 'Will you get married again and will you raise a baby with me?' I now think, 'Do you know what a big leap that is? That's really love.' Because I know what's it like to be fifty-seven now. And you're not really in the mood. But what's really magical is that this amazing thing happened, which is that having a baby together, first of all it brought us very close."

"It narrowed the age gap a little," Paul added.

"He's an incredible father," Winnie continued. "But also, it brought him youth."

"I brought her 'oldth' and she brought me youth," Paul responded, taking her hand.

Winnie used one of the best lines I've heard to get Paul to have a baby with her. "She wasn't breaking my balls about it," Paul told me, "but she's telling me it would be nice to have a child." But he wasn't even sure he wanted to get married again. "So she says to me, not her exact words, 'I know you'll kick off before I do, but I just want a piece of you left behind for the rest of my life.' Now really, what man is going to say 'Nah, no thanks'? It really touched me."

They got pregnant on the first try.

Agreeing to have a child with Winnie was only the first part of Paul showing up as a parent. He had no idea that he'd also end up being the primary caregiver for a while. When they had their daughter, Savannah, Winnie was not working. Paul was the breadwinner for all of them.

"Then around the time Savannah was three or four years old," said Winnie, "I met the guys from [the very popular eighties TV Show] *thirtysomething*, and they were interested in having me write for them full-time. That was a huge change in my life and my big, big break. And Paul just made it work."

Paul explained some of the nuts and bolts of being a freelance character actor, even one as successful as he was. "You're not working half the time. You may not be working a third of the time. You're not working nine months of the year. That's a lot of time to be able to spend at home." This also meant he had the time to be a very hands-on father.

As Winnie tells it, though, Paul's contributions went far beyond chauffeuring their daughter to preschool. "He really just freed me. He completely showed up as a father, but another level of it is that he freed me mentally and emotionally, he was clearly proud of me. He wanted me to succeed. He was thrilled. I never had the feeling, 'Well maybe I better not get too successful.' I couldn't have seen that coming. I don't know if I intuited that. When he met me I was in a completely different place." Now, Winnie's career was booming, and Paul was staying home with their child. Twenty-five years later the stay-at-home dad is much more common, but for Winnie and Paul it came as a surprise.

Not many people talk about the challenges of showing up for a spouse's career success, about what happens when your spouse's work life explodes, demanding a lot more of their attention. You wouldn't think this would be cause for concern, because isn't this good news? Yet it can absolutely cause some tension in a marriage. Any dramatic change in the dynamic of a couple's success takes adjusting to, not only in terms of how available you are to each other, but, as Winnie points out, it can also mean a mental adjustment of expectations of who was going to play what role in the marriage.

What was interesting to me about Winnie and Paul's thirty-plus-year history together was that unlike many of the other long-standing couples I spoke with, it was the husband, Paul, who did the lion's share of showing up in terms of absorbing the biggest changes to support the family. Although he was being funny when he said that Winnie "brought me youth," that's no joke. It wasn't until I was driving home from the interview and tallied up how old Paul was when they met to the number of years they'd been married that I realized I had just spent four hours talking about timing, faith, listening, and sex with an eighty-four-year-old man and his adoring wife.

Before we finish talking about how showing up is essential for marriage, I want to circle back to something I mentioned at the beginning of the chapter, which is showing up for the simple, day-to-day moments of a shared life. Not the parties, the in-laws you can't stand, or any surprise children. I am talking about the low-fanfare task of just being there for each other. There is no substitute for this kind of consistency for creating intimacy and trust that yields what one couple— Dan Bucastinsky and Don Roos, together for 22 years—called an "unspoken sixth sense." Over time you come to know how important something is to the other person and are able to respond without having to be asked. This is not to be confused with the passive-aggressive non-tool of hoping your mate will read your mind and figure out what you want. No, the "unspoken sixth sense" is a knowledge of the other person and how best to support them that can come only from continuing to show up for each other, respecting what I call "The Three T's": tenacity, tenderness, and timing.

As for me, I have become much more sensitive about showing up in my own marriage. Which is not to say that I show up for everything without question, but I do my absolute best to be there for moments that are important to Tod. When I can't because of children or work commitments, I don't ignore his possible disappointment, hoping that if I don't draw attention to it he'll get over it faster. We talk through these challenges because I understand in a way that I didn't before how much not doing so can chip away at your connection to each other.

TIPS FOR SHOWING UP

- Go to functions with your spouse even when you don't want to. Just put a smile on your face and do it. You never know who you will connect with, what you will learn, or, at the very least, what fantastic stories you'll come home with.

- Keep showing up every day for each other during temporary challenges, like jobs that require long commutes, periods of unemployment, or just plain stressful periods of life. Be loving toward one another despite your "mood." Trust that the marriage is bigger than temporary stresses.

- Remember the concept of "Hineni," which means not only "Here I am," but also "I am ready." This is echoed in the Christian idea of marriage that you come into it prepared to serve your spouse. Incorporating some version of either of these ideas is a great way to approach your marriage, because instead of resenting each other for how hard it sometimes gets, you can always put your attention on how you can help your partner and what you can do to make the marriage better.

- Showing up is also a daily awareness of and sensitivity toward the other person. Allow an "unspoken sixth sense" to grow between you, where you know instinctively how to respond to the other person. It can only develop over time, with patience and care. Keep in mind the three T's: tenacity, tenderness, and timing.

2

Listen

NOT JUST TO WORDS—
YOU HAVE TO TAKE
IN EVERYTHING

I wish that science, if there is a science, would come up with
a brain ride where you could take a ride in someone's brain
where you could see all their thoughts, and their memories
and why they do the things they do and why they feel the way
they feel, and I know there's a low-tech version of this just
called listening. . . . this would be so much . . . easier."

— MARIA BAMFORD, *The Special Special Special!*

It was 2003 and I was waiting for a babysitter to come and watch my
two-and-a-half-year-old son, Gabriel, so I could go see one of my students perform at the Laugh Factory on Sunset Boulevard.

I had this baby at forty, a miracle in itself. As soon as I saw him, I
wanted another. Since I was not young, we had been trying for over
a year and a half to get pregnant with no luck. Once you start using
fertility drugs, which I had, your moods are all over the place and

usually not the "happy" one. I was definitely in need of a laugh. I put
on real clothes—no stained T-shirt and stretch pants—a red silk shirt
that felt luxurious on my skin, and pants with a zipper and a button!

The babysitter was late, put her bag down and mumbled something about horrible traffic.

"Mamma don't go!" Gabriel shrieked from the floor, clinging to
my leg. I kneeled down to meet his eyes. Uncurling his fingers from my
calf I said, "Sweetheart, Mommy loves you very much, but she needs
to go to work."

"No, Mama!" he shouted, and his little hands grabbed me again.
My heart sank. I looked up at the sitter. "Um, can you . . ." I whispered,
"distract him?"

"Hey Gabriel, do you have Legos we could play with?" she asked.
He looked back at her for a second and released his hold just long
enough for me to dash off.

"Love you, sweetheart!"

"Maammmmaaaa!" I heard through the closed door. Nothing
rattles me more than that sound. Except maybe LA traffic. And my
sitter was not lying: Sunset Boulevard was a parking lot. I checked the
clock on my dashboard; I was a good forty-five minutes away and the
show started in thirty. I can't stand being late. My mother was late to
everything and I had vowed to myself never to follow in her high-
heeled footsteps. But having a child had messed with my timing. There
were too many variables keeping me from getting out of the house on
time now: a late babysitter, the clinging factor, the unexpected Play-
Doh handprint on my shirt that would have to be changed, and then
there was the always unpredictable L.A. traffic.

When I finally got to the club the emcee was already onstage. The
room was packed. "Hi, Dani," the hostess whispered. "Not many seats
left," she continued, leading me toward the front of the showroom. I
tapped her on the shoulder and tried to communicate that I didn't
want to sit near the stage, but it was obvious she didn't hear me when
she pulled the chair out for a seat at a table at the foot of the stage.

"Thanks," I said, and sat down quickly, knowing that a single
woman walking in late would be an easy target for any comic who's a

fan of crowd work. Fortunately, a couple across from me at the table couldn't stop pawing each other. Must be a date, I thought. Distracting as it was for me, I was hoping they'd keep it up all night and give the comedians something to make fun of other than me, a single, exhausted woman.

A waitress came and took my order. I could practically hear the jokes the comics would lob at me if they noticed my choices.

"Salad, huh? And I bet that's a *Diet* Coke. You're here alone, right? Your big night out? Go nuts, have a butter patty!"

My student was sixth on the lineup. The first comic came up, a young woman, and she did some funny material about (who else?) George W. Bush, and (what else?) LA traffic and then, randomly, how much she hated mothers who use cloth diapers. How they make the baby lie there screaming while they wrestle with their non-toxic safety pins. To illustrate her point she imitated a crying infant. I'd only recently stopped breastfeeding and I swear I felt my milk coming in. I looked down. No wet spots—all clear.

The next performer came up. The waitress approached with my food, but just as she was in arm's reach, the lovebirds had untangled themselves and the woman stood up, right under the server, upending her tray at an angle that landed my food, including my side of ranch dressing, on my formerly dry chest. My red silk shirt looked like a Jackson Pollock painting, if he made art using salad dressing.

Oblivious to the chaos at his feet, the comic continued right on with his joke, "So I say, 'Dude, I'm really into your sister' and he says, 'That's not my sister you asshole that's . . .'" I missed the punch line because my head was under the table while I wiped liquid off my shoes. Which is my point here. Not that I didn't hear the punch line, but the fact that he was continuing to try to land it after three women— me, the waitress, and the hottie girlfriend—had all gasped loudly, ducking left and right, while the boyfriend stood up to get out of the line of fire. All this activity was happening live and yet the comedian acted like nothing was happening, continuing with his scripted bits. Mind you, this was not an audition for a late-night comedy spot where you have to deliver a tight, six-minute set. This was instead a regular evening at a comedy club, where people come out specifically for the spontaneity of it all, that you-never-know-what-might-happen feeling in the room.

What a missed opportunity, I thought, even though personally I was grateful to have dodged a humiliation bullet. But the comedy enthusiast and the teacher in me couldn't understand this guy's failure to listen to what was going on right in front of him and put it to good comedic use.

I spend a lot of time with students talking about this aspect of being a comic, the importance of being "present" in the room, engaging with your audience, every time you perform. As soon as you walk onstage as a comic, the audience becomes your partner in an interdependent relationship. Which may not sound funny, but I promise you it's true. You need them to appreciate your work and they need you in order to have a good time. For this relationship to be satisfying, you must work off what they give you, not as a generic "audience," a faceless mass of chicken-wing (or salad) eaters, but as people who have paid hard-earned cash to see the world from your hopefully highly entertaining point of view.

You do your part by being truly "present" in the room with them, which means seeing them, and listening to them—often even more important than seeing them because the stage lighting may blind you. If you don't do this, as was the case on my big night out at the Laugh Factory, there is going to be a noticeable disconnect between what is going on in the room and the words coming out of the comic's mouth. Not to mention the fact that as great as your scripted jokes (or plans) may be, there is real, live comedy happening right in front of you.

In a club this denial of, or obliviousness to, the present moment is annoying. In a marriage, not hearing or seeing what is happening with your spouse in the moment or in your life can be deadly.

According to Patricia Love and Steven Stosny in their book *How to Improve Your Marriage without Talking about It*, "Lack of connection is the true source of resentment" in a faltering partnership. Connection comes with listening. After you commit to showing up for each other, the next most important promise in the pursuit of a happy marriage is to listen to each other. Why make the effort to show up for your spouse and then not listen to them?

If, as Love and Stosny assert, connecting with each other is a sure-fire way to nip resentment in the bud, and listening to each other creates this connection, then why don't we all listen to each other more? It seems easy enough, right? Not always. Sometimes, like that comic ignoring what's happening in the room, we are not interested in listening. Regardless of what is going on with your spouse, you have something you really, really want to say, so you're just not up for listening. You may be so invested in expressing yourself that you don't notice your partner is exhausted, or is preoccupied waiting for the phone to ring with the results of a big job interview, or even worse, is about to play the winning letter on Words with Friends. So you plow ahead with your own "material."

Or perhaps the shoe is on the other foot: Instead of ignoring that your partner is not in the mood to listen, you ignore the fact that your partner needs to talk to you. You're the one who doesn't feel like listening because you're too hungry, your favorite show is on—of course you could record it, but you need the one-hour of schadenfreude that only *The Bachelor* can deliver. It's not that you don't want to listen to what your better half has to say, you just don't want to do it in this moment. Other times, listening isn't just a matter of eliminating distractions; sometimes it takes real courage because you suspect that what your spouse has to say may be hurtful or, even harder, may involve making some changes. You may be afraid of what you are about to hear, but listen anyway!

Many marriages float a long time on the river of denial with two people either unwilling to risk expressing how they genuinely feel or unwilling to listen to the other person's truth. But these marriages run the terrible risk of one partner waking up one day and, seemingly out of nowhere, saying, "I'm done." Marriages where spouses don't listen to each other, don't notice when the other has something to say, are not happy marriages—and happy marriages are what we're after here.

It is possible when you don't feel like listening to your spouse, he or she can sound to you a lot like how a heckler feels to a comic, someone you wish would just be quiet. Or even like a buzzing sound coming out of the mic that you are trying to ignore. You may try nodding, tossing out some "Uh-huh's" or "Ummm's," hoping this will pass for listening. Be advised, this is not going to be any more effective for you than for an irritated comic in a club. It doesn't work for comics because in stand-up more than any other art form, acknowledging what is happening in the room is part of the entertainment. A comedian who does not respond truthfully in the moment is not fun. It's too much like being at school, too much like being at the office, too much like the masking of the truth we all have to do to "work well with others."

In the real world, we often have to engage in low-level denial ignoring certain realities to keep our jobs, get along with coworkers, or keep peace with extended family. But live comedy is supposed to be a better experience. So is marriage, without the two-drink minimum. Denial of our true feelings with our spouse is not helpful. You have to listen to each other and then risk giving your authentic response. And make sure you have heard each other. If you don't take the time and focus to tell the truth and listen to each other in a marriage, the two of you can get swallowed up in one big ball of unheard feelings that congeals into an impenetrable orb of resentment. I've never heard of anyone laughing from inside a congealed ball of resentment.

> If my father wanted to tell my mother something during the game she had a better chance of him hearing if she bought a ticket and went down there and held up a banner in the stands.
>
> —RAY ROMANO, *Live at Carnegie Hall*

As you are about to learn, happy couples approach listening in many different ways. The first couple we hear from had the good fortune to be friends for nearly a decade before they took the romantic plunge. Even before they married, there was no way Tracy Vilar and Eric Daniels were going to let their marriage turn into a congealed humorless orb. In fact, making each other laugh was so important to Tracy that she wrote it into their wedding vows. Tracy is a direct descendant of a bad listener, her mother, so she was determined to behave differently.

TRACY VILAR AND ERIC DANIELS
Vowing to Laugh

Tracy and Eric met while working on Spike Lee's movie *Do the Right Thing*, she as a casting associate and he as a production assistant. Tracy was twenty and Eric was twenty-one. They have been together twenty-three years, and married for thirteen. Tracy's a tiny, saucy woman from a big Puerto Rican family in East Harlem and Eric is a six foot three African American teddy bear of a man raised in Michigan. They credit the ten years they spent getting to know each other, first as friends and then as a couple, with giving their marriage a solid foundation. This, and having a shared sense of humor. Since leaving casting, Tracy has worked as a comic actress in television and film. Eric became a screenwriter about ten years ago. They have two children, Lucy, eleven, and Milo, two. Eric explained their listening style:

"Keeping it real, we don't argue that much, which is good, but you don't want to pretend that everything is perfect all the time. Especially at our daughter's age, because she understands there are things we need to talk about and decide and agree on. That's how relationships work. You have to really listen to each other. It's not always going to be everyone on the same page. When it's not, you have to try to get there."

In addition to the importance of listening, Eric brought up another great point: accepting that your relationship is not going to be perfect all the time. Happy couples don't expect this. Time and again I found that what's important to people who are content together is not being a perfect couple who never has conflict, but rather being able to communicate a point of view and then listening to your spouse's point of view without killing each other. Ideally, you exchange ideas, even opposing ones, in a way that makes you still want to be married when you climb into bed that night.

Tracy was hugely affected by how bad her mother was at listening to her father growing up. She explained to me, "My parents had a rocky marriage, but they stayed together. It definitely made me see that if I don't want that, I need to create what I think a marriage should be. I make deeper communication and understanding a priority with Eric. My mom wouldn't go deeper into anything. They would fight and I would think, 'That is not what Dad is saying! You're not looking deeper into what is going on. You're yelling. You're not even looking at him.' If I catch myself doing that I know I am on my own agenda and then nothing is really being said."

In a way it was fortunate for Eric that Tracy had been given a very clear example of how not to listen in a marriage. Her fear of becoming her mother keeps her actively working on listening. Not everyone has this same commitment to listening, however. In which case, at the very least, you had better learn how to laugh about it. And that is exactly what our next couple does.

The amusingly, self-aware Danny Greenberg doesn't blame a dark past for his limitations when it comes to listening. Fortunately, after seventeen years of marriage, his wife, Michelle, has learned to mostly laugh about Danny's weak listening skills. Figuring out how to laugh about Danny's shortcomings in this area, precisely my prescription when all else fails, reflects Michelle's acceptance of Danny's acknowledged problem with listening. Let's see what this feels like in practice.

DANNY AND MICHELLE GREENBERG

A Question of He Said, He Said

The Greenbergs are an energetic twosome who met in 1991. Danny works as a film agent and Michelle is a full-time mother to their three young boys. These two clearly enjoy each other. Despite some potentially joy-tempering obstacles in their life together—including having a son with learning difficulties (who they both say brings the most laughter to their lives) and Michelle's highly challenging relationship with Danny's mother. Their effervescent, finish-each-other's-sentences energy is compelling.

Danny described his marriage unlike any other man I interviewed. "I have a little bit of a 'separation of church and state' mentality when it comes to work," he said. "I prefer to keep work friends at 'work' and then have a different set of friends with Michelle that are kid-related."

Michelle interrupted him, laughing. "By the way, this is not always the best! You tend to—what is that word?"

"Compartmentalize," Danny answered. "Only because I put so much into my work in terms of my brain that I like to get away from it."

Danny's listening problem may stem partially from his "compartmentalizing." He fully cops to the fact that when he is at work it's hard for him to hear anything that isn't business-related. Regardless of the reason, Danny's bad listening is a genuine challenge for Michelle.

"Even when I e-mail him, it's a fifty-fifty, less than a fifty-fifty shot that something is going to get done. For example, he will go to the store and ask me, 'Do you need anything?' and I'll think, 'That's so nice,' and I'll say, 'How about some soup?' and he'll come home. No soup." Michelle gestured to him, as if to say, "Explain yourself to the lady, please."

Which he did: "I've got a lot on my mind all the time, I'm juggling a lot of stuff."

"Like, I don't? You see what I'm talking about?" she said, smiling.

Playing off each other's humorous frustration, these two sounded like siblings telling their mother what the biggest problem is with the other one. It's possible that the subject made them so uncomfortable that what I was really witnessing was nervous laughter, but because they were both so willing to put Danny's listening handicap out there, there certainly wasn't any seething, underlying resentment. Which is interesting to note: If you can call out the problem together and accept it, you can almost always find a way to laugh about it.

There was a pause in their dialogue, and Michelle added, as if she had just remembered this, "But then, if something is bothering me, and I need to talk to him, that's when he'll listen to me."

Danny looked across at his wife, if not exactly contrite, at least moved by her appreciation. "I don't listen well to individual tasks but my macro—you know, when you pull the lens back and see the whole landscape of what is going on—I'm good at that. Then, I listen."

Michelle confirmed this. "If it's my emotions, then he will listen, he's good at helping me with that." And then, in case I'd forgotten, she proceeded, with the zeal of a trial lawyer summing up his case for the jury, "But if it's anything else, anything to do with the house or the kids, anything, I have to tell him ten times. The emotional part, which is the most important part for me, he gets. There's times when literally something is bothering me so much and he's not listening, not listening, not listening' and then I'll yell at him to try to get through to him and about twenty minutes later he'll call me and say, 'I heard you, I know what you're saying.'"

"All true," he said, picking a thread off his pants.

This exchange was a rich example of how a marriage with a sense of humor can work. She has shortcomings, he has shortcomings, but at the heart of it, he is able to show up for what matters to her and she can get what she needs from him when she needs it. Michelle accepts the fact that she may have to yell to get Danny's attention, but she is willing to do this, and rather than be put off by the yelling, Danny hears her and responds. This understanding of each other and acting accordingly until everyone gets their needs met, despite the repetition and yelling involved, works for them. If it didn't, they definitely wouldn't be laughing about it.

FINDING YOUR LISTENING STYLE

Being an active listener is part of what makes a comic good. Apparently this is also true in marriage.

—KAREN BERGREEN, married twelve years

When it comes to listening style, you and your spouse may find yourselves somewhere in between these two couples, neither fiercely committed to earnest listening on a deep level, like Eric and Tracy, nor with one partner resigned to being amused by the other's perpetual distractedness, like Danny and Michelle. Wherever you fall on the spectrum, it is guaranteed that you, like all couples, can use some basic strategies to help you listen to each other better.

I sat down with Jan Jorden, a marriage and family therapist for over twenty years, to hear her take on the value of couples listening to each other. Jan is an almost six feet tall, a blue-eyed blonde from Cincinnati who herself has been married for almost thirty years. With her graceful hands, a blond bob framing her delicate features, and her easy laugh, you can see why she made a nice living as a model and actress in the 1970s. But as soon as she starts to speak about matters of the heart, it becomes equally clear how passionate she is about her second career as a therapist.

Looking at me through glasses that made her eyes appear even larger and bluer, she told me with absolute certainty, "Listening is the only thing you have to give to another person, ever, your presence. Show up in the present. Pay attention to what has heart and meaning. Deep listening is the single most valuable gift you can give your partner."

Jan then made an analogy between a spouse and an audience, expanding on the comparison I offer at the beginning of this chapter. "You are the audience for your partner and your partner is the audience for you," Jan said. "You are the witness to his or her life. Listen to him. Pay attention to him (or her) in the moment right now. Yes, you will fail sometimes. That's OK. I'm not suggesting that you do this twenty-four/seven. But if you do this kind of listening for just twenty minutes a day, it is truly honoring another human being."

I like any suggestion that has the possibility of failure built in—it takes the pressure off doing it perfectly, which can suck the joy out of anything, especially marriage.

I asked Jan for suggestions to help people listen better during an argument.

"Ask your partner to repeat or clarify what he or she has actually said and make sure that you get it. He or she will be honored by your effort alone. Look for points of agreement. Say you agree, out loud, when you do. Look for small points where you could change. The smallest point of change could lead to a beginning of a shift in energy. That shift in energy could change the conversation, and change your marriage. That's what I strongly suggest doing in your day-to-day relationship."

It takes a concerted effort to listen this way, but the good news is that if you do manage to pull it off, it certainly seems like a great safeguard against thoughts and feelings being ignored or misinterpreted. Looking for a small point of agreement rather than more stuff to be mad about was something I definitely needed to hear. I had to consider the possibility that sometimes I am looking to blow off some steam. And interpreting something Tod says or does in its most negative light gives me exactly the justifiable anger I am craving. This was not a happy epiphany.

If I could do what Jan recommended, stop the rage train and take a different action, like putting my attention on a small change that I could make, even a minor shift in point of view, there's a chance I could shake myself out of it. I could even ask Tod to repeat what I thought I heard, the thing I am so mad about, to make sure it is actually what he said. This alone would be a positive choice. Because Tod is a good guy, but sometimes the way my brain listens to what he says when we're in a fight makes him seem like the villain in my drama. According to Jan's wisdom, it's up to me to get clarification before I blow a gasket. I am allowed to react to my husband, but it's not OK to react to a fictitious, sinister interpretation of him.

NEWSFLASH

Listening Is Still Better Than Assuming

It's no big reveal to say that Tod and I have had our share of listening challenges. I like to think some of them are a function of our different backgrounds—he's East Coast; I'm West Coast—and family history and our different ways of being in the world in general. By "ways of being," I'm talking about our instinctive communication styles. Tod is thoughtful and deliberate; I'm impulsive and emotional. Neither of us is like this 100 percent of the time, of course, but it's who we are unless someone tells us not to be this way. Add to this the fact that he's almost ten years younger than me, and it is safe to say we are definitely not cut from the same cloth. Our marriage is more like trying to weave strands of kelp and hemp together into something durable. Both are natural materials, and if you could do it you'd have a remarkably versatile fabric, but getting it to hold together can be a little taxing.

This is one of the reasons why listening is crucial for us. I can't assume I know what Tod is thinking without asking him what he is actually thinking. Whenever I do this we end up in trouble.

In my house growing up, when someone was quiet, it meant one of three things, either they were seething with rage, brooding from deep disappointment in you, or depressed. It took me a while to adjust to sharing a home with someone who grew up an only child and likes quiet. Every time he chooses to lie on the couch reading, I have to remind myself he's not secretly wishing he never married me.

On the other hand, when I am upset about something, I get "animated" about it. I raise my voice, I gesticulate, I might froth at the mouth a little (or it could be a latte mustache), and when I express whatever my peeve of the week is to Tod, inevitably in the middle of my rant he will say, "I don't know why you're screaming at me—what did I do?" Then I have to say, "You didn't do anything, I'm not screaming at you, I am screaming around you. You are scream-adjacent!" Sometimes I wish I'd married someone more like me so we would have exactly the same thoughts and I wouldn't have to explain myself and apologize so often. But in saner moments I know this would actually be much worse. In fact, we'd spend more time apologizing because we'd both be ranting lunatics who never listened to the other person because (a) we'd assume we already knew what they were going to say and (b) we'd be screaming too much ourselves to hear the other person.

So we're not that couple who know each other so well that we can finish each other's sentences—not yet, anyway. In case you are similarly challenged, as I discovered many couples are, I put together suggestions of some concrete actions to take for better listening.

Give Your Undivided Attention

The simplest listening tool may be to turn off machines and media when your husband or wife is talking to you. Put your device down, or, if you're old-fashioned, put the newspaper down, put a bookmark in the book, and look up.

Eye contact is a great setup for successful listening. Not that it's necessary—in fact, you could make the argument that not being able to see would heighten your sense of hearing. But for people who have trouble focusing, looking at the person talking to you is a great beginning for either saying what you need to say or hearing the other person.

One couple I met came up with a great idea for setting each other up to listen better. Michael and Hutch, a fabulous dual-actor, single-sex couple who have been together for seventeen years, both acknowledge how hard it can be for Michael to unplug and listen. Hutch came up with a great idea to alleviate stress around this with something he calls, "the five-minute warning."

"I can't expect him to just shut down the minute I need to talk to him," Hutch reports, "so I give him a five-minute warning. I say, 'Michael, can you be available to listen to me in about five minutes?' And unless the house is on fire, or he's in the bathroom, the answer is almost always yes."

"What can I say? It works," Michael admitted with a sly smile. "I get the five-minute warning, I wrap it up or pause it, whatever it is, and I listen." At six foot four, Michael is a big guy with a big voice—the night he and Hutch first met, at a bar in New York City's West Village, Michael threatened bodily harm to a poor soul in pursuit of Hutch. I wouldn't want to have to tell him to turn off his iPod and listen to me, so I was impressed and inspired by Hutch's boldness.

Say It Again, Sam, Out Loud

Once your spouse has your full attention, another great trick for making sure you are listening well is to repeat aloud exactly what your partner said to you, using his or her own words. Both Jan Jorden and Marc Sholes, a couples counselor for twenty-five years who is based in New York City, recommend this exercise. Sholes swears by this technique for deepening partners' understanding of each other. He explained to me by phone how this technique works:

> The first person makes a statement about how they feel. Then the other person repeats it back and asks, "Is that what you meant?" If the first person feels understood, they say, "Yes, that is what I meant." If the first person does not feel understood and says, "No, that isn't what I meant," the other person tries again to state what he or she heard until the first person feels understood. Once the second person has understood, they then express their subjective experience of what the first person said. Then the first person repeats that back to them to make sure he or she heard that right. This back and forth repeating continues until both spouses feel understood. That's the entire exercise. The goal in not to discover whose perspective is objectively correct—the goal is to feel heard. This exercise helps couples begin to appreciate the other's subjective experience, their separateness. In many cases couples are merged and are already assuming what they think the other means without really listening. This is bad as it perpetuates a cycle of old patterns being repeated.

Sholes was describing an exercise that the couples therapist Harville Hendrix calls "mirroring." It shortstops people from wasting time trying to solve whatever problem they thought they heard, allowing them to focus on what is real. It also forces both partners to slow down and really listen to the other, which leads to a deeper understanding of the other person.[1]

What surprised me about this technique is that it is the exact exercise I spent two years trying to perfect in my early training as an actress before becoming a comic. The curriculum at New York's William Esper Studio, where I studied for two years, came directly from the legendary acting teacher Sanford Meisner. Meisner's "repetition exercise," which requires you to repeat back exactly what your acting partner just said to you verbatim, is the foundation of the Meisner technique. At the Esper Studio you spend an entire academic year fine-tuning your listening through exercise. This gives you a better understanding of the subjective experience of your scene partner, just as Sholes and Hendrix get their couples to do.

Doing this exercise I not only learned to give my full attention to a person when I am listening but also became highly aware of my own communication. When you start practicing this kind of focused listening, whether in a class, on a therapist's couch, or out in the world, you can't help but become much more aware of tone of voice, because you see how much a change in tone can affect how people hear what you are saying. This would not be news to comics who know that tone is just as important as the words they say. Would Chris Rock's jokes have the same impact delivered in the deadpan style of Steven Wright? Of course not. I doubt that Tig Notaro's brilliant, dry words would sound as incisive if delivered in the baby voice of the veteran comic Rita Rudner. Not surprisingly, tone also has a great effect on how we speak to our loved ones.

It's not hard to illustrate the power of tone. Take this simple question, something either you or your spouse might ask each other weekly: "Did you load the dishwasher?" Now think of all the ways you might ask this question.

Depending on the tone you use and where you place emphasis, the question could imply anything from "You have no understanding of space," to "Apparently I'm your domestic slave," to "That was so sweet of you, thank you!"

For successful couples, as for successful comics, the act of listening takes some effort and awareness. But like the best comedy, it will keep your marriage from feeling like it's on autopilot. Without active listening, you and your spouse will begin to feel disconnected, the same way an audience senses something is off when what is happening in the room is not acknowledged by the comic. They may still get obligatory laughs, but the magic will have left the room. This is also true in your marriage: you can certainly stay in it, but if you're not listening to each other enough you are going to miss the magic.

HELPFUL HINTS FOR BETTER LISTENING

- Be in the present moment when you are talking to each other. If you cannot be present in the simplest conversations with your partner, you will never build the foundation you need for complicated conversations.

- Look up. Eye contact is a great aid for quality listening. At the very least, looking into each other's eyes sets you up not only to hear each other but also to engage your other senses to better understand what your spouse is saying and feeling.

- If listening is not one of your strongest skills, set aside a specific time with your spouse to talk. We all lead busy, frantic, distracted lives, but it's important to stay connected, so schedule communication into your day if you have to. If you can't plan ahead, try giving each other a five-minute warning when there is something you need your mate to hear.

- Make sure your own listening is accurate. Before you fly off the handle at something you thought you heard, check it out with your spouse. When in doubt, repeat back exactly what you heard your husband or wife say to make sure you got it right.

- Become conscious of your tone of voice, particularly when you are asking each other questions. Tone is just as much a part of our communication as the words we use. Sometimes it says even more. If you use a kind tone—the tone you would use to talk to a dear friend who you know loves you and whom you love very much—you will be a hundred times more successful in having your thoughts heard by your spouse than using an unkind one.

3

Give the People What They Want

Sex Is to Marriage What Jokes Are to an Audience: Without It, the Natives Get Restless

No matter what else you do, if you throw your husband a sincere and enthusiastic bone at least twice a week, you can almost take the long-term success of your marriage for granted.

—ERIN B., married for fifteen years

"Where do you put this stuff?" I asked Tod, straining to read the fine white-on-black print on the tiny piece of paper folded like origami that came with the tube of massage gel.

"I don't know, honey. Why are you asking me? Let me read it," he said, reaching across the bed and grabbing the instructions out of my hand with the specific impatience of someone who is ready to get it on, but also wants to help his wife.

"It says to put it on the places you like to be touched most." We looked at each other.

"Sounds good to me!" he said.

"Okaaay," I responded, squeezing a small amount onto my finger and rubbing it on my inner thigh. "Certainly they don't mean for me to put it 'there,'" I thought, "and even if they did, I'm not doing it because from the heat I'm feeling on my thigh I'm pretty sure it will burn my whole business right off."

"My thighs feel like I've rubbed cinnamon fireball candies on them," I reported.

"Uh-huh." Tod said, trying to kiss me.

"What's that's stuff that athletes use when they get a cramp? It feels just like that . . ."

"Bengay," Tod mumbled, still heading for my lips.

"That's it! It's like Bengay! Only cinnamon-flavored. Scented."

"Yep."

"It feels kind of nice, actually."

"That's great, I'm glad."

"But it's not worth twenty-nine ninety-five for that little tube. That's a big turnoff."

"I hope it's not too big a turnoff because that would kind of defeat the purpose here, right?" Tod responded.

I realized that I had been talking the entire time I should have been . . . well, *not* talking. I let the instructions fall to the floor to allow for a deeper appreciation of the product.

In retrospect, buying this "essential female arousal oil" wasn't a total waste of money. After all, it did get us where we wanted to go. It also gave us a new shared experience and something to laugh about, even if I was intermittently distracted, reminiscing about the joys of cinnamon-red candy balls. Not exactly the foreplay the packaging promised.

Why did I pay thirty dollars for a tube of gel the size of my index finger just to have a slightly new experience in bed with my husband? Especially when it turns out a dollop of Bengay would probably have had the same effect? The simple answer is: good marketing. The real reason they hooked me, though, is because I believe having sex with my spouse and keeping it interesting are essential for staying happy together. That is what we are going to talk about in this chapter: uninhibited, unadulterated, and unapologetic sex. In comedy clubs, this might be called "working blue." Except, I'm not going to be using relentless profanity to make my point, what I'm going to say is definitely not going to be indecent, and you don't have to wait until after 10 P.M. to read it.

In the same way that live comedy audiences expect to hear jokes when they come out to a club, the vast majority of people who marry expect to have sex with their spouse. So is sex. In both cases, if too much time passes without those expectations being met, people get restless. Audiences in a club will put up with a rambling setup, some storytelling, and some "crowd work," but they come out to hear jokes and laugh. And yes, your better half cares about you and loves you, but we're human, and intimacy is a significant part of why most of us marry.

Like long-term comedy fans, spouses also get excited about fresh material. What if every time you shelled out big bucks to see Seinfeld live he was still doing his bit from the Merv Griffin show in 1981 about lifting up the hood of his car and trying to look like he knows something? Or if every time you saw Louis C.K. he did the same Cinnabon bit about how no one's happy in the Cinnabon line? Personally, I still laugh at this, but if it was the only bit I heard for the next forty years, at a certain point I think I'd probably stop.

MARRIED PEOPLE ALSO LIKE NEW MATERIAL

Having the same type of sex over and over in a marriage is not all that different. But let me make myself absolutely clear: even having the same old sex is better than no sex at all. If I am making an audience laugh consistently with my jokes, even if it's mostly oldies, they are a lot more attentive and patient with my bloopers, my rambling stories, and my frizzy hair. This is also true of my husband: Tod is a lot more patient with my eccentricities when we are behind closed (and since having kids, locked) doors regularly. Throw in a little creativity and suddenly he's emptying the dishwasher with gusto and taking out the trash with a skip in his step. This isn't just a "man thing," by the way. I feel happier too, more connected physically and emotionally. The give and take of naked bodies doing what they are inclined to do, much like giving and getting laughs, makes you both feel better.

Just in case you're one of those people who think that focusing on keeping sex interesting is primarily for the husbands, according to Daniel Bergner, writing in *What Do Women Want? Adventures in the Science of Female Desire,* women in long-term relationships are just as apt to get bored as men, if not more so. Bergner looked at numerous studies of women and desire and concluded that men are not the only ones vulnerable to the lure of new and different sex partners. Women can get bored, too.

As Bergner tells it, the scientists conducting these studies went to great lengths to collect their data, in some cases having researchers hook up sensors to women's genitals—yes, you read that right—and then showing them porn. Some women were shown the same clips a second time. After seeing the same clip repeatedly, these ladies showed no physical signs of excitement, whereas when men were shown these same clips twice, their reactions stayed constant. Apparently, for women a repeat incarnation of the sex act was not sexier the second time around. His extensive research led Bergner to conclude that despite what laypeople and scientists have asserted for years, "Female eros isn't in the least programmed for fidelity."[1]

If you extrapolate this insight regarding female response to years and years of the same bodies doing the same things in a long-term marriage, it appears that at least for some women, being bored in the bedroom is something we should take seriously. And not for the oft-cited reason that men have wandering eyes because they are always looking to spread their seed and therefore cannot be expected to control themselves, but also because if we're not careful, we are all going to get bored.

I always assumed it was men who needed shiny new toys, reflexively scanning the road for newer, sleeker models, and that we women were deeper, seeking emotional connection and lasting intimacy, and possessing admirably longer attention spans. Turns out that with the women these researchers observed, there's more of a teenage girl's "been there, done that," sensibility in play.

I couldn't stop thinking about the women who let people clip sensors to their clitoris. Boredom might be a life problem for them. I would have to be bored in every aspect of my life to let anyone put a clip on that part of my body. I wondered if Bergner's conclusions would ring true for the kind of women I had access to. Real-life, non-clinically-monitored-via-clitoral-sensors married women. Was it possible that there were some who were not bored? Who were in fact happier with their spouses, and their sex lives, over time? So during my interviews, when husbands were out of earshot, and promising anonymity when desired, I asked the wives about the boredom factor in their marriages. What I came up with are some first-person testimonials, no machines or sensors in sight. Most of the women who shared their experiences with me took me up on my offer for privacy, which I respected by not including their full (or real) names.

> I never find sex boring, I am sorry—maybe that is a boring answer. Orgasm is something that thrills me even fifteen years into knowing [my husband]. Do we spice it up? Yep. Are hotels, dressing rooms, fantasies, and even an occasional trip to a sex shop involved? Yep. For me the secret is so lame and New Age-y I am tempted not to say it but . . . it's "Be where you are." I am in a long-term marriage with a great guy who loves me. This alone is rare and amazing. If I focus on that when I am having sex . . . if I just feel his lips, feel the love, and goodness follows.
>
> —ALYSIA, married seventeen years

There isn't anything more fun than saying, "Let's have sex this afternoon," and anticipate it and plan for it and think about what would make it different and what would make it fun. Don't wait for it to just be continuously magical and when it's not, then feel "Just fuck it, this relationship is never going to work."

—DEBORAH, married thirty years

Monogamy *is* a turn-on. The thought of sex with another man makes me a little nauseated.

—DONNA, married forty-three years

We've been together since 1981. . . . My one and only. . . . It gets better and better. We can't wait to be together after work. Not bored, not restless. I would say blessed.

—TRACY, married thirty years

I have to say that not only am I not bored, it's better. It may seem cliché, but sex with someone you truly have shared intimately your thoughts and fears with, and the life experiences being together presents, make the sexual connection that more intense. Jim and I can't speak for anyone else on this, but for us, it has only gotten better. Not because the mechanics are different but because the honesty and the full expression has become truer.

—MELINDA, married thirty years

Hearing all these positive sentiments motivated me to delve a little deeper into this boredom theory. I started to poke around—pun possibly intended—to see what the experts and some of these happy wives advised for keeping the home fires burning.

It didn't take long to find some specific advice. Sonja Lyubomirsky is a psychologist who has devoted her career to the study of happiness. She has done a significant amount of work exploring the causes of, and remedies for, boredom in marriage.

In "Making It Last: Combating Hedonic Adaptation in Romantic Relationships," Lyubomirsky and her colleague Katherine Jacobs Bao found that it's not contempt that familiarity breeds in long-term relationships—it's boredom. In line with Daniel Bergner's findings, Lyubomirsky also notes that from the mid-eighties to early nineties, "Boredom was one of the most frequently given reasons for divorce."[2]

But, Lyubomirsky and Bao are optimistic. They recommend two specific ways for couples to keep boredom at bay, and not just in the bedroom: variety and appreciation. As we've already established, it's very hard to laugh at the same thing over and over again; even diehard fans want new material. Lyubomirsky has found the same to be true of long-term couples: Keep it fresh. She's not suggesting that couples come up with new jokes (although it couldn't hurt), but she recommends doing things together that you don't normally do. The anthropologist Helen Fisher, an expert on romantic love, strongly agrees with this outlook.[3] In her book *Why We Love: The Nature and Chemistry of Romantic Love*, she makes three simple-sounding suggestions for the health, happiness, and hotness of a long-term marriage: "Marry the right person, have sex with them regularly, and go out and do novel, exciting things with them." Asked what she means by "novel," she said, "Anything that's new or interesting—or even slightly dangerous—will help sustain feelings of romantic love."[4] Visions of toys, lacy thongs, and airplane bathrooms with Luther Vandross piped in danced through my mind.

As to Lyubomirsky's other suggestion about cultivating appreciation to stave off boredom, this might not be something you instinctively think of for goosing your sex life, and yet, it makes good sense. Sometimes feelings of appreciation spontaneously well up for your spouse, but what a great idea not to leave that to chance. Like the comedian who can only write jokes when they feel "inspired," and who end up with a lot of blank pages, don't wait for that moment of inspiration to express appreciation for your spouse. Making the effort to do this when these feelings are not necessarily gushing out of you spontaneously will pay off not only in your day-to-day life but also no doubt in the bedroom, too. It will compel to you to actively identify what you love about your partner. By taking this action, you will be reminded of the specific ways your spouse brings comfort and love to your life. Reminding yourself of your spouse's fantastic qualities will rekindle your passion and (hopefully) drive you to grab them and throw them on the couch for a big wet kiss, or anything else the spirit moves you to do.

But what if you're still skeptical? What if you know that no matter what an expert says—about getting some new bedroom gadget or going hang-gliding instead of out to the local sushi joint, or making lists of all the reasons you married your spouse—it isn't going to make you feel any better about the ho-hum sex you're having (or not having)? Is there anything else out there to do to get your heart racing? Well, one of the longstanding sources for variety has been to seek out other sex partners, creating an open marriage. Sam and Rosalind, married forty-five years, had valuable wisdom to share on this subject.

SAM AND ROSALIND
Three Is Not Company

Sam and Rosalind[5] met in the winter of 1967 and married in the summer of 1968, when she was nineteen. She was an undergraduate at SUNY Buffalo and Sam was a graduate student. Today he's a proudly bald man in his late sixties who wears fluorescent paperclip earrings, has a passion for soul music and Jesus, and likes being described as eccentric. He's also an accomplished writer.

Rosalind is a complicated, soft-spoken, gentle woman, a mother and grandmother of great depth, intelligence, and sensitivity. When I talk to couples like Sam and Rosalind, I get a visceral understanding of why marriage is referred to as "an institution." Sitting with them was like witnessing a living, breathing piece of American history.

True to late-1960s evolution, Rosalind's parents were very upset that she wanted to marry so young. She wasn't so excited about the idea at first, either.

"My parents had an awful marriage and I was very gun-shy about getting married. So when he asked me—"

"It was a maybe," Sam interrupted.

"Yes, I said maybe and he said, 'What?' I said, 'I need to think about it.' He said, 'How about tomorrow morning?' I said, 'That's too soon.' Finally we set a deadline, five o'clock the next day. Way before the deadline I said yes."

There is an ease between Sam and Rosalind when they talk about their shared history and the life they have now that makes it easy to be in their company. They were open about their experience with sex—specifically, "variety"—in an era, the sixties, when practicing monogamy was not at the top of anyone's list of fun things to do. As such, they did their share of experimentation, but they wanted me to be clear that their experimentation was not unique for the time. Sam recalled, "We had an open marriage briefly in the seventies, and it was kind of a catastrophe. So it isn't that we haven't toyed with those ideas, but I think overall, my feeling is, at least with Rosalind and me, that monogamy provides a simplicity that a relationship needs. Everything else is just far too complicated."

Rosalind agreed. "I love the use of the word 'simplicity.'"

Sam had more to say about monogamy. "It might not be the most perfect thing in the world, but if you introduce Alvin, or I introduce Marylou, into this equation, it's way too complicated. Not to mention jealousies, insecurities, and money. I know as a writer my guiding principles are simplicity and clarity. In a relationship these are also really important. And monogamy aids that. It doesn't guarantee it, and it's taken me a while to come to that conclusion. We've tried [the alternative] and it just—"

"It's fraught with problems," said Rosalind. "And ultimately it can't help but dilute the intimacy within a couple."

"Your energy is quite literally being pushed to an outside presence," Sam concluded.

I can't say I'm surprised by what Sam and Rosalind shared with me, but I am very glad they were so honest with me. Rachel Sussman, a psychotherapist and author who wrote *The Breakup Bible*, agrees that opening up your marriage sexually is not a great choice.[6] In 2012 there had been a surge of interest in open marriages after Newt Gingrich's ex-wife revealed that he had asked her for one. Sussman wrote an article on the topic for the *Huffington Post* in which she stated, "In most cases someone is going along with another person's desire to have an affair and a safety net. Once in a while a couple comes in to try to work out the terms of an open marriage. Once the conversations get going, I often find that many of these couples really don't want to go this route, but they are having a hard time communicating their sexual or emotional needs to each other. And when those needs are [satisfied], the desire to seek sex from another is often alleviated."[7]

If we take Sam and Rosalind's experience and put it together with the expertise of Sussman and Lyubomirsky, it doesn't seem that people necessarily want multiple sexual partners to be happy. What they need is the courage to ask for the variety we all want within a monogamous relationship. The results of a 2004 Scandinavian study of 16,000 Americans reinforced this conclusion, finding that married people have more sex than those who are single, divorced, widowed, or separated and that the "happiness-maximizing" number of sexual partners is one.[8]

Tod told me before we were married that having an affair was a deal breaker for him, so I hadn't given a lot of serious thought to the pros and cons of an open marriage, but all this information made sense. Opening up your marriage to multiple partners may solve the problem of boredom temporarily, but it swings the door wide open for a whole bunch of other headaches. Besides the ones already articulated, I also know that if Tod ever changed his stance and decided he needed to have sex with other women too, I would feel the utter heartbreak of having given myself fully to someone who can only be happy if he gives himself to others, too.

Let's assume open marriage is off the table. Is there anything else you can do—if, say, you are too busy to create variety, you already feel you appreciate your spouse, and boredom still threatens to shut down the love train between the sheets? Or if a lack of interest in sex is already solidly in place? Wouldn't it be great if there were some kind of pill you could take? Funny you should ask. Yes, there is. Or there will be very soon.

In the near future, a pill to stimulate women's sexual appetite will be available by prescription.[9] (Some pharmaceutical company is going to clean up!) Leaving aside the boredom factor, hormone depletion in women as they age also contributes to their waning interest, so as the population ages, there is a very large untapped market for such a pill to appeal to. This pharmaceutical has been dubbed Lybrido, which I guess the inventors chose because Sexpill was a little too obvious. The manufacturers are banking on its being as transformational to women's sexuality as Viagra was for men. I just hope they iron out the kinks, which so far include side effects equivalent to a ten-hour erection for men, during which no matter how many times you have an orgasm you are not satisfied, creating the sexual equivalent of an itch that cannot be scratched enough. As someone who scratches a mosquito bite until I draw blood, I don't want to imagine the effects of this pill on my body. In the meantime, there're plenty of other sex enhancers like arousal oils, gels, lotions, and potions. They may or may not work, but you can definitely have fun trying.

There are also hundreds of boutiques and websites full of sex toys with black lace–corseted salesgirls at the ready to explain how the toys work.

Now, if variety within monogamy, expression of appreciation, orgasm pills, or fancy sex toys don't appeal to you, and yet you are still concerned that boredom might be lurking behind the curtains of your bedroom, there is still one option for you to get your juices flowing. According to couples I spoke with of all sizes, ages, and genders, the best aphrodisiac they've found is laughter.

One woman who has been married for thirty-five years put it to me this way: "Something I've noticed is that often what starts as talking, then laughing, moves to sex. Not planned, but a result of being available to the other person. Laughing is a bonding experience, intimate in its own way."

This didn't surprise the longtime marriage and family therapist Michael Latimer: "If you have people who can feel connected with a laugh, it can lead to sex. When someone feels embraced by humor, when they are laughing, it takes him or her off the defensive and opens them up. Laughing literally opens up the chest and heart chakra, if you believe in that kind of thing."

I do believe in laughter opening the chest and heart, I've felt it. The chakra part? Well, I've never studied chakras, but millions of yogis can't be wrong, so I'm sure there is truth there. What's interesting to me is the connection between laughter and sex: two humans laughing together makes them, particularly women, want to get it on. I mentioned this to Tod at dinner one night and he looked at me like I was informing him that our children are both boys.

"Why are you looking at me like that?" I asked.

"How do you think I got the ladies in college?" he said. "I would make them laugh in class, and then . . . well, it always worked."

Come to think of it, he made me laugh the night we met. He had a shaved head, was wearing a black leather jacket, and smoked cigarettes. Not exactly my type. But he was funny, so I agreed to go out with him when he called me a month later. Like I've learned about most women, when a man moves us to laughter, we begin to wonder about the other ways he might move us.

I also found research to support the fact that being able to make us laugh is something that women actively seek in a partner. Robert Provine, a neuroscientist and professor of psychology at the University of Maryland, was curious about the different relationship to laughing that men and women have in the pursuit of a mate via that twentieth-century relic, the personals ad. This is what he found: "In 3,745 ads placed on April 28, 1996, in eight papers from the *Baltimore Sun* to the *San Diego Union-Tribune*, females were 62% more likely to mention laughter in their ads, and women were more likely to seek out a 'sense of humor' while men were more likely to offer it. Clearly, women seek men who make them laugh, and men are eager to comply with this request."[10]

According to Provine, laughter is also contagious. He cites what sounds like a crazy "outbreak" of laughter at a girls' school in Tanzania in 1962. Three girls got the giggles in January, and by March all ninety-five students had to be sent home because they couldn't stop laughing. So, not only does laughter turn women on, it's also contagious.

This is good news for couples looking for a nonchemical way to stimulate their sex lives. Someone needs to start laughing, because if one of you does, it's almost guaranteed that the other will follow. Once everyone is laughing, chakras will be opening left and right, and soon enough clothes will start flying off!

How about this uplifting fact? Laughter doesn't even have to be genuine to be contagious. There is an international yoga movement called—not ironically—laughter yoga, that gets people in studios to laugh together for healing purposes. The founder is an unsurprisingly ebullient Indian physician, Dr. Madan Kataria, also known as Dr. K, who has made it his life's work to educate the masses on how to laugh better and more often. One of the main tenets of laughter yoga is that you don't need to hear jokes, or find anything funny, to laugh. You just have to start making the sounds and facial expressions of a person who is genuinely laughing. At his website, Dr. K has instructional videos of himself sitting alone talking into his computer camera demonstrating this in what he calls "laughter meditation."[11]

Though I was skeptical, within three minutes of watching one of his videos I, too, was laughing. This proved not only the contagious nature of laughter but also the fact that it can be stimulated without anything notably funny happening.

After twenty-eight years of marriage, comedian Ray Romano relies heavily on being able to make his wife laugh for keeping their relationship honest. He recently told David Letterman about how, in the beginning of his marriage, he was driven to satisfy his wife in the bedroom, but now, over twenty years later, what he really wants to do is make her laugh, which is easier than trying to figure out if she's really enjoying sex. He told Letterman, "The thing with a laugh is, I know it's real, it's genuine. My wife, she can't fake laughter, she won't fake laughter, she'll tell me, she'll look at me and say that's horrible, that's a horrible joke. But in the bedroom . . . look, I'm not going to call her on it, but . . ." Well, apparently you can fake laughter too! But not to worry, Mr. Romano, because even if your wife does happen to (one time) fake it, real laughter is not far behind the fake kind, and as we now know, real laughter can often lead to really good sex.[12]

I'm going to recap some of the key points of information here about the benefits of laughing together, and creating laughter, with one essential caveat: No amount of forced giggling is going to fix a "we-need-to-think-about-divorce" crisis. But if you find yourselves in a somewhat apathetic, static, uninspired-heading-to-bored phase of your marriage, there is real hope to be found in laughing together. Among other reasons:

- Because women find laughter hot.
- Because laughter is highly contagious.
- Because you don't have to wait until either one of you finds something funny to do it. Just start being silly and making the sounds of someone laughing. (Trust me, it works.)

You don't need expensive ointments or an endless-orgasm pill or three other people you're schtupping on the side to create excitement and fulfill desire. You could just start laughing more.

If there is any couple that truly appreciates the power of laughter as fine foreplay, it's Ira and Anthony, a gay black couple who have been together for forty years. When I approached Ira about being interviewed he immediately agreed. "Of course I'll talk to you. If we don't tell our story," he said, "who will believe it ever happened?"

IRA AND ANTHONY

Trailblazers Who Are Still Hot

Ira and Anthony couldn't be more devoted to each other. You can still feel their romantic love more than four decades into their relationship. Sitting with them, I felt a little like an extra in the diner scene from *When Harry Met Sally*. Not because they were moaning in rapture, but because of how they relate as a couple. I kept thinking of that line, "I'll have what she's having!"

Ira and Anthony talked with me about the connection between laughter and sex after years with the same partner. "There are things communicated in laughter," Anthony said, "and a coming together that happens in laughter that has more importance than people think. If you are able to bring each other to laughter, to me that says, I still find you sexy, fascinating, interesting and all of that."

"That's what I was going to say," Ira chimed in. "He doesn't make me laugh. I make him laugh, but Anthony is a turn-on to me. A total turn-on to me sexually. All he has to do is walk around the house with his shirt off."

"He objectifies me," Anthony said.

"I do, I do," Ira responded with a Cheshire cat grin.

Later in our discussion they brought up an important point about sex with a long-term partner having nothing to do with boredom and everything to do with being human, which is aging together, a fact that no long-term couple escapes. "We've accepted that our sexual relationship has evolved. It's not what it was when we were twenty or thirty," Anthony said.

"But we still love being intimate," Ira clarified.

"Of course, I'm not saying that—I'm saying it's changed," Anthony said. "I don't have an expectation that it's going to be like it was when we were twenty. We don't look twenty, we don't think the way we thought, our hormones are different. And all of that is different. It's a bit of an adjustment, but this is where we are now."

Time and again, I found that in long-term happily married couples—with the emphasis on happily—staying physically connected remains a priority for them. There is a huge perk of hanging in there with the same person when it comes to sex that Ira and Anthony wanted to make sure I understood. "We have an advantage in the bedroom because we experienced each other young. Because we communicated that way early on, we still kind of see each other that way. If he were meeting me for the first time now . . . "

Anthony jumped right in: "Oh, he's still hot and sexy. Are you kidding me?"

"The brain is always sexy, right?" Ira said.

Anthony looked at me. "I'm not just talking about the brain."

This aside made Ira laugh. "Oh, Anthony! Younger people look at me like I'm a grandpa. They're not looking at me like some hot sexy man." Then he looked back to me. "But Anthony can still see me as a hot sexy man. Part of the reason is he knew me when I was hot and sexy. Other people have said, he's older, and whatnot, and I think, how can they think he looks older? He looks like he's twenty-seven to me. I see him as Anthony."

It wasn't just a lack of boredom I heard from these two—and, frankly, from all of the men in decades-long heterosexual marriages I spoke with as well—that I found compelling. It was the heartfelt gratitude men seem to have for their spouses that struck me. Maybe it's just because they were speaking on the record, but no man I interviewed for this book sounded bored or restless. Their eyes didn't dart around the room when I asked them about sex, as if they were trying to avoid answering or were looking for an answer, nor did they try to change the subject. They were very clear, and just as the happiness expert Sonja Lyubomirsky advises, they were appreciative.

For instance, whenever Rosalind's husband, Sam, hears men "boasting of multiple orgasms with women half their age who they met only a few months ago," he becomes incredibly grateful for a marriage that gives him the opportunity for "loyalty, maturity, and not having to be that guy."

Winnie and Paul, the May-December couple who shared with me the importance to their marriage of showing up, were also very forthcoming about the importance of maintaining their physical relationship. I loved listening to Paul's take on it, since it's rare to hear about the value of sex from an octogenarian. Sitting in their sweet kitchen with a picture window overlooking the yellow brick pathway he had made for Winnie after the success of *Wicked*, Paul revealed what he values most about their sex life now: "The pillow talk. All that relaxed, cuddling, postcoital communication that goes on after the fact is very important. It is the essence of intimacy, and sometimes the only time there is any between a couple. One of the bonuses of being in your eighth decade is you can finally admit how cool it is to cuddle."

Not all couples were able to say it so simply, but postcoital affection is yet another reason to keep having sex. Sure, it's great to get all hot and sweaty together, but don't underestimate the value of those quiet moments in our otherwise fast-paced lives. And please don't stop this short by leaning over to check e-mail. Think afterglow, not iPhone glow.

We've been talking a lot about, and to, couples who are having sex, even if there is concern about how exciting it is. But what about couples who are not having sex? What if one person is putting him- or herself out there for physical intimacy and night after night they are being shut down? If you told me about a situation like this directly, I would respond the same way I would to any comic who was going out to perform every night and hearing crickets. As painful as it may be to hear, you need to find out why whatever you're doing is not working.

I interviewed one couple who told me point-blank that after seven years of marriage, they were no longer having sex. Let's call them Sally and Rex.

"I used to be the aggressor," Sally said, "but I'm not going to do that anymore, and so . . ." She tucked a loose curl behind her ear. Her sad-eyed husband clasped his hands together, and nodded, looking down.

"Yep," Rex said. "It's true."

That's it? I thought. I didn't feel I could dig any deeper on this, since they weren't paying me to analyze them, but I wanted to ask so many questions. It was unbelievable to me that the wife didn't want some answers to questions like, "Why do you never initiate sex with me?" for one. And "What is going on with you that you don't want to have sex anymore? Why do you think it's OK to not be fulfilled in this way?" It reminded me of that well-known Dr. Oz quote, "The penis is a dipstick of the male health." Sex gives us a clue to how healthy an individual—and a relationship—really is.

The combination of Dr. Oz's vaguely prophetic words and the lack of communication in this sex-free couple motivated me to ferret out some specific ways for couples to talk to each other about sex. Here it is plainly stated: If you are not happy in your sex life together, get curious about what is going on, and talk frankly about why either one or both of you are unhappy. It's probably going to take some courage to be honest with yourself and your spouse, but after you get that out in the open, think of the brainstorming you can do to improve the situation, keeping in mind that when brainstorming, there are no wrong answers. As they say, knowledge is power, in this case the power to get each other all hot and a lot less bothered.

STAY CALM AND BE CURIOUS

Just in case there is any doubt in your mind about the effectiveness of curiosity for creating happiness in and outside the bedroom, I stumbled across an article entitled "What Happy People Do Differently" that put curiosity number one on its list.[13] They reported that people who felt curious in their day were also the most satisfied with their life.

Curious people, according to a 2007 study from the University of Colorado, "are willing to venture outside their comfort zone and that ultimately contributes to their happiness." For most of us, talking about sex usually falls outside our comfort zones, so discussing your sex life with your spouse is a great opportunity to flex your curiosity muscle, just like happy people do! If you're a couple that's having sex, fantastic, but you, too, can stay curious. Don't just accept the status quo in the bedroom. Keep asking each other how to make it better.

> For normal people, marriage is certainly not about getting the most laughs from your spouse, but the comedian Steve Skrovan is not normal. "If I walked in on my wife having sex with another man I'd probably say, 'Aha! Was he making you laugh!? Were you laughing at him!? No? OK. Just thought I heard some giggling. Sorry to bother you.'"[14]

If you're not having sex at all, it's time to start working blue, my friends. Please challenge yourselves to ask those very hard questions about what you can do to reconnect in this way. A marriage without sex is like comedy without punch lines: not very much fun. No need to overwhelm yourselves, I'm not suggesting you have to "kill," in the bedroom right off the bat. You don't have to throw each other against walls, hang from chandeliers, or do a striptease using a dishtowel as a boa (although, why not?), but for the sake of your happiness and your spouse's, make staying physically connected a priority.

TIPS FOR SEX IN A HAPPY MARRIAGE

- Have it. Regularly. It doesn't have to be the most amazing sex of your life every time, but make the effort to stay connected physically.

- If you're bored, shake things up. Variety is the spice of sex too, baby. Experiment with great new enhancing products—they may not necessarily make sex better, but they might make you laugh. Which, as we learned, definitely turns the ladies on.

- Avoid considering having an open marriage. And extramarital relations are also not good. Both are setups for confusion, hurt feelings, and the erosion of intimacy with your spouse.

- Laughing together is sexy! And you don't even have to wait for something to strike you as funny. Faking laughter can stimulate real laughter, which can lead to real sex.

- If you're not having sex together, find out why. Be curious and have the courage to ask questions. Don't be too afraid or too "busy" to sit down together and face this issue. You have to make this a priority for a happy marriage. (You may decide to get some professional help. We discuss this in detail in chapter 13, "Get Help to Get Better.")

4

Know Your Audience

I fell in love with the right person, a person I know and who
knows me.

—BILLY CRYSTAL, O magazine, June 2004

In August of 1992 I landed in Guam. A friend of mine had to drop out
of a show sponsored by Miller Lite beer, and she recommended me for
the gig. I would be the opener for Bernie McGrenahan, a successful
road comic, in a show at the Westin Hotel. I met with the producers.
They wanted a woman and needed someone quick. By then I had been
doing stand-up for a few years, and I had three qualities that show producers who are up against the wall love: I was eager, available, and
cheap. I got the job.

I had never been to the South Pacific, although my father had
been stationed in Guam at one point in his army days. In the few days
before I left, I spent some time learning a little about the island and its

people so I could get a sense of what the audience might like. The morning of the flight, I folded my futon back up to couch position, threw my dad's silver army dog tags around my neck, got a ride to LAX, and boarded a very crowded plane to Hawaii. In Maui I stared at wet coconut trees through the glass of the airport atrium and waited for the decidedly smaller plane that would take me to Guam.

When I got to the hotel, which was also where the show would take place, I went looking for Bernie to introduce myself. I found his room, and like many comics I worked with on the road, he answered the door with a towel around his waist.

"Oh! Sorry to bother you, I can come back—"

"It's fine. What's up?" he asked, his hand on his hip drawing attention to his tanned and tattooed physique.

"Oh, I'm Dani. I'm opening for you!" I said.

"Good to know," he said.

"Um. OK," I said awkwardly. "See you later, then."

I left, walking backward, tripping over a copy of the *Pacific Daily News*. Which I immediately picked up. I wanted up-to-date information about the crowd I'd be playing to. The amount of mileage a stand-up comic can get out of one or two specific references to an audience's town, a local politician, or some recent news event is worth the time it takes to learn about it.

The next morning, I went down to the beach to swim, where I ran into Bernie, lying out on the towel he'd previously been wearing. Before running into the bluest water I'd ever seen in person, I pulled out my *Pacific Daily News*. I'd brought a pad with me and was taking notes.

"What are you doing?" Bernie asked, squinting at me.

"Looking for material," I said.

"That's funny. I come to gigs with my jokes already written."

"Me too, just, you know, checking things out . . .," I said, hiding my blushing face behind the paper. Within the first five pages I found out about construction causing crazy traffic on the island and a drug scandal that had just broken involving a local politician, Governor Ada. Found art.

That night I walked onstage and did my standard opening bit

about having a boy's name and how people always ask me if my parents wanted boys. Then I moved on to local fare. "Who here tonight is high?" I asked, adjusting the microphone. The room was quiet except for one or two "Woo-hoo's!"

"Only a few of you. Makes sense, I mean it's a Miller Lite–sponsored show, you're not gonna brag about your *drugs*. Plus, it must be harder to find the good stuff since Ada is controlling it." There were a few "Oh, no, she didn't!" type reactions, and then the room erupted with laughter. I then brought up the traffic problem. "You have insane traffic here! Took me forty minutes just to get here from my hotel room. On the fourth floor." The audience's appreciation that I knew what was going on with them and had the nerve to make fun of it was exactly what I needed to break the ice.

I have used this tool, of learning as much as I can about the audience I am playing to, my entire career. Whether I'm prepping for a law firm roast, a school fundraiser, or an *Afterbirth* show in a new city, I always take the time to find out as many details as I can about the people I will be entertaining. There's a term for this in comedy: "knowing your audience." It might seem obvious, but this rule of comedy is remarkably effective in long-term marriages, too.

There is something about a person's saying "I see you," be it a comic with their audience, or your spouse sitting across from you at dinner, that draws you in and makes you feel valued.

Talking to a well-known comedian recently about her marriage, I was hoping she'd have some great gems for me about how being funny is such an asset to her marriage. She flat out shut me down.

"My husband is very private, so I can't contribute to your research, but thank you so much for asking, and, yes, laughing matters."

Despite my disappointment at not extracting some fantastic inside secret, she couldn't have given me a better answer. Sure, it would have been more titillating to learn that she swings from a rope on a swing in a G-string reciting George Carlin routines in the bedroom, but practically speaking, for a marriage built on mutual respect, this is the perfect response. She knows her husband the way a smart comedian knows their audience, presumably even more so, and acts accordingly.

Which is different than pandering to him. She is not compromising her own integrity by not revealing details of her marriage publicly. She is responding appropriately and respecting her husband.

Knowing your audience also helps you avoid alienating and/or insulting them. It allows you to be sensitive and responsive to the situation, so you set yourself up to be successful. You can do the same thing in marriage, by making an effort to know your husband or wife and taking actions that reflect this knowledge.

Karen and Dan, a couple for fifteen years and married for twelve of them, provide a great example of how knowledge of one another can help them be more loving and happier together.

KAREN AND DAN
Twelve Years of R.E.S.P.E.C.T.

Karen is a stand-up comic and author. Dan is a lawyer. Karen is a smart woman with a deceptively goofy, impulsive manner. Dan, on the other hand, is an intellectual who expresses himself in a thoughtful and commanding way. They are not a couple you would instantly imagine together. Yet when they met at a party fifteen years ago, despite both being ready to leave right before they saw each other, they decided not to let the evening end. "It was three A.M.," Karen told me, "but we went for drinks because I wanted to show I was interested." Karen didn't hear from Dan for several weeks. She had mentioned to him that she would be opening for Lewis Black during Christmas week. Remembering this, Dan appeared at the show one night. With a woman. But she was a friend, not a date. The friend gave Karen the big thumbs up, and she and Dan have been together since. They have two sons, ages eight and ten.

Speaking with Karen about their twelve-year marriage, it was clear how well they know each other and also how they each make a concerted effort to use that knowledge to keep each other happy.

"I need to exercise every day, *every* day, or I get too angry," Karen told me. "I'd have to be on pills and go to therapy. Dan knows this and never gets in the way. He encourages it. He even asks me about it. 'Did you have a good time at the gym?' He has no idea what I do there. He doesn't care, he just knows that I'm happier if I go."

There are also aspects of Dan that Karen knows to respect, like his love of superheroes. "It's not a joke," she told me. "In fact, there is no joking about it. Superheroes, and superhero lore hold a sacred space in our home. For instance, Dan and the boys loved *Man of Steel*, they thought it was the best movie ever. I hated it. I have to bite my tongue whenever they talk about anything superhero-related. I don't make fun of it, even though sometimes I desperately want to, because I don't want to hurt his feelings."

For just this reason, not wanting to hurt your spouse's feelings, "knowing your audience" in a marriage is more complicated, and more important, than it is for a comic. As a comic, you can know your audience and still say whatever you want onstage. You run the risk of alienating them, but so what? It's not like you're getting into bed with them that night, at least not all of them. You're certainly not building a life together. In fact, as a comedian you actually *can't* worry about hurting people's feelings. You won't be free to be your funniest if you're worried about this.

One of the best examples of a comedian knowing his audience and deciding *not* to aim to please is Stephen Colbert's 2006 White House Correspondents Dinner "tribute" speech to George W. Bush. If you've never seen it, I recommend watching this performance online. Ninety percent of the audience in that room had no idea what to make of his sarcastic and scathing assault on the President, nor did they find it funny. Though it was certainly not Colbert at his most relaxed, he persevered, before a very cold crowd, and gained even higher status in the comedy community at large who were watching him from their living rooms. Colbert and his writers knew exactly who President Bush was and what he believed in, but in no way did they concern themselves with whether or not they were hurting his feelings. Colbert hadn't made a vow to love and cherish him, nor did he have any investment in keeping him happy. Although Colbert's performance counts in elite comedy circles as one of the most widely admired, I'm pretty sure Colbert and Bush haven't spent much time together since.

Karen brought another aspect of the sensitivity of humor between couples to the surface when she mentioned not mocking Dan's love of superheroes. A study entitled "Bad Humor, Bad Marriage: Humor Styles in Divorced and Married Couples" is a wonderfully comprehensive analysis of the different types of humor and how they affect couples.[1] The researchers break down humor between couples into four categories, two positive and two negative. They call the styles that are positive for relationships "affiliative," which they define as social and "self-enhancing." Affiliative humor is used positively to cope with stress or to break tension. It "involves the use of joking and friendly humorous banter to facilitate interpersonal bonds." For example, a husband might say, "I know my mother is critical, honey, but on the other hand, she's also selfish!" as the wife dreads yet another demoralizing brunch with her mother-in-law with whom she seems to be stuck in a game of find-the-flaw.

Self-enhancing humor is "characterized by the ability to find amusement in life's stresses." Like, "Hey, honey, it could be worse. Instead of screaming at each other about how we're going to pay the mortgage, property tax, and insurance premium on the same day, we could be screaming good-bye on a plane crashing into the Pacific!"

You can see how the positive uses of humor, those that lend perspective or relieve tension, are helpful to couples. But let's not fail to flesh out the negative and destructive ones for couples, for instructive purposes, of course. Two categories of negative humor were labeled "aggressive," and "self-defeating." They include heavy doses of sarcasm and excessive self-deprecation, which can be very damaging.

The couples therapist Jan Jorden (see chapter 2) confirmed the findings of this study in her practice. "Humor can be bonding or it can be destructive. It can be the most extreme point of contact or it can be completely deflective. Using humorous exaggeration puts things in perspective. But sarcasm is veiled anger. Like baring your teeth. Having someone reflect back to you what you are going through in a humorous way gives you some perspective. When I start seeing a couple for therapy and in the first couple sessions I see that they can use humor appropriately, not in a negative, putdown sort of way, it is a sign that they can externalize the problem. Not saying the problem is in you or it's in me, but the problem is out here and we can solve the problem."

I'm pretty sure Karen never sat down and analyzed the effects of affiliative and aggressive humor on her marriage, and yet she instinctively knows to keep her marriage happy by not mocking *The Justice League*.

By now, if there was ever any doubt, I am certain we can all agree that knowing your spouse goes a long way toward making each other happy. I wish knowledge alone were enough, but alas, many times it isn't. Because knowledge in marriage can be trickier than it sounds. For the long haul, in addition to knowing the ins and outs of who you married, you also have to *accept* what you know about them. Practically speaking, this means not spending precious years trying to change them.

Trying to change your spouse is like doing your retirement account material to a room full of college kids and then blaming them for not getting your jokes and stomping off the stage cursing. Getting angry because you can't accept who people are, and where they are, whether it's an audience or a party of one, your spouse, does not work.

I loved what Pete Cook, a high school economics teacher, said to me about the need for acceptance in marriage. He and Lisa, a writer and the owner of a kids' swim school, have been married for sixteen years. "If you're going to marry somebody, you have to marry them in character," Pete said. "We're in this sixteen years, right? Lisa didn't get that guy over there, she got this guy, me. And I didn't get that woman, I got Lisa. I can't walk around wishing that she would act like someone else for the rest of my life and vice versa. I tell young couples, I understand when you say 'You have to make the marriage work for you,' but if what works for you isn't the other person, then you can have all kinds of prescriptions, but all you're doing is putting Band-Aids over a bad match. You have to really know that person and he or she has to be the right person."

Pete's idea of marrying a person "in character"—which for him means knowing and accepting exactly who the person is—is a great safeguard against being disappointed in your spouse, particularly when he or she is just behaving in a way that is consistent with who they are. This is a level of maturity that, honestly, took me years to understand.

What I didn't mention in my list of qualities that make Tod's character different from mine is that he's also an introvert. For an embarrassingly long time I refused to accept not only that this was true, but also that being "an introvert" was a real thing. Until recently, I responded to this idea in the same expansive way I used to respond to all the people who wanted to lose weight and suddenly announced they were allergic to gluten: *Prove it.*

Yes, that's the kind of generous wife I was, despite evidence that this was Tod's nature. Unlike me, who feels energized by other people, for Tod, being around masses of people for extended periods of time is exhausting. Big events—kids' birthday parties with strangers and forced small talk, sometimes even dinners with more than four people—can drain him of energy. He'd always prefer a quiet dinner to an evening with multiple conversations happening simultaneously around him while people stab each other's plates for tastes of spaghetti Bolognese or Cajun grilled fennel. For years, it would frustrate me nearly to tears when we were invited someplace and I'd joyfully thrust the invitation at him only to see his face drop while he asked, "You really want to go to this?" I would think (but thank God did not say aloud), "What is wrong with you? Here's a chance to ditch the sweatpants, be social, and meet new people."

It took me awhile to appreciate that the thought of making small talk with people he didn't know, after being around people at work all week, made him want to curl up with *The New Yorker* and take a nap.

This reaction is as authentic for him as my daydreaming about eating muffin tops during conversations about the stock market.

Before I understood and accepted Tod's introversion, I didn't think I could ever stop being mad at him for not liking lots of parties. Because that's how deep I am. I mean was. I'm much deeper now. Here's how it happened.

One day our ten-year-old son spent the night with a friend who, according to my son, at around their twenty-second hour together completely stopped talking to him. He was telling me about it while we were unpacking from the sleepover when the phone rang. It was the boy's mother, who wanted to explain to me, in case Gabriel had said anything, that her son reaches a maximum with people and he just shuts down. She didn't want Gabriel's feelings to be hurt. She asked me to put the phone on speaker so she could talk to Gabriel directly.

"It's not that he doesn't like you, Gabriel," she said. "He's just an introvert, and the weekend was a lot for him."

"OK, thanks, no problem," Gabriel said. And they hung up. It was that simple. Her explanation was clear, and it put him at ease that he hadn't done anything wrong. When I asked him if he knew the specific definition of the word "introvert" he said no. Since I had never defined the word myself, this seemed like the ideal time to learn it. I found a definition geared for children.

An introvert is a person who is energized by being alone and whose energy is drained by being around other people. Introverts are more concerned with the inner world of the mind. They enjoy thinking, exploring their thoughts and feelings. They often avoid social situations because being around people drains their energy. This is true even if they have good social skills. After being with people for any length of time, such as at a party, they need time alone to "recharge." When introverts want to be alone, it is not, by itself, a sign of depression. It means that they either need to regain their energy from being around people or that they simply want the time to be with their own thoughts.[2]

"That's cool," said Gabriel. And then he walked away.

"Totally," I said, to the back of his head. But my stomach had tightened and I felt nauseated, that queasy feeling you get when you were certain about something and it turns out you were wrong. And you hurt someone in the process. That simplified definition sounded awfully familiar to me. Forget Gabriel's friend apologizing for shutting him out, I thought, I'm the one who owes someone an apology. For years I thought maybe Tod struggled with some kind of undiagnosed depression and that's why he didn't like being around lots of people. It was so obvious to me that if only he could resolve his "issues" we'd have a happier marriage. As Gabriel ran off to torture his little brother, the error of my ignorant ways stabbed me. Our happiness wasn't about Tod changing, it was about me accepting that I had married an introvert.

After that I stopped pressuring Tod to go to parties with me. And maybe because I'm more relaxed about it, he actually goes to a lot more of the social outings we are invited to these days. And even has a good time.

Neither of us has changed the essence of who we are in this minor evolution. Tod still needs to retreat to recharge and I still go nuts if I'm alone for too many hours. But over time we have come to accept more who the other one is and to modify our behavior as best we can to make the other person happy. Or at least try to.

To be clear, expecting one's partner to modify behavior for a happier marriage does not contradict Pete Cook's point about accepting our spouse's character. Changing behavior, like putting shoes in the closet instead of leaving them on the floor for your loved ones to trip and twist an ankle on, is a reasonable request. What does this mean in reality? It is not hoping that your conservative accountant spouse will sell all your worldly possessions and take a world cruise that ends in a hut in wilds of Madagascar.

If you know your spouse can't concentrate when he is hungry, wait until he is fed to launch into a big, intense talk. If she likes her car clean, make sure your stuff goes with you when you get out of it. If leaving plans to the last minute reminds your spouse of a high-anxiety childhood and causes undue stress, be sensitive about this and make every effort to plan ahead.

What you believe in deeply and how you conduct yourself in the world is what makes up your character, it's who you are and what you must know and accept about your partner. But almost everything else in a respectful and happy marriage can (and ideally should) be a collaboration. This is what I have learned from the experts and people at the marriage game much longer than me.

Ironically, given the premise of this book that the rules and tools used by comedians can help your marriage, comedians are not known for collaboration. This, then, is the exception that proves all the other comedy rules in this book, because although comedians are notoriously bad at it, collaboration is a terrific approach to marriage. In the PBS special *Pioneers of Television*, in the "Standup to Sitcom" episode Jerry Seinfeld calls stand-up the "least collaborative medium there is." He even goes so far as to say, "The reason you become a comedian is, you're not a good collaborator, you're not good with people, you're not good in social situations." This was in contrast to his experience with his sitcom—he calls situation comedy the most collaborative kind of storytelling. Seinfeld has been married to his wife, Jessica, since 1999, so I would venture to say that all those years working collaboratively on his hit television series have paid off in ways even bigger than the fame and fortune the show has brought him.

Collaboration means figuring out compromises so that you can both be happy. To me the oft-used "negotiation" sounds inherently adversarial—fine for boardrooms and legal battles and who gets to eat the last red velvet cupcake, but not for couples' happiness in the long haul.

I heard many stories of collaboration, but Heidi Levitt and Charlie Hess, who have been married twenty-five years, shared one of my favorites. These two seem to drive each other with their aspirations; rather than responding to their goals with fear or resentment, they both come at them with an impressive can-do spirit. According to Heidi, Charlie has mostly been the initiator of the major changes in their life together, "otherwise we'd never have gotten married." But once he brings a new idea to her, they consistently sit down and figure out how to make it happen together.

Before they married, they were living in Manhattan, but Charlie wanted more affordable space, so they moved to Brooklyn. Heidi, born and raised in Montreal, had never been there, "but Charlie thought it was a good move because it was near all the major subway lines. He knew the city would develop along the lines, so we went for it. I was the only white person getting on the subway. I literally had to swat away little boys on the train. 'Lady, give me your money!' they'd yell, and I'd say, 'Get the fuck off of me!' It helped me become much more fearless."

Then Charlie decided he wanted to move again. They discussed Los Angeles and San Francisco. "I had just worked on a film set for the first time," Heidi said. "So I looked into film school at the American Film Institute in Los Angeles, because it was prestigious but less expensive, a conservatory full of working people, and the second year was optional. So if I hated it, or we hated LA, we could leave." At the time, Charlie was working for *Print*, a design magazine. He had taken classes at Parsons School of Design, but realized he needed to learn how to design on a computer. He heard about Art Center College of Design of Pasadena and decided to go there. He talked them into letting him enroll in a one-year program they didn't have.

They put their furniture in storage in Heidi's grandmother's basement and made their way cross-country.

They each got accepted by their respective schools and established their life in Los Angeles, where they have lived for the last twenty-nine years. They still collaborate on everything, from raising their two children to supporting their constantly evolving careers. Today Heidi's work has grown beyond casting film and television to producing independent movies. Charlie continues to work as a graphic designer with his own company, and, no surprise to Heidi, has developed a strong passion for urban planning. Given all they have created together, they are a fine example of two heads being better than one, particularly when they work together and keep saying yes to each other.

The best illustration of the concept of collaboration versus negotiation was offered by a woman who requested that their names not be used. Through raising three children, and a cross-country move early in their marriage, they had many opportunities to confer with each other, but their need to collaborate became particularly intense in the last five years. She described their experience for me.

"My husband was offered a job that required a two-hour commute each way, so we had to sit down and figure out what this meant for the family and if it was going to be worth it. It was with a tech start-up, which would be exciting for him and have a potentially huge payoff for the family, so we went for it. We have found over the years that when we sit across from each other it becomes a negotiation where each person is advocating for his or her needs, but when we take a breath and see ourselves as two people sitting side by side, looking toward our future together, we are able to work together to clarify a vision of what would be best for both of us, and then create the steps to realize this vision."

Collaboration requires knowing all that each of you brings to the other and then approaching your marriage as a masterpiece of thoughts and actions that you are creating together. And you don't have to have the genius of Cezanne or Mozart or Seinfeld to pull it off. You simply have to take the time and effort to know who your spouse is and then use what's there right in front of you to make him or her happy.

TIPS FOR KNOWING YOUR AUDIENCE IN MARRIAGE

- Do your homework! Pay attention to what is going on with your spouse not only in the moment, but also on a larger scale. Stay on top of what he or she cares about.

- Use your knowledge and sense of humor responsibly. Don't use sarcasm and teasing as a weapon. Use humor to make your life together better, by lending perspective and breaking the tension with some silliness once in a while to lighten the mood.

- Unlike knowing a live comedy audience you are going to say good night to an hour after you meet them, knowing your audience in marriage means more than just knowing who your spouse is. You also must genuinely accept their character. Which means you can't keep hoping that with enough nagging he or she will become a different person. I mean, you can, but it will be a painful waste of time. So don't do it.

- Know yourself, too. Become aware of the behavior you engage in that isn't so pleasing to your spouse.

- Forget about "negotiating" for what you need or "deserve," and start collaborating to create a marriage that makes you both happy.

5

Pay Attention to Timing

WHEN YOU SAY (AND DO) WHAT YOU SAY (AND DO) MAKES A HUGE DIFFERENCE

I was ready to get married nine years before my wife was.
It was only later I realized that she was using all those years to
    train me.
And that's why I know she will never leave me.
She doesn't have that kind of time to train somebody else.

—STEVE SKROVAN, married twenty-eight years

In comedy, timing is all. It's a familiar saying, and it is true. Knowing when to hold for laughs, when to drop the punch line, when to deliver the unexpected image in a way that slays your audience is the whole game. The comedy legend Jack Benny built his entire career on pauses. If you are familiar with Stephen Wright's laconic monotone, or the rapid-fire delivery of Chris Rock, or the throw-away approach that

Sarah Silverman uses on some of her most lethal punch lines, you know exactly what I am referring to.

I never thought about timing and marriage when I was single. I didn't think much about marriage in general. The only thought I had about timing in romantic relationships was when to leave.

In my thirties, though, I started to think about timing in relationships beyond just when to exit. I suddenly became exceedingly aware of mortality. Maybe because my father had been diagnosed with terminal cancer. Witnessing his illness and death eight months later, it was as if I understood for the first time that the words "life span" and "life time," these were actual, limited measurements. There is no "life forever." I was thirty-four then, so the idea of baby making was also starting to seep into whatever crevices of my brain weren't preoccupied with morphine doses for him and gossip from the *New York Post's* Page Six, which I read to my father daily. It's not that I was dying to have a child. But I was becoming aware that if I didn't acknowledge the years ticking by, I could die without having one. What if I regretted that? Not having a child when you wanted one felt, even to my non-maternal self, like one of those deep, intractable regrets. It was also hard not to think about witnessing my once-workaholic father, now at the end of his life, desperate to be with his children. Apparently, we were very important to him.

For the first time I found myself interested in the role of timing of my life. Which was surprising, since my livelihood now rested almost completely on my understanding of timing onstage.

My father died, and after a hedonistic year of grief during which I decided, since we're all going to just die anyway, what's the point of doing anything that doesn't feel good, I took an extended trip to Los Angeles. A year and a half later, in 1999 I met Tod at a birthday party in a bar on La Brea in Los Angeles. I was introduced to him by a friend and I still remember the first time I looked in his eyes. They were clear blue and drew me in with a look that said, "I'm a smart-ass, but I'm worth it."

The hostess of the party informed us that we had gone to the same college, but I quickly realized it was not at the same time, since he had graduated a decade after me. I'd had enough of younger men, so I wished him well and went home alone.

A few months later he called me at an office where I was temping and asked me out to dinner. I truly was done with twenty-somethings, but I agreed, thinking he was cute, we'd have a nice dinner, and I'd end the night by assuring him that I would find him someone age appropriate. Which is, in fact, exactly how the night played out.

Several weeks later a card arrived in the mail from him. It had an artsy picture of a typewriter on the front and a beautiful handwritten note tucked inside. It genuinely impressed me. He'd made such an effort, how could I not take him seriously? So I called him, and we started dating and fell in love. Then I broke up with him one night after a brief conversation about David Lynch and the genius of his taking a paper route while making the movie *Eraserhead* so he could have his freedom to create. I became convinced that Tod needed a more bohemian lifestyle than I could handle at my more *mature* stage of life.

Then I missed him terribly. So I begged for him to take me back, plying him with a roast chicken and wearing a knit wrap dress and boots. In our brief time apart, I realized I had to stop throwing men out because they didn't fit some fantasy that didn't exist. A year later we were married.

The reason I shared the basics of our history together is because it is relevant to the subject we are about to tackle, the tool of "timing" in a couple. Our relationship is a classic example of how timing can affect couples. As far as my ovaries were concerned, we had to start trying to have a baby ASAP. But Tod was just getting adjusted to being married. It was very important to him that we meet with a financial planner before trying to conceive. Planning was very much not my style. I hadn't planned one aspect of my life since applying to college. This was the first moment in my adult life that not only did I have to think ahead, but I had to align the timing of what I wanted with what someone else wanted.

To make Tod happy, I agreed to meet with a financial planner before we started trying. To make *me* happy, the financial meeting happened quickly. But it didn't happen easily: these were the days of our first big fights, and they were absolutely about timing. Unlike Tod's, my instinct is usually to act quickly and alone. It's great for being a comedian, but is not very couple-friendly. I'd like to think my impatience with Tod during this time had a lot to do with how dependent I felt on him. Moving at a pace that was comfortable for him made me feel vulnerable to him and feeling vulnerable is never a party for me. In the past, timing my life with another person's wasn't a consideration because I didn't care enough to think about it. I traveled when I wanted, took leases on apartments when I wanted, moved when I wanted, with no regard to another person's life. But now I loved someone, so I had to time my life with his. This made me very uncomfortable. But what I've learned from my own experience now, and couples together decades longer than me and Tod, is that this kind of vulnerability, weighing when you do and say things as a couple, is exactly what makes for the happy marriages I admire.

In this chapter we will look at timing in a couple in two ways, using simple concepts I've hijacked from basic economics: macro-level timing and micro-level timing. Micro-level timing is more about the behavior of one individual in a couple—the everyday business of when to reveal sensitive information, when to stop talking about something and give the subject a rest, when it's OK to joke about a spouse's disappointment, when to give a much-needed hug, or when to give your spouse some space. One woman who had been married for twenty-three years gave some good examples of micro-level timing: "I don't talk about property taxes during the Super Bowl, and Steve doesn't talk to me about where the boys are going to middle school when I've lit my vanilla soy candle and am up to my neck in bubbles."

Macro-level timing refers to the big decisions you make as a couple and can start before you're even married, with decisions about whether to take a vacation together, when to move in together, when to tie the knot, when to buy a house, or, if you're lucky enough to be able to plan it, when to have a child.

Interestingly, a lot of couples I met with talked about the role that luck played for them when it came to macro-level timing deci-sions. Long-term couples citing luck for why something works always makes me bristle a little. Certainly there is some luck involved with getting pregnant, or in finding a great place to live, and unless you grew up together, even in meeting your spouse. If I hadn't gone to that birthday party I would not have met Tod. But I don't buy "luck" as the whole story. Calling it luck overlooks all the active choices we make to steer our lives. After all, Tod had to do some snooping to track me down several months after that party. An initial stroke of luck, being at the same party, after nearly fifteen years has resulted in hundreds of deliberate decisions to keep showing up, staying together, and doing our best to make each other happy. Or at least not killing each other.

For some couples, such as John and David, it could be argued that macro-level timing is a function of fate. Had they fallen in love during a different era in U.S. history, the early years of their relationship would have been very different. Being a gay couple in the eighties, when this was still something you kept to yourself, had a profound effect on them. Perhaps that experience strengthened their total appreciation and enthusiasm for their life together today.

JOHN RIGGI AND DAVID WENDELMAN
All in the Timing

John Riggi is a dark-eyed, compact man with the energy of a coiled spring. In conversation you can almost see the thoughts darting through his brain behind his eyes. He is also very funny and surpris-ingly emotional. He began his career as a stand-up comic. He has since gone on to be a director as well as a writer for a number of shows, in-cluding *The Comeback* and *30 Rock*, for which he won an Emmy. His husband, David, is a filmmaker with vivid blue eyes, and a slower, more contemplative presence. He is also delightfully guileless. The two have been together for twenty-eight years.

They met in 1986. John was working on the road as a comic. He was in Kansas City visiting a man he had been dating secretly—no one knew that he was gay. They went out with a few of this guy's friends. One of them turned to John and said, "So, Ryan, what do you do?" John's date quickly jumped in with "Oh, this isn't Ryan." John suddenly realized that they were not in an exclusive relationship. This was when awareness of AIDS was first breaking through, and, as John put it, "I just didn't know anything and it kind of freaked me out."

He decided to make a fast exit, which resulted in a life-changing chance encounter with David. John said, "This guy I was dating had a night job at a liquor store, and as soon as he left for it, I showered and went out to a bar. I was just about to leave when David walked in."

Hearing this, David laughed. "He talks about it like it was this casual thing. This was Kansas City in 1986, it was a gay bar. It was a brick building and the windows were smoked over. You only knew about it if you knew about it."

John nodded in agreement, but was eager to get on with the story. "We danced and it was very country. I looked at his eyes and I said, 'You have electric eyes, electric blue eyes.' Then we spent the night together. The next day I went back to 'liquor store guy' at five A.M. and started packing my things."

The timing of John walking into that bar in Kansas City on that night and meeting David at that moment now seems divinely inspired. David was in his first year of coming out. He had gone to Kansas City to escape from his family and from suburbia, and had just been jilted by his lover. Despite the sense that their meeting was fated, however, their future would not prove to be all hearts and flowers. David decided to move in with John, and John introduced David as his lover to many of his friends, thus coming out to them. The fact that John was gay seemed to his friends to come out of nowhere. Many of them were not happy.

"I had friends who weren't speaking to me because I had come out that way and they felt betrayed," John said. "They were freaked out that I was gay and hadn't told them first."

"So they figured it must have been me that made him gay," David said, taking a bite of some coffee cake John had baked.

"Yeah. During that time, he kind of got blamed, absolutely," John said.

"Yep," David said.

"Without a doubt. I caught it from him," John said, and they both smiled wicked smiles.

Although they can laugh about it now, for John the timing of meeting David was way off. He was not out and still felt a lot of shame about being gay. David didn't have any shame at all, and it was hard to deal with what they both call John's baggage. They reflected on their early years.

"What I should have done, although I'm glad I didn't ultimately because we probably wouldn't be together," John said, "is, I should have said to him, 'I'm not ready to do this. It isn't fair to you and it isn't really fair to me.'"

"And that you need to go to Fire Island," David interrupted.

"Yes! And I need to go to Fire Island and have sex with nine thousand dudes and really get this. I wasn't ready to be with somebody. I can't tell you how many times we would go out and I would coach him on what he should and should not discuss with any given group of people."

"Especially with friends and his family."

"I would say to him, 'Don't touch me,'" said John.

"I was just a roommate," David recalled.

John told me later that he would snap at the love of his life: "'Don't talk about this, don't do this thing, and don't do that thing.' The bottom line was that I had jumped into a relationship when I was not one hundred percent ready, not emotionally ready. The fact that he stayed is mind-boggling. Because if it had been reversed and he had done that to me, I would have been like, 'Adios, buddy, I'm outta here.'"

"I stayed because I loved him," David said.

Within a few years John became more comfortable being out, and today, hiding his early love for David is one of his few regrets. Sitting in their dining room in LA in August 2012, we couldn't help marveling at how much had changed in the quarter century they'd been together. Just one year later, in August 2013, gay marriage was made legal in California when Proposition 8 was overturned.

Nowhere is the change in society more evident than in John's profession as an actor-writer for television, where the stigma of being gay has all but disappeared. "When we were coming up," he explained, "especially for me, since I was a comedian, you did not tell anyone. Stand-up was such a boys' club and it could really affect your career. They were so touchy about things and weirded out by that kind of stuff you couldn't come out. If you would've gone to [legends of Boston Comedy such as] Lenny Clarke, or Don Gavin, or Kenny Rogerson, and said, 'Hey, guys, I'm gay,' your life would have been ruined, it just would have imploded."

Because of the early history of their relationship, today John and David take every opportunity to enjoy life together. They have many friends, both gay and straight, whom they go out with, John talks openly about his life with David when he does stand-up, and they have even become collaborators on the documentary work that David does. They are true partners.

A WELL-TIMED PUNCH LINE

John and David told me of one romantic trip they took together not so long ago that was a humbling reminder that despite the amazing strides in gay rights, they still have to keep up their guard. It's also an illustration of the gift of a well-timed punch line.

John was looking forward to having a quintessential Southern California weekend with David and planned the entire event. They would stay at the acclaimed Surf and Sand Hotel in Laguna Beach, shop at kitschy stores, eat fresh seafood, and take long, romantic walks on the beach. David was not quite so gung-ho. He was concerned they wouldn't feel comfortable as a gay couple in the upscale suburban town. "But I convinced him to go," said John. "Sure enough, we were walking home after dinner the first night, arm in arm, and a pickup truck with kids drove by and one of them yelled out, 'Faggots!'"

David was beside himself with rage. "See?" he fumed.

They walked in silence for a good five minutes until John took a breath and said, "Well . . . they're not wrong."

David couldn't help but laugh. They walked back to their hotel and finished out a lovely weekend, despite their brush with gay bashing. John's tagline at the end of a genuinely upsetting experience illustrates the affiliative humor we learned about in chapter 4. This is a perfect illustration of the huge benefits of being able to find the humor in a situation and say something at just the right moment to relieve a tense situation.

The timing of being a gay couple before it was acceptable is a very specific macro-level timing issue. But many other timing issues can affect couples, involving business opportunities, unexpected pregnancies, or even the rise and fall of the economy, to name just a few. What about when a job offer comes in that is too good to turn down, but taking it means relocating to a new city where you know no one right after you have had a baby? That's what happened to the ad executive David Gassman and his wife, the writer Johanna Stein—and it turned out to be great for the whole family.

DAVID AND JOHANNA
Opportunity Knocked

David Gassman and Johanna Stein have been married for twelve years. They met fifteen years ago at a dinner party in LA, where both lived.

Johanna gave him her number, which to her surprise, David didn't use right away. "I was out of town," he said, a little defensively, when asked why. David, a creative director in advertising, is not a man of many words. He has self-diagnosed ADD, but when he stays in one place long enough and does talk, what he says is succinct and often wry. David's dry temperament is just the right yin to Johanna's warm, expressive yang.

In 2008, a few years after he and Johanna had married and become the parents of a baby girl, David was offered a job in Chicago. Deliberating whether to take this job and relocate from California was one of the macro-level-type decisions they made together. At the time, both of them were unemployed, which was not a comforting thought as they shopped the aisles of big box stores for cheap diapers.

"Then this interesting job came up," Johanna said, "and we were like, OK, let's go. Best thing, we love it and find a new life there. Or we don't and we come back." They sold their house, packed up, and made the move.

"And then the world collapsed," David said, suddenly animated. "The recession hit, the whole world collapsed. And yet I had a job."

The timing of David's job offer, prompting them to sell their house just before the housing market crashed, could not have been better. And even though he didn't love the work, his company offered him the chance to get his MBA, which he did. As for Johanna, being isolated from friends and family gave her the quiet she needed to sit down and start writing, something she had always wanted to focus on. With no one close by to share her early parenting stories with, she had a lot to write about. These stories were the material that eventually became her first book, *How Not to Calm a Child on a Plane: And Other Lessons in Parenting from a Highly Questionable Source.*[1]

Remembering that time, Johanna reflected on the impact of the many changes that hit them so quickly. "What could have been a horribly precarious situation became a really great time in our marriage. You know how when you get married, that's a project, then you have a baby and that's a project, and then the move was so huge, it was such a great project to do together. It solidified us . . . into a family."

When the job in Chicago ended, the three of them hightailed it back to Los Angeles. David, now with an MBA, Johanna with a new career as a chronicler of family life, and their daughter with memories of playing in real snow. All of them closer than ever as a family.

Now what about the less dramatic stuff, the little picture, or micro-level timing? This timing happens daily and comes into play for everything from coordinating the scheduling of our days, to when we talk to each other about matters of the heart, to helping each other laugh with a well-timed joke like Mr. Riggi's when we need it. We tend to have a lot more control over this kind of timing.

MICRO-LEVEL TIMING: ASK A SIMPLE QUESTION

David Basche and Alysia Reiner, a couple that's been together twenty-two years (and has a great story in the upcoming chapter on surprise), learned early on to respect timing in their communication. During wedding prep, before either one asked the other about monogramming, cutlery, buttercream, or any other urgent issue, they first had to ask, "Is this a good time to talk about this?" The other person could respond yes or no. To avoid stalling on a topic indefinitely, if the answer was no, the naysayer had to offer a time that would be good.

This is a great, simple way to avoid an intense conversation that one person might not have the energy for, if you can remember to do it! By taking this extra step to ask your spouse before you launch into a topic that has some weight, you also have the added bonus of ensuring that when you do sit down to address it, you will have your spouse's undivided attention. It's also a great tool for avoiding tackling a subject before both of you feels ready to talk about it.

TIMING IN THE HOUSE

I woke up thinking about timing the morning after my fiftieth birth-day. Not just because I'd hit the half-century mark and realized no one would ever call me "young lady" again, but because I'd gone to bed angry with Tod the night before.

No magic sleeping dust had cleared the air in the morning, so after one-word hellos and no kiss good-bye before leaving each other for the day, I sat down to figure out how the train went off the happy track. The previous evening we'd had a celebratory birthday dinner with friends, and even though some of the toasts sounded like eulogies, it was a lovely evening. But still I couldn't shake my dark mood. It wasn't about wrinkles or sagging. My upset around growing older had to do with facing the fact that I had a finite number of years left on earth. I finally had this sweet life with beautiful kids and a husband I loved, and something about the number fifty made me see how little time I had left with them. Being a late bloomer was feeling like it came with a high price tag.

It was in this melancholy state that I opened my computer when we arrived home and saw a picture of me on Facebook taken at the dinner we had just left in which I looked exactly like my eighty-nine-year-old aunt Thelma. I shut the computer down and tried to erase that image with some light conversation with Tod about a web series I'd shot that had launched. "It's pretty good," I said, putting on my T-shirt-slash-lingerie. "Maybe someone will see it and ask, 'Hey! Who's that girl? She's funny!'"

"You mean 'woman,' right?" Tod said, his face in his phone. Then he looked up. "'Cause I don't think anyone would call you a girl any-more."

"Right," I said, turning toward the wall.

"What? I mean because you're a *woman*," he said.

I buried my sad, humorless, fifty-year-old face in my pillow.

"Yep. That's true. Good night."

"What? What did I say?" Tod asked.

"Nothing. I'm tired. Good night." I closed my eyes and prayed for sleep to knock me unconscious.

What does this have to do with timing? On another day, or maybe postcoitally, or over a bagel and espresso, Tod's minuscule word clarification probably would have rolled off my middle-aged back. I might even have burst into Helen Reddy's "I Am Woman," laughing. But not that night. That night in that moment, I just couldn't take it.

A day or so later, when I pulled my self-pitying head out of my ass, we talked about it. Tod's bad timing wasn't intentional. He didn't think he was being insulting. His mother started the First Women's Bank of California, not the First Girls' Bank. He doesn't know why any grown woman would want to be called a girl. As far as my overreaction to turning fifty, he's one of those "consider the alternative" people when it comes to aging. Doesn't get upset about it at all. Later that day, he e-mailed me a few links to long-term healthcare plans, "because I think we both know where this is all headed," he wrote with a winking emoticon. He may not have understood the sting of his "woman" comment at the time, but the joke told me he'd heard me. It also made me laugh.

THREE QUESTIONS BEFORE OPENING YOUR MOUTH

Our whole exchange reminded me of a technique someone suggested I use in conversation with my mother, who frequently frustrates me. Before you begin to speak you ask yourself three questions:

1. Does this need to be said?
2. Does this need to be said now?
3. Does this need to be said by me?

These are extremely helpful questions to ask yourself before sharing any opinion you are burning to express. "Does this need to be said *now?*" speaks directly to the question of timing. "Does this need to be said *by me?*" is also invaluable for the health and well-being of a marriage. Because although you definitely look to your spouse, and only your spouse, for certain insights—such as "Don't wear that shirt with a frayed collar to an interview, honey," or "Maybe balancing a checkbook would help, instead of just writing checks and hoping for the best!" or "That friend does not have your best interest at heart"—there's a fair amount of commentary, particularly of the negative sort, that we don't have to say and that if left unsaid might spare the feelings of the person we care most about in the world. Pausing to ask yourself these three questions before you speak gives you time to confirm that what you are about to say brings added value to the discussion and also to formulate your thoughts in a way that will be most effectively heard.

If I bring up a topic at the wrong time because of my own inner fears and anxieties, I will blow it every time. And I've done that a million times with Paul. But I'm in my late fifties and now I have finally learned, maybe I should not bring this up now, it's twelve midnight. We'll talk about this another time.

—WINNIE, married twenty-eight years

As a performer you figure out the concept of "holding for laughs" pretty quickly. This means waiting and letting the audience settle down before you move on to the next joke. If you don't pause, and you go into the setup for the next joke when they're still laughing at the last one, you run the risk that half the audience misses the setup and your next punch line does not land.

Although timing in the context of marriage isn't about getting the maximum number of laughs from your spouse, the concept of "holding for laughs" is highly applicable to marriage, because sometimes as a mate you have to hold for the other person. It might be waiting to make sure your mate understands a point before you move on to the next one, or holding on an action you want to take, such as my meeting with the financial planner before getting knocked up. In happy marriages, people strive to be in sync.

Whether they're tackling big-picture issues or managing their daily lives, people in it for the long haul know how much timing all aspects of their lives together matters.

TIPS FOR TIMING

- Timing is as important for a couple offstage as it is for comics onstage. Prepare for big-picture, "macro-level" timing issues, like moving, having a baby, and making long-term work commitments, to name a few, by talking through them together.

- Ask yourself those three important questions before expressing an opinion on a sensitive issue to your spouse: Does it need to be said? Does it need to be said now? Does it need to be said by me?

- Before broaching an intense topic, try asking, "Is this a good time to talk about this?" If the answer is no, make sure you set a definite time to follow up.

- Do your best to check in with your spouse after a loss or disappointment so you can use humor positively to help your spouse gain a different perspective on it. Or maybe send them a cat video.

6

Keep Surprising Them

} DOING THE UNEXPECTED: {
} ESSENTIAL FOR COMEDY, {
} ALSO GREAT FOR MARRIAGE {

Relationships: easy to get in to, hard to maintain. Why are they so hard to maintain? 'Cause people stop talkin' . . . Why? 'Cause at a certain point you have heard everything this person has to say and it makes you sick to your stomach. You know what they gonna say before it even comes out they mouth and you just wanna stab them in the neck with a pencil . . . They're like, "Remember that time?" "Yeah I remember that time . . . stop tellin' me the same shit over and over! Why don't you go out and get kidnapped and have some new shit happen to you?

—CHRIS ROCK, *Bigger and Blacker,* 1999

In 1915, Charlie Chaplin opened in a movie called *By the Sea.* In the first minute, he walks down the street eating a banana. He finishes it, throws the peel on the pavement. Within three seconds he slips on it.

I wasn't in the theater to hear the laughter when *By the Sea* first screened, but watching it in my office, even seeing the banana in his hand and knowing it was a setup, it still surprised me when he actually fell. Right on cue, I laughed.

Surfing the web nearly a hundred years later, I saw that one of my favorite comedians, Maria Bamford, has a new comedy special titled *The Maria Bamford Comedy Special.* The picture accompanying the link is of her standing in front of a microphone, a brick wall behind her, pretty standard for a comedian. Or so I thought until I bought it and started watching *Maria Bamford: The Special Special Special!*, a comedy performance shot in the apartment in Eagle Rock, California, that she shared with her pug. The audience is not the usual faceless throng of fans, but a party of two, her parents. Even before she starts telling jokes, with the camera following her from her bathroom, through a cramped hallway, to the microphone, where a lone pianist tinkles on a keyboard, I'm already laughing. But the surprises don't stop there: at every turn Ms. Bamford delivers the unexpected, including a brilliant description of her families' gift for something she calls "joy whack-a-mole," which, on this show, she delivers directly to her parents. I expected to laugh, but not this hard.

A month later I was sitting at the Wiltern Theatre in Los Angeles. A large, imposing African American comic with a huge Afro strode across the stage with purpose. Nothing about Reggie Watts says delicate or sentimental. And yet, after a few brief introductory comments, he launched into a highly sentimental story about a tiny lost cat trying to find its way back to "Ameowica." I can't tell you the story of the tiny cat's travels for two reasons. One, I don't think there were any plot points, and two, if there were, I couldn't hear them. The entire audience and I were laughing too hard from the surprise of this huge, bearded man with a naturally basso profundo voice, modulating it into falsetto, and waxing prophetically about a tiny cat's journey to "Ameowica."

Another time I was in Boston with an evening to kill, so I wandered into a place called, what else, Giggles. It was a weeknight, so no headliners were on the bill, but there was an audience, and they were happy. A pretty young girl wearing a short pleated skirt and pale blue cardigan sweater walked onstage. She gazed out at the audience and batted her big brown eyes. She appeared to have something to say, that she was working up the courage to get out. Finally she looked down and raised her right hand,

"Have any of you ever been high-fived after giving head?"

Everyone erupted into peals of laughter. Everyone but me. After my twenty years in comedy, it no longer surprises me when a pretty young woman talks about blow jobs in a comedy club. But for reasons beyond my ken, audiences still find a girl talking dirty in a comedy club surprising, and so it makes them laugh.

What do these four scenarios have in common? Paul Dooley, the elder statesman of comedy who loves pillow talk, commented, "The element of surprise. That's practically the definition of comedy!"

I knew about the importance of surprise for making people laugh before I heard Paul say this, but what I didn't know before I started doing this research is how important the element of surprise also happens to be for a happy long-term marriage. Obviously, one big concern for being with the same person year after year after year is that you will grow bored with each other. As with sex, one surefire way to head off boredom at the pass is to make an effort to surprise each other once in a while. Just like a comic might do something unexpected when he feels he's losing his audience—whether it's some unplanned crowd work, taking off his shirt, or pulling out a phone to take pictures of them (all of which I have seen work to good effect for winning an audience back)—you can and should also do the unexpected in your marriage to wake each other up now and then.

And it doesn't necessarily have to be done by talking dirty, either, although I wouldn't discourage this if it works for you. There are all kinds of ways to surprise and be surprised. The happiness guru Sonja Lyubomirsky (see chapter 3) has more to say about this:

> Variety goes hand in hand with another tip: surprise. With time, partners tend to get to know each other all too well, and they can fall into routines that become stultifying. Shake it

up. Try new activities, new places, and new friends. Learn new skills together.[1]

Just like any comedian worth the price of admission, you don't want to let yourself and your marriage fall into a rut. You don't have to jump out of a plane—just challenge yourselves a little. Or, as the comedians say, write some new material.

THE UNPLANNED SURPRISE

When Tod and I went to New York City some years ago, I wasn't thinking about the importance of surprise for couples, I just knew we'd have free babysitting for New Year's Eve. Our youngest son was six months old, and my mother, always eager to be with her grandson, lured us there with the promise of a mini-vacation. Come December 31, Tod and I had no idea what to do with our night out. I had a postpartum body so I wasn't excited about a fancy meal, and Tod enjoys theater even less than I like watching golf, which is to say, not at all, so Broadway was out. I opened up a copy of the *New York Press* and saw an announcement for the Emerald Nuts Midnight Run in Central Park.

"Hey," I yelled out to Tod, "we could do the midnight run in Central Park!"

"I didn't know you liked running," Tod answered, "particularly with me." It's true, I hadn't enjoyed our previous jaunts, where he felt compelled to yell "Stride out! Stride out!" in response to my short-legged, pigeon-toed style.

"But it's Central Park. It's a New York tradition! It'll be fun."

At around 9 P.M. we started to prepare ourselves for our winter adventure of running in twenty-degree cold. We smeared Carmex on our lips to keep them from chapping, and dressed ourselves in layers of sporty silk and wool separates—in my case, my father's old silk underwear and high school ski pants. Tod had prepared himself for New York with his cold-weather gear from college. Stuffed into clothes from our youth and feeling like a couple of Michelin-tire men, we left the apartment ready for a baby-free good time.

And it would have been, if my dormant competitive nature hadn't burst forth, transforming me into a competitive freak, annoyed by the runners who had the audacity to party and celebrate the New Year instead of seriously running.

"Don't they know this is a race?" I spat at Tod, my inner Jackie Joyner hijacking my New Year's Eve partier, as I wove in and out of the revelers and he tried to keep up with my determined hippo-in-sneakers trot.

I'm pretty sure I finished 4,076th, no surprise there—what was unexpected was Tod's reaction. "I had no idea you'd be like that in a road race," he said, slightly mystified. Although I didn't know this then, I understand now that the surprise of seeing his wife suddenly become a competitive runner, albeit without much natural ability, allowed him to see me in a slightly different light. Maybe that twinkle in his eyes was hope. Like, "I didn't know that about you. Interesting. Maybe there's other stuff I don't know about." Many couples echoed this idea of discovery and mystery and never wanting to feel like, "Yeah, I know everything about you. My work here is done."

I have not run competitively since, but last December when our boys were asking about New Year's Eve plans, Tod smiled and leaned in like he was telling them a secret. "One year your mother and I did this race in New York City, a midnight run in Central Park. You should have seen her out there, leaping past people, like a gazelle."

"Yep," I said. "Only human and a little heavier."

When I first mentioned the importance of surprising each other to the couples I interviewed, almost all of them asked, "You mean, like surprise parties?" Which actually wasn't something that any of the articles I read offered up as a good solution for staving off boredom, with good reason, as you will see from the experiences of two long-term couples.

LEW AND LIZ

Thirty-Three Years of Marriage, One Surprise Party

The writer-producer Lew Schneider and his wife, Liz, have been together since she was a freshman and Lew a sophomore. He's a feisty five foot eight and Liz, at over six feet tall, is, as my father would have said, a tall drink of water. It's clear from the way Lew looks at Liz that he cherishes every inch of her. After creating a home in Pacific Palisades— a surprise in itself, since neither one ever thought they'd end up in California—and raising three sons, Lew put together an unexpected celebration for Liz's birthday. Things did not go as Lew planned. Liz wasn't afraid to cut to the chase: "He threw me a terrible, horrible, surprise party for my fiftieth."

"Not entirely my fault." Lew defended himself. "A friend in our circle had killed himself the night before." I could see where that might have affected the mood. Lew explained. "The day of the surprise party Liz and I were at a school function, and I was using that as a way to distract her while the guests assembled at our house. But then, during this event, we heard about this friend's suicide the day before. Meanwhile, the cake order was screwed up and the food guy flaked, so while we were dealing with this tragic news, I was trying to manage the party snafus via cell and text with my friend. I was upset about the cake and tacos and the suicide, but I only told Liz about the suicide, which was my excuse to go off and deal with the cake and the tacos. I got the cake fixed, but the taco guy never showed. When we finally got to the surprise birthday party at our house I was walking around offering Advil and toothpaste as snacks. Our dear friends finally ran out to Baja Fresh for takeout."

"I actually *will* divorce him if he ever throws me another one," Liz said.

Surprise parties are tricky because there are always a lot of variables. And not everyone likes them, or likes them after a certain age, as Liz made clear: "No fifty-year-old woman wants a surprise party. A woman this age needs time if she is going to be presenting herself to people, she needs some advance notice, she needs to be able to do a little spackling." But there was a silver lining in the almost taco-less cloud when Liz added one more important detail to the story: "I had already had a nice surprise: Lew flew in some old friends for my birthday weekend and they met me on the hiking trail. It was great and, really, enough of a surprise!"

Fabulous point, Liz! Often the less dramatic surprises go over best, as I learned in even more painful detail from another couple. For our purposes, what's as important about this story as the plot points, is that they were laughing about it when they told it to me. Bringing together people in a new location to unexpectedly celebrate your spouse without a high-pressure "Surprise!" moment seemed like a nice, low-impact way to keep things interesting. I couldn't imagine how that could backfire. Until I heard this story from that fun-loving pair of actors, David Alan Basche (*The Exes*) and Alysia Reiner (*Orange Is the New Black*; *How to Get Away with Murder*).

DAVID AND ALYSIA

Surprise Party of Three

I met with David and Alysia in Los Angeles in an apartment they rented so the family, including their young daughter, could be together while he shot the TV show *The Exes*. I hadn't seen them since our first meeting, in New York, and being in their company reminded me again that they are way more attractive than real people should be. What makes them even more compelling, though, is how willing they are to laugh at themselves and each other. More than willing, they're eager. "We have the best surprise story ever, can I tell it?" Alysia asked David, giddy with excitement.

"Sure. Tell whatever you want. I have nothing to hide."

So she did. "It was David's thirtieth birthday. The surprise was that we were going to have drinks at the Hudson Hotel in New York City, one of our favorite places, and all of our friends would just show up and it would be, like, 'Oh, my god, what are you doing here?' and then at the end of the night, I got us a hotel room. Also, I'd got my first 'Brazilian wax.' So after cocktails, I'd be upstairs waiting in a hotel room with 'the Brazilian.' I had to figure out how to get David upstairs. The surprise had two levels, first the friends, then me. But how to get David upstairs? I decided I would have my friend Porva, an actress, tell David she had an audition upstairs in a suite, not that unusual in New York, and that she would just feel more comfortable if he came upstairs with her. So she does, and as he's going up with her in the elevator—"

David couldn't contain himself. "Can I take over?" he asked.

Alysia ceded the floor to him.

"I've caught on now when all the friends showed up that Alysia is trying to surprise me," he said. "I got it, I got the surprise. So when Porva tells me about her audition and even though that's plausible I think it's part of my surprise, that it's some kind of a mislead. What I know is, my wife has disappeared from the restaurant saying 'I'll be right back.' I assume she's gone up to a hotel room, I figured out the surprise. But now there is one of our very attractive friends coming up to the hotel room with me, so naturally in the elevator I assume that my surprise is a threesome."

David has a way of speaking in an understated tone, making me wonder for a second if I'd heard him right. And if I had, holy moly, he just confessed to hoping for a three-way with his wife sitting across from him. I froze for a second, not knowing how to react. Until Alysia burst into gales of laughter.

David continued. "However, I was incorrect."

Alysia cut in. "Yes. So when he opens the door to the hotel room he's like 'Porva, aren't you coming in?'"

"She says, 'I don't think so!' and pushes me in the room and locks the door."

"I'm spread-eagle on the bed with my Brazilian," Alysia says, wide-eyed.

"Which, believe me, was no disappointment," David stated matter of factly.

"Then of course he has to tell me what he was thinking, and I just start sobbing because I went through all the pain of that fucking Brazilian, and then, it wasn't enough because, you know, I wasn't a 'three-way,'" Alysia said.

"No, but it was a great night," David said, apparently still backpedaling years later. "Awesome. One of the best."

He touched Alysia's bare knee. There was an awkward moment of silence while I took it all in, still not sure if it was OK for me to laugh. But within seconds they were laughing again.

"Can you believe that? Isn't that amazing?" Alysia asked.

"Amazing," I said, a bit distracted, wondering what I would do if Tod walked into a room where I was laid out on a bed, still throbbing from torture-by-hot-wax, and he started looking around for a third player. It's hard for me to imagine on almost every level. Which made hearing this story from a happily married couple that much more incredible.

These are just two of hundreds of stories I heard from couples where one of them behaved in some devastatingly embarrassing or humiliating way and yet, where I would have given in to my impulse to flee, they were able to sit with their spouse on a couch and recall the whole debacle together and laugh about it. How could figuring out ways to laugh together at our human frailties not be the secret to making a marriage last?

Once we moved beyond discussing surprise parties, couples shared other surprises with me, some intentional and some not, which had kept their lives interesting. One couple had a surprise pregnancy ten years after their daughter was born, which shook up their household. One husband surprised his wife by renting out their house for two years, relocating them to the beach to avoid the empty nest syndrome after the youngest child left for college. Although resistant at first, his wife now sees those years as some of the happiest and rejuvenating of the forty they've been together.

Another husband had a spiritual awakening and became a Methodist pastor fourteen years into his marriage, a real surprise, since he and his wife had had a Buddhist wedding. Another announced on his fortieth birthday that he was done with drinking alcohol and watching television. One woman I know surprised her husband fifteen years into their marriage, after their son was diagnosed with autism, by choosing to leave behind a life in the performing arts to get a master's in clinical psychology with a focus on children on the autism spectrum.

Although not always smooth transitions at first, these life-altering and unanticipated changes are actually good for marriage for a number of reasons. One, we learn something new about our spouse. Two, we can be doubly surprised by our own reaction to their change. The second surprise is probably more enlightening, since it shows us what we are capable of accepting, and even embracing, because of our love for another person.

Here is where we begin to see the fork in the road between using the tools of comedy as a comic and using them in your marriage. Because unlike the audience-comedian dynamic, where you're surprised, you laugh, you have a few drinks and go home, the surprises we experience in our marriages can be quite a bit more profound. When a comic surprises you, it does not usually involve them opening up their heart, making themselves vulnerable, and hoping the audience will respond with compassion.

Granted, there are exceptions. Tig Notaro made herself vulnerable to her audience to great effect when she revealed her cancer diagnosis onstage in Los Angeles in August of 2012. Vulnerability is Maria Bamford's greatest asset.

But for the most part, surprises in comedy make the audience laugh but do not change anyone's life. Surprises in life as a couple, however, absolutely can. Nobody goes to a club hoping to hear a compassionate comedian, but because of the curveballs life throws, everyone at some point hopes they have married a compassionate person. Being able to enjoy, or at least endure, surprises as a couple, the intended ones and the unintended ones of human error that challenge our compassion, is a hallmark of marriages that last, where couples find their way to being able to laugh about the surprises together.

All this talk of character breakthroughs and deepening compassion is great, but what happened to using the element of surprise in marriage the way comedians do, to make each other laugh? When I sat down with Patricia Heaton, the multiple Emmy Award–winning actress best known for playing Debra Barone on the CBS sitcom *Everybody Loves Raymond,* and her husband, David Hunt, they shared some great stories with me about their twenty-three-year marriage.

PATRICIA HEATON AND DAVID HUNT
Art Imitating Life

Patricia Heaton is a petite, feisty brunette who is unapologetic about her love of Jesus, family, and comedy. She's also not afraid to express a conservative point of view in notoriously liberal Hollywood, which certainly takes moxie. Politics aside for the moment, the woman is fiercely committed to marriage and to making people laugh, which is the main reason I wanted to meet with her and her husband of twenty-three years, David Hunt. Dave is a blond, blue-eyed, English-born, Julliard-trained actor, director, and producer with a lot of energy. He loves to engage in passionate, detailed conversations about everything, from the perils of raising four boys in Los Angeles to the recent wins and losses of his favorite soccer team. In fact, when I met with them, there was a game playing silently on the TV behind us.

"Is that going to stay on?" Patty asked, walking into the room wearing a sweatshirt, stretch pants, and a headband. If I hadn't known she was a TV star, she could have been mistaken for a very fit mom from Cleveland, which is where she's from.

"The sound is off, it's recording. I'm not going to watch it, don't worry." David said.

"Uh-huh," she said, her expression just shy of an eye roll. Then she did a quick assessment of the room and curled up on the couch, strategically placing herself so that David would have to have his back to the set in order to be in the conversation. There was her sixth sense in play. No need to have a fight over something silly after twenty-three years—just make a minor adjustment.

Heaton has spent the majority of her adult life working in situation comedies, most of them about family life. "Which has been surreal at times," she told me. "There were times when we'd do a read-through of the script for that week, and I'd think, Did they put cameras in our house? All of us, the actors, writers, most of the directors, we were all living exactly what we doing on the show."

Even before David married a woman whose livelihood would be making people laugh, he knew he would have to be with a woman with a sense of humor. Pushing up his shirtsleeves like the coach he's been to each of his athletic sons over the last seventeen years, he told me, "The gel, the connective tissue, the connective fluid in friendship, which is what a marriage has to be first and foremost, is humor. Life will smack you in the face at every opportunity, and if you can't make light of it and ride the wave of it, the crashing wave, you are going to come unstuck. If I don't have humor to rescue me I know I will go into narcissism, self-involvement, and depression."

Fortunately, David married the right woman, as this story they told me shows. It's a great example of Heaton using what she learned about comedy and marriage, specifically the element of surprise, to take what could have been an ugly moment and, by doing the unexpected, make it an exchange she and David could laugh about. I'm going to let you be a fly on the wall to this exchange between these two natural storytellers.

Patty: Dave was watching the *Victoria's Secret Christmas Show* because what better way to celebrate the entrance of the savior of the world than a woman in a Diamante-encrusted push-up bra?
David: It was merely a channel surfing situation—
Patty: And he paused it for quite a long time.
David: I just lingered.
Patty: Uh-huh. I walked from the closet, past the TV, he's on the bed and I ask, "What are you watching this for?" and he says, "I just wanted to see what this is about," and of course I'm thinking, "I think we know what it's about." I go in to the bathroom and I'm getting a little peeved. I was getting ready to get in the shower so I had no clothes on, had my hair in a towel, so I just walked naked back through the room like one of the models like this (*she thrusts her hips forward and does a supermodel strut across the room*) past Dave and walked into the closet. And we just laughed about it.

Dave: She didn't stay in the closet.

Patty: I think he switched it a few minutes later. I don't remember, but I had to do that for myself. Because I had a choice, I could get really like, "Screw you, why didn't you marry one of them if you blah blah blah, that's what you like." Or I could try to make a joke out of it and know that humor is sexier than that.

Exactly, Ms. Heaton! Nothing is sexier than making someone laugh!

The element of surprise has so many fabulous uses for the health and happiness of long-term marriage. And it doesn't have to be about throwing a party, whisking someone off in a jet, or talking dirty, not that any of this can hurt. (Unless you have a smokin' hot friend escort your husband to a hotel room where you're waiting.) There are opportunities to surprise each other every day in very simple ways, too. An unexpected kind word can do it, or any gesture of generosity, including making the choice not to be so quick to anger, but finding a silly way to break the tension instead. Keeping an eye on doing little unexpected pleasures for each other, and remembering to dance off the beaten path together once in a while, will go a long way toward keeping your marriage a happy one. As I like to say: No ruts, all glory.

TIPS FOR USING SURPRISE IN A HAPPY MARRIAGE

- Like our most revered comics who keep writing fresh material to stay relevant and keep their fans happy, don't just do the same things over and over. When you feel yourself wanting to say no to your spouse's suggestion to do something new, say yes instead.

- Stay open to new ideas and activities, even when, at first, they seem too hard. A move, a career change, or even a change in life philosophy can reveal new strengths neither of you knew you had. Stay open to each other's life-altering surprises.

- Think through your surprises and be empathic when you plan them. Make sure they are the right one for your spouse. You don't want them to be too shocking, unintentionally humiliating, or one-sided. Surprising your spouse doesn't have to be a grand gesture.

- Consistent small, thoughtful actions are just as meaningful as large gestures, if not more so.

- SURPRISE! AN EXERCISE: Make a list of adjectives to describe the least favorite aspects of your character. In a column on the other side of the page, make a list of their opposites. Brainstorm activities to do either individually, or as a couple, to bring out the attributes you would love to see more of in yourself. Go do them.

7

Don't Quit after a Bad Night

> DON'T LET ONE OR TWO
> BAD EXPERIENCES TAKE
> YOU OUT

Marriage definitely has its ups and downs. I mean, sometimes I *hate* my husband and lie awake in bed at night thinking of ways to kill him, but we've been together long enough now that I know I just have to ride it out and we'll be fine. That said, I think if I had it to do all over again I'd marry someone with a nut allergy.

—BONNIE McFARLANE, comedian/filmmaker, married nine years

"Nice dress!"
"Get off the stage!"
"Go get married!"
These comments and suggestions were coming from the audience.

It was 1 A.M., my first time onstage at the Comic Strip on Second Avenue in New York City, in the nineties. I was not, as they say, "feelin' the love" from the crowd. The club was about three-quarters full and nine-tenths drunk. I'd heard that audiences in New York were tough, and my Los Angeles–centric jokes were clearly not going over. I had a joke about the crazy anorexic women of Hollywood holding up the lines at the frozen yogurt stores, making a meal of tasting all the flavors.

"Can I taste the peanut butter fudge?"

"Can I taste the chocolate?"

"Can I taste the vanilla?" Does anyone above the age of three not know what vanilla tastes like?

People in Los Angeles in the early nineties, the height of the frozen yogurt craze, loved this material. Nine times out of ten it got solid laughs. But in New York City, on a cold December night, clearly I'd landed on that tenth night. This audience had no interest in Hollywood ladies and their eating disorders.

As a gal who loves being onstage more than free shoes, I was shocked to be up there counting the minutes until my set was over. I was still basically a new comic with a thin skin, so the fact that these people didn't find me funny was making me feel physically ill, like I might throw up on the stone-faced person sitting at my feet. I gripped the mic a little tighter and scanned the room for the red light that tells you it's time to get off. Looking out into the dark room, I felt like Tom Hanks in *Cast Away*, gripping Wilson and looking for a rescue team. The red light finally blinked on, I walked offstage, grabbed my knapsack, walked straight for the door, and didn't look up until I hit First Avenue.

When you're working as a comic, some sets are going to be insanely fun to perform and laugh-out-loud funny. Some, on the other hand, are going to be like the night I just described, filled with some combination of stuttered words, forgotten jokes, or drunk hecklers. If you are going to have a long and fruitful comedy career, you have to know that no one set is ever the final word on your talent.

I walked home licking my wounds. And a lot of Tasti D-lite cones,

New York's answer to frozen yogurt. But because I had actually been invited by the then-owner of the club, the late Lucien Hold, to develop my material there with guaranteed spots, something that truly is priceless for a beginning comic, I pulled myself together, wrote some New York–centric jokes, and returned to the club two nights later. And at least four or five nights a week after that, getting more and more laughs, each one putting greater distance between me and the searing memory of that first New York experience.

I bet you know by now where I am going with this. Because not giving up after a night when you really, really want to is also something vitally important to remember in marriage.

After my father died and I was packing up the house where my parents had lived, I came across a picture of him I had never seen. He was looking seventies slick, in white pants, a button- down shirt open at the neck, tan with a few gold chains, and slim.

"Wow, look at Dad! When was this?" I asked my mother.

She made a snorting sound and said, "Pfft, yeah, those were the bad years."

Years? What? I was single at the time and I remember being shocked that you could be in a marriage with someone and have some bad *years*. But they did, and managed to stick it out for forty of them. I wouldn't describe my parents' marriage as blissfully happy, but they taught me a lot about loyalty and love for sure.

Not unlike stand-up, in marriage some days/conversations/texts/ car rides/gifts/dinners with in-laws are going to be spectacular and some of them are going to be crappy. The trick is learning how to get through the tough ones, and how to use everything you learn from the bad experience as information to work on your craft, in this case your marriage, to help you do better the next time.

When I have a show that isn't great it stings, but I don't quit and I don't hold on to it. I realize I just had an off night. I'm committed to the bigger picture—that I'm a comedian—and I chalk the setup to experience and use the information to work on my craft and do better next time. Doing stand-up is like an experiment every time. Prepare, show up, do my best, learn for next time. In stand-up there's no dress rehearsal, it's always the show. But it's also a work in progress.

—WENDY LIEBMAN, comedian, married eleven years

Speaking of which, there's one more relevant piece of that first disastrous New York set that really did help me squeeze the learning juice out of it. After the set I was pacing up and down outside, looking at the ground, talking to myself, "That was awful. I have to *never* do this again," when suddenly from behind me I heard, "Dani, is that you?"

I turned around and there stood a friend of a friend of mine from LA, a brassy woman with a big voice and lots of teeth.

"Oh, hi!" I said, trying not to look like someone who had just been having a conversation with the pavement.

"What are you doing here? What's going on? Were you just working?" she asked, seeing the neon sign of the club over my shoulder behind me.

"Um, yeah," I said, and then, relieved to be talking to another human, I blurted out, "I just had the worst set of my life and I am never doing that again. But otherwise, I'm fine," which was a tough sell, since tears had squirted out of my eyes and my hands were shaking.

"That sucks! Poor thing. But you'll be fine!" she said, grinning ear to ear. Even her molars were supporting me. "Everyone bombs, that's part of the job."

"Well, it's not for me," I said, still embarrassed, avoiding eye contact.

"You need to lighten up! It's one night. Aren't you a comic? You'll be fine." She turned away and hailed a cab. "See you soon!"

I stood for a second in her wake, annoyed at first. I don't like it when people tell me to "lighten up." I never tell people who insist on talking about what's trending on Twitter and their ab work that they should be deeper. But since she's not the first person to tell me I'm a little intense, and since I was feeling terrible, I was open to hearing it this time.

Walking the thirty blocks downtown to my sublet, my nose turning red and my mittens stiffening in the freezing air, I considered what it would mean for me to "lighten up." Sidestepping urine-soaked sleeping bags, bottles of Colt 45, and rats sniffing take-out cartons under the Fifty-Ninth Street Bridge, I realized I must have some investment in being intense—there must be some payoff for me in responding to life this way or I wouldn't feel so threatened by the mere suggestion that I lighten up a little bit. What came to me is that being intense made me feel safe, impenetrable, and less open to attack. The problem with this, for someone who wanted to be a comedian, was how not funny it was to be around.

I continued to think about that night and that exchange for at least the next seventy-two hours. Then I went back to the club. Choosing to go back there had a lot to do with something that woman had said right before she told me I had to lighten up, the line about it being "only one night." This was not subjective interpretation, it was fact. It was one night, actually even shorter: it was one fifteen-minute set. It was my choice to either allow one performance to define my talent and my commitment to my work, or to see it for what it was, one bad show, bummer. Time to let it go. I could heed the advice of my Jewish grandmother: "This, too, shall pass."

This more accepting, and yes, lighter, perspective did not come easily to me in my stand-up. So it's not a surprise that I am similarly challenged in marriage. For years, every time Tod and I had a fight, I'd think it's surely the end, or it should be. And yet we've hung in there for thirteen years. In fact, now, usually two days after a fight, I can't tell you what 90 percent of them were about. I've heard this from other married people, too. Fighting in marriage for some of us must be like giving birth for most women: we forget the gory, painful details so we can keep doing it.

Now we get to enjoy the story as Joan Rater and Tony Phelan

recount all the gory, glorious details of a trip to Niagara Falls early in their marriage when Joan was certain, or at least hoping, it was the end of the line for them.

JOAN AND TONY

A Story with a Good Ending

Joan Rater and Tony Phelan met at a show in New York's East Village in 1989 and got married in 1993. Joan is a highly charismatic woman with an easy laugh, a quick mind, and an open heart. A shock of white hair frames her face and her piercing blue eyes can go from warm and inviting to tough and uncompromising in a blink. Her husband, Tony, is a perfect foil for her. His steady, quiet, and yet no less articulate presence seems to be the rudder for the full life they have together as the parents to two daughters and cowriters and coproducers for television. Being in their company makes it very clear how well they function as a team. Which makes this story that Joan told that much more compelling.

Early in their marriage they were living in New York City. Tony was working as a theater director and Joan was pursuing acting work, which meant they were both working as waiters. They had a three-year-old daughter, Maggie, and they were broke. They had decided to spend the summer writing a screenplay together while staying in Tony's parents' ski condo in Ellicottville, a small town in western New York State. Tony bought a book called *How to Write a Screenplay in Thirty Days*, which they were trying hard to do. It was not going well. According to Joan,

> Our goal was for each to write ten pages a day, then at the end of the day we'd read each other's stuff. Well, I'd write a few sentences, then scribble them out. Rewrite them, hate myself, take a bath, write some more, hate some more, bathe some more. By the end of the day I'd have maybe one shitty paragraph and really dry skin. Tony, the achiever, would have his ten pages. He'd hand them to me.

"I think it's pretty good," he'd say.

"Pretty good?"

"No, it's good."

"Do you think I'm gonna like it?"

"I don't know, Joan, just read it."

"I'm scared to read it because you don't seem all that excited about it. Are you excited about it?"

"Yes, Joan, I'm excited about it!"

"You don't have to get mad. I just asked you a simple question."

This was how it went. By day thirty, not only did they not have a screenplay, they were exhausted, almost to the point of not being able to handle their daughter. They decided they needed a break and drove Maggie to Tony's parents' house in Cleveland so they could have a little rest. On the way back to Ellicottville, Tony suggested they go to Niagara Falls, since he knew they loved being in nature. Unfortunately, they took a wrong turn and ended up on a local road, passing mile after mile of cheesy motels. Joan thought about checking into one—if she was in a different mood it might have been fun to have a quickie with Tony. She wasn't interested. "I knew if we pulled over to one of these motels in this moment it would break us," Joan said. "To look across the heart-shaped bed at Tony, who I hated, would break me. We wouldn't be able to fall asleep and we'd feel like failures at trying to have a kitschy, funny, motel kind of day."

The pressure of using Niagara Falls to fix things between them grew stronger the closer they got to the falls. There was an unspoken thought that if they could just get there and see this amazing natural phenomenon together, their faith would be restored and everything would be fine. When they arrived at the falls however, they had to park in a high-rise mall parking garage that was very hot and smelled like crap, literally. Joan wasn't sure she was going to make it to the waterfall. But she kept going, determined. They passed a lottery ticket vendor and decided to buy a ten-dollar ticket. Maybe they'd win. They didn't, which in her heightened state further sealed their fate as "losers." Then they walked across the street to see the falls, and were completely un-derwhelmed. Joan, being the gifted writer she is, told me this story, which could easily be a soliloquy from a great American play.

> The falls looked like a sprinkler to me. I'm thinking, this is it? I want them to be bigger or faster. I look around at the other people and they seem impressed. They're eating ice cream, they're smiling and posing for pictures. And we look dirty and we just lost the lottery. And Tony tries to take my hand and I can't believe he would try to touch me. Why would he want to touch me and why would he think I would want to touch him? I appreciate the gesture, but I'm annoyed at how horribly he's misjudged the moment. I was at the end of the line. Because my screenplay was difficult to write? Because we were short on money? All these things had happened before. Because it was hot out? We sat under a dead tree in a section of burned-out grass. We picked at the dirt. We stared at the falls. I asked Tony what he was thinking. "Nothing, really," he said. "What are you thinking?" What I didn't say was that I was thinking about leaving him and the thought made me feel good be-cause leaving him was something I could actually do. I didn't say that. Instead I said, "I don't know. Nothing."

The summer finally ended, and Joan and Tony had no screenplay, no money, no plan. Driving back from Ellicottville to New York City, they stopped at a McDonald's in Binghamton. Joan and Maggie got in line. There were two workers taking orders, and a manager. They knew she was the manager because she was wearing a polo shirt with her name on it, Cindy. She filled orders quickly and effortlessly. Then, the drive-through attendant called out to her, "Cindy, your mom's here." Cindy answered, "OK, Brenda. Just go ahead and fill her order." By then Joan and Maggie were at the front of the line and they heard a small voice behind them, "Cindy?" It was Cindy's mom. She had stringy gray hair and was wearing jeans and a Mickey Mouse sweat-shirt, both too small.

Cindy's mom said, "I ordered my food at the takeout window but I just came in to make sure it was OK . . . because you know . . . I can't pay."

"Just go. I'll see you at home later," Cindy said to her mother. The woman left.

"It was just a second, a split second," said Joan, "but I saw Cindy start to collapse, kind of shrink, all the efficiency was gone, and all that was left was hopelessness. She shook it off, looked me dead in the eye, and said, 'Welcome to McDonald's! Can I take your order?'"

Although Joan didn't know it at the time, witnessing this exchange would have a huge effect on her marriage. She went back to her car and told Tony everything she had seen. Instead of brushing it off, he was genuinely interested and wanted to hear every detail. Again and again. As they were talking about Cindy and her mother, Joan felt a shift, "not just because Cindy had a worse life than me, although it was inspiring to see someone up close and personal with amazing perseverance." It also lent a little perspective to her disappointment about their writing and not "winning the lottery." More important for their marriage, the two of them were talking and excited in a way they hadn't been in a long time. When they were close to home, Tony blurted out, "That's it. That's Annie. That's our main character. She isn't a dog walker, she's a manager at McDonald's who gets fired for giving her mom free food. Annie is Cindy."

That unexpected experience driving home, and the insight they gained about their work, reconnected them and reminded them of their shared passion for storytelling. It also gave them the confidence to become a solid and highly successful writing team. Not that it's been twenty years of sunshine and flowers, but, Joan says, "Now we're at a point where we know that sometimes the only thing you can do is walk away and let time pass because you have faith that something will shift."

People go over the top with marriage vows. You spend three months working on words that you'll say to them and you'll never say those words to them again for the rest of your marriage. Save it. Don't blow it all up front. Use one of those lines every seven years. Don't get up there like Shakespeare, like, "And . . . your breath is the soul . . . and the wind under my wings and the FIRE!!" And then the married people are going, "Oh, shut up!" Because you know in a week they're gonna be, like, "Hey, where's the mayonnaise?" "I don't know, where'd you put the mayonnaise? Look, sweetie, you're the wind under my wings, but where'd you put the fucking mayonnaise?"

—GREG FITZSIMMONS, comedian, married sixteen years

TAKE A BREATHER

Joan and Tony's strategy of "walking away," creating a temporary physical separation when part of you is sure that leaving for good is the only option, is one I heard time and again from other couples and marriage therapists. Allowing time to pass helps. Getting out of the eye of the storm and allowing it to pass so you can come back together in a calmer state is always a good idea.

Figuring out ways to fight civilly can also keep arguments from escalating to the point where one of you slams the back door screaming "I am so done!" and breaking a few glass panels. Not that I ever did this six years ago . . .

Managing expectations is very effective for helping everyone stay cool, too.

Fortunately for Wendy and Nancy, a couple who have been together for eighteen years, they already had a great grasp of this tool before Nancy got laid off for two years. Nancy is a hard-driving finance manager for commercial real estate deals and her wife, Wendy, is an accomplished painter. I loved what Nancy had to say about this: "You're a happier person in your marriage by far if you manage your expectations. It can sound unromantic, but it is romantic because you're being respectful by being thoughtful and not putting false expectations on a person just because you think they ought to be able to do this thing."

Accepting your spouse's limitations helps you avoid having the same fights over and over. Nancy had something helpful to say about fighting, too: "You have to know when to throw in the towel on something—and not after you've beaten a dead horse. You have to stop before you've beaten the horse."

Being sensitive about when to stop a fight is a great suggestion. If you get out before it gets ugly, you will avoid the one thing that all couples, married and divorced, say can strike the hardest blows to relationships: cruel words uttered in anger.

IN A FIGHT, LOOK BEFORE YOU LEAP

Reading a room and reacting on your feet is a necessary skill for comics (part of listening, as described in chapter 2). The logical next step for comedians who are fully present is to respond freely to what they see and hear, with no internal editor impeding their creative juices. That impulsive, take-no-prisoners form of expression is what we love about comics. But in a marriage, this kind of hair-trigger communication— used for anything other than giving hugs, kisses, and compliments— can have some devastating results.

When I sat down with Dan and his wife of seventeen years, Shawn-Catherine, Dan, with his bulging muscles and several references to his Porsche, impressed me as a high-testosterone, macho guy. I never would have expected the sensitivity he showed about the perils of talking before you think. It was clear from the passion with which he spoke that Dan's wisdom was born of personal experience. When we talked about communication between couples, his macho bravado disappeared and he spoke quietly and from the heart. "Take a couple minutes to think about what you're going to say, especially in an argument, in a heated discussion, because what you say leaves your mouth and it then becomes, 'Oh, wait, I didn't mean to say that!' and you're trying to grab the words and put them back in your mouth, and you can't."

Lew and Liz, the couple who survived the disastrous surprise party, also feel very strongly about thinking before you speak in the heat of the moment. Lew can always tell when he's in trouble because Liz's jaw locks, an expression he was eager to imitate. It doesn't surprise me that Liz's mouth snaps shuts when Lew does something to piss her off, given how passionately she believes that "you'll never regret what you didn't say, but you may regret what you did say."

Although all of the couples I met with agree that it's essential to bite your tongue when you're angry, no one said it was easy to do. Michael Latimer, a marriage and family counselor in Los Angeles, who has been working with couples for more than twenty years, advises people to try a technique that seems like it's lifted straight from a handbook for new parents. Basically a highly structured version of the time-out, it's very similar to what Joan said works for Tony and her, because it gets people physically separated in the heat of the moment. When I mentioned to Latimer that people associate "time-outs" with children and wondered whether his clients don't find this suggestion a bit patronizing, he smiled and explained how it worked:

> Often in a fight, people are responding from an emotionally young place. They can get stuck at emotional adolescence. A time-out in this context is not just five minutes to go in your room and color. I have them set a timer for an hour or a half hour, and then they commit to coming back together. They might not continue the conversation because they can't, but if not, they take phase two of it, which may take another thirty minutes. It's not a way to get out of having the conversation, it's a way to prevent the conversation from escalating. It creates space between them and also opportunity to soothe themselves.

The writer Emmy Laybourne, married twelve years, puts a personal spin on the time-out. Her favorite motto is "When the going gets tough, the tough clean the kitchen." I like to clean up when I'm feeling stressed or anxious or angry. As I put dishes in their places, I put my mind in order. Once the kitchen is clean, I've cooled down and am ready to be rational.

Latimer also talked about helping people become aware of the meaning we assign to exchanges with each other, especially those impulsive ones that can be lethal for a couple. "If you stay in a marriage long enough, there's going to be pain," he said. "Conflict is unavoidable. The conflict is not the problem, it's how we deal with it. It's the meaning we make of it."

When we are able to see that we're investing too much meaning in something, we become much more able to let it go and stay in the game, whether it's our career or our marriage. I couldn't help but be reminded of my disastrous set at the Comic Strip in New York City— my "bombing," if you will. That's the lesson I learned that night: My success or failure in my career did not hinge on that one night. My intense desire to succeed that night had caused me to take that one gig *too* seriously. I had invested too much in one isolated experience. As a comic you are going to bomb at some point; it's the meaning you make of it that affects whether you will persevere and survive. This is also true in marriage. You must make the effort to see the moment in its proper context, to pull the lens back a little and see the bigger landscape. When you do so, there is usually hope and enough reason to stay.

GOOD NEWS!
Your Marriage is the Only One You Have to Worry About

Something I always tell comedy students—and frankly, we all hear it ad nauseam but it is as true for your marriage as for any other part of your life—is, don't compare yourself to anyone else. As an artist you can certainly admire talent and craft and hard work, but not from the perspective of "Look what he or she is doing and I'm not!" Once you start seeing your peers in this way, the thoughts that follow can veer way too easily to "I must suck. I should just quit." But as anyone who has ever sung "Rudolph, the Red-Nosed Reindeer" knows, we're all special in our own ways. This holds true for marriage, too. Don't compare your marriage to anyone else's. No matter what you see at dinner parties, school functions, or Saturday night movie dates, none of us has any idea what is really going on between two people.

It doesn't matter where you are in life, what level of success, fame, and money you have amassed, you're still vulnerable to the instinct to compare yourself to others and think they are playing the marriage game better. Patricia Heaton told me a story illustrating how she has learned this over the years.

"I'll show up for a school function by myself and think, 'Oh, look, Sandra's husband once again has attended the function with her,'" she told me. "I will build this up in my head and decide that everyone else's husband cheerfully goes to everything.

"Then I'll say to Betsy, 'I love the way Jimmy just comes along to events.'

"And she says, 'Ugh, we have a huge fight every time beforehand. He hates it! He's always saying, "I don't know any of these parents, what am I supposed to say? How long is it going to be? Who's going to be there? What do we have to do, is there going to be food?"'

"Then I think, 'OK, that's exactly like every fight we have. They are doing exactly the same thing and her husband isn't perfect.' So often we look at others' marriages and we make assumptions about them. There was one other couple who always seem to be having so much fun. They would go to strip bars together, and the husband was always around. One time I said to her, 'Your husband is so fabulous!' She said, 'Ugh, he doesn't do a damn thing. I run around, I get the food together, make the plans and then he walks around being the big host, like he set it all up.' I felt like, 'Wow. The grass is not greener.'"

Interesting, that "The grass is always greener . . ." saying dates back at least to the sixteenth century, so it's safe to assume that the instinct to look at others' lives and think they have it better is no new phenomenon. Which is to say, remember this bit about the grass being greener whenever the desire to compare your marriage to other people's marriages hits you.

An important downside of comparing your marriage to others is that you're taking precious attention away from your own marriage. With some effort, you could use the time and energy to make your own better. For instance, instead of envying how affectionate Steve is with Linda, be more affectionate yourself.

Comedy tools can also come to the rescue in the comparison game. When I am feeling irritable and find myself obsessing about other couples and how much more in love and happy they must be, I think of one of the exercises that always made my UCLA class groan: "Write down ten things about the life you have created for yourself as a comic that you love." Back then my list used to include things like "I make my own schedule"; "I don't have to wait for the phone to ring to work"; "I get to feel useful by making people laugh and maybe feel less alone." Now, I write about my marriage. I get to list all the good parts of my life as a wife and mother. They often feel too earnest to say out loud, but on the page I will confess to some highlights here:

1. I love Tod and I know he loves me, even on bad days.
2. Tod is not interested in lying.
3. I have a spouse who is open enough to let me write about our marriage.

The best way to make your list is to a brainstorm. Comedians love brainstorming as a creative tool because there are no wrong answers in brainstorming, so it frees the mind to find exactly the words and thoughts you are looking for. Don't hold back. Write down anything that occurs to you that is a plus of being married, or of your own marriage, from the smallest perk, like having someone to tell you when a piece of kale is stuck between your teeth, to having someone to plan the twilight years with, to the comfort of getting into bed with someone who has warmer feet than you.

As I have discovered in a long marriage, there will be bad nights, weeks, or even, unfortunately, months (and according to my mother, even bad years!). But if what you ultimately want is a long-term happy marriage, you have to keep your eye on the prize. This means showing up (that's why it's chapter 1!), continuing to be honest, not only with your spouse but with yourself. Have manageable expectations of each other, and, as often as possible, find ways to lighten up. And if you catch yourself looking longingly at another couple, get specific about what you envy about them and set out to create it yourself. Then stop looking over there, and start looking at the person next to you.

TIPS TO HELP YOU NOT QUIT

- Marriage is better when you manage your expectations. Knowing and accepting your spouse's limitations is a great way to keep fights from getting out of control.

- Don't say words you will wish you could take back. Hold your tongue in a fight. Literally shut your mouth if you have to. Protect your most precious relationship by thinking before you let your rage speak for you.

- Get some space from each other. During a fight, there is nothing wrong with creating actual physical distance between you until you both calm down. Time-outs are not just for five-year-olds.

- When a situation such as a fight or hurt feelings occurs, try to get enough distance from it to do a reality check. In other words, ask yourself, "Am I reacting to what happened or am I reacting to the meaning I gave to the situation?" Be open to the possibility that it doesn't mean as much as you think it does. It could just be a bad night.

- Comparing what you know about your marriage to what you think you know about someone else's is a waste of your time. Use that same mental energy to make a list of ten things you love about your marriage and your spouse.

8

Find Ways to Relax

It's fun to complain with someone. Nothing brings us together
more than complaining about other people. That might be
the thing that holds us together more than anything.

—LEW SCHNEIDER, comedian, married thirty-three years

By the sixth week of my stand-up class, my students start going out to
clubs to test their jokes, so we begin to learn about ways to deal with
the anxiety they might feel before a show, ways to relax and center
themselves. Everyone lies down on the floor and we do a meditation
exercise.

"Take a few minutes to feel your breath. Feel your chest move.
Breathe in and out, in and out . . ."

That's when the giggling starts, followed by the comments.

"What's funny about this?" I ask.

"I think I got gum in my hair," one student replies.

"I don't think Seinfeld lies on the floor," another quips.

Maybe not, but he swears by Transcendental Meditation (TM) to keep himself clear-headed, energized, and überproductive for the last forty-one years. And he is not the only TM enthusiast. The radio-personality-turned-reality-show-judge Howard Stern is also a TM practitioner, as was the late comedy legend Andy Kaufman. Seinfeld started practicing TM as an undergraduate in 1972. He told guests at the 2013 benefit gala of the David Lynch Foundation, which was founded to bring TM to a wider public, that the twenty minutes a day he spent meditating during his lunch break, while everyone else was eating, had enabled him to handle the extreme pressure and the monumental workload that came with starring in and being executive producer of a network television show. And that was before he started doing morning meditation, too. Now, at sixty, he has more energy than he thought possible. According to him, "It's just a dumb way to live, not doing it." He told the audience there that the practice of TM is like "you have a cell phone but no charger, and someone gives you the charger. And you go, 'Oh, now I can keep using this thing and it will work all the time.'"[1]

Years ago when I read about Andy Kaufman, the genius comedian and performance artist of the seventies and early eighties and his Transcendental Meditation practice, I began to appreciate the need for taking a few minutes before a show to take some deep breaths to relax and center myself. So although I have not yet made the commitment to TM, I do make a conscious effort every day to engage in some activity that relaxes my mind and my body. A dance class, a spin class, or even just stretching on a hotel-room floor and breathing helps me stay on top of my energy when I am working and performing. Sometimes even that small ritual makes me more relaxed, more comfortable, and, most important, more present and aware of what is happening in the room when I walk out onstage and thus more available to my audience. Little did I know when I started out doing stand-up that a similar kind of commitment to relaxation would also help in my marriage.

Before I met Tod, I never thought about the need for relaxation with a boyfriend. There was always time to relax after one of us left. But then we met, and we both stayed. And then we started planning a future together, and I found that even when I wasn't about to face a crowd, I could feel heart-racing anxiety. The thought of spending the rest of my life with one person was making me a nervous wreck, and I'd stopped drinking years before, so that wasn't an option. I had to find ways to relax. Counting my breaths for five minutes on the way to meeting Tod's father helped me, but as the wedding date approached and the stress around that piled up, taking some deep breaths by myself in a bathroom stall wasn't enough. When Tod and my mother were going head to head at an outdoor mall about how the wedding invitation should read, I knew I had to bring in some bigger guns to calm myself. I knew I had to make a commitment to relaxation in my marriage.

Just as you cannot entertain a crowd when you are gripped with anxiety and tension, there is also no way a relationship can flourish when either one or both of you is in a state of constant tension. Building a life with someone, you are bound to experience stress—caused, I daresay, by a lot more than what font to choose for your wedding invitation. In order to be happy, you have to create ways to relax so you can be more present, be more available to each other, and simply said, have a better time.

Tod and I have known about the importance of relaxation from the very beginning of our marriage. We're just not good at it. In October of 2002, we were in Santa Barbara celebrating our second anniversary. We were at a low-end hotel whose name had the word "Cliff" in it, probably something like "Cliffsedge," since the establishment, featuring prison-cell-like rooms and mildewed carpeting, was located on a cliff jutting out over the ocean. This was why I had booked the place. For me as a native New Yorker, hotels perched on top of the ocean still give me a thrill, even ones that look like they might rent out their rooms by the hour.

Tod, however, being from Southern California, wasn't quite as excited when he opened the door to our room. Hit with a blast of chemically freshened air trying hard to mask the odor of cigarette smoke trapped in the faded yellow curtains, he quietly asked me, "Where did you find this place?" He gripped his bag in his hand, hoping he could turn around and leave as soon as I gave him the go-ahead. I was five months pregnant, so the place smelled even worse to me than to Tod, but I was willing to hold my nose for a few days for the chance to stare out the one large window framing a piece of dark blue ocean where the waves crested and broke. I've always been a sucker for moving water. I used to drag my father to the window of a Jacuzzi store on First Avenue when I was in preschool just to stare at the swirling eddies in the bathtubs for sale.

"Tod, we can't leave, it's our anniversary."

"This place is gross," he said, dropping his bag with a thud.

"I guess," I said, my eyes transfixed by the ocean outside the window.

"Fine. I'm going to go check out the pool. I hope there's nobody floating facedown in it."

Ten minutes later, still sitting in front of the glass, I heard his footsteps.

"There's a Ping-Pong table, honey. Pong!" he said, followed by what looked disturbingly like a fist pump.

Tod is a former member of a fraternity. I married a frat boy. There, it's in print. I wasn't the sorority type. I did go to a few rush meetings my junior year, but mostly for the free cake and Diet Coke. Tod, on the other hand, knew Greek life intimately. Fraternity life for him was a lot of drinking, chasing girls, and playing beer "pong." During his fraternity years Tod had honed his Ping-Pong skills, and now the game would hopefully salvage our weekend. He could now relax knowing we'd be a carefree, frolicking couple playing Ping-Pong. He'd get to nurse a Coors while his pregnant wife sipped cranberry juice and soda, the two of us playing table tennis overlooking the Pacific Ocean. What could be more relaxing?

Ten minutes later I was standing at the Ping-Pong table. "Did you just slam the ball into my stomach?" I snapped, trying to stay calm after my fetus had just been assaulted by a small, white ball.

"What are you talking about? That was nothing. Come on, let's play! Eight to seven, my serve."

Since we had only been together a little over three years, I hadn't yet seen the full extent of my supposedly "California-boy" husband's competitiveness. Playing Ping-Pong with him *while carrying his baby* would not have been my first choice for the best time to discover his killer instinct.

"You just slammed the ball at my stomach," I said swerving my middle to the right to avoid being hit by the next ball. "You do realize there's a baby in here, right? I'm done. I'm not playing with you," I said, laying my paddle down.

"What? Come on, don't be like that," he said, bending his knees and leaning into the table, in proper "Pong" position for the next serve. "You're being ridiculous. I didn't slam the ball—that's how you play the game, I mean, are you playing or are you playing?"

I started walking back to our hotel room, making it pretty clear I wasn't playing. Here's a little bonus advice for the menfolk: Don't ever say "You're being ridiculous" to a woman bearing your child if you're interested in having sex again with her anytime soon.

Ten years later, my chest still tightens thinking about that game of table tennis. I wasn't one of those happy pregnant women with my first child. I felt overtaken and out of control. I didn't plow through dozens of pregnancy books in joyful anticipation of this new life I was creating. I was very scared. It was truly unbelievable to me that all you do is have sex and eat and you make an entirely new human being. I wondered a lot about what I would do if my baby died. Being pregnant felt like the biggest setup ever to screw up in some unforeseeable way.

So a ball, even one weighing less than three grams, careening at my stomach, possibly the baby's head, made me nuts. I was also not very good at "managing my expectations." I couldn't believe Tod didn't (a) know this was how I felt and (b) feel exactly the same way. Wasn't that the whole point of being married? To have someone who knows you well enough to read your thoughts and who feels exactly the same way you do about everything? Never mind that every women's magazine I'd read had advice columns telling me not to expect this. I was convinced that my husband and my marriage were going to be different.

I went back to the room, this time oblivious to the soothing ocean. I packed what little I had pulled out and lumbered to the parking lot. When I got there, panting, I saw a film of sea salt and dust had already settled on our car. If I left in this car, Tod would be stuck in Santa Barbara, three hours from our apartment. I couldn't do it. He was, after all, the father of my fetus. I dragged my bag back to the room, spread myself out on the bed, and ate Saltines until I passed out.

When I woke up, Tod was getting out of the shower, wrapped in a seedy hotel robe, the moonlight reflecting on the water behind him. "What can I say? I'm a competitive guy," he said, coming over and sitting next to me on the bed. "And I'm kind of fantastic," he added, smiling and wiggling his eyebrows.

"Come on, don't be mad at me. Let me rub your feet," he continued after a beat, grabbing one of my bloated hooves, which he somehow didn't find repulsive. I surrendered to the foot massage, took some deep breaths, thought about ordering room service, then remembered there was none, and sent him out to the nearest 7-11 for cottage cheese, green apples, and chocolate chip cookie dough. We did end up relaxing a little in the next twenty-four hours, but—typical of us—not without a lot of kicking and screaming.

Over the years, we've figured out that relaxing together isn't one of our strengths, particularly when it involves sports since it's always possible that one of us will unexpectedly turn into a competitive freak. So we have other ways. Sometimes we find a TV program we can both enjoy. One where no babies or children are held hostage so I can sit through it, but there's enough history or action or science fiction to keep Tod interested. For those one or two shows a year, we curl up on the couch together, fingers entwined, and enjoy at least twenty minutes of it before I fall asleep.

We mostly relax on our own with yoga, running, or reading the paper. Some nights we read in bed side by side, which is good for us. It's not competitive and there's no threat of anyone being hit in the head with a ball.

Unlike us, most couples I interviewed for this book enjoy relaxing together. The most common ways to do so were watching television, going to a movie, or eating a meal together. All good ideas, and although these activities don't exactly adhere to the happiness expert's advice for finding variety to keep your marriage happy, I think when relaxation is the goal, routine is actually OK. I see no need to look for excitement in your relaxation. I'm going to go out on a limb here and say that relaxation activities should be . . . relaxing. But when I pressed couples to go beyond the obvious in describing what they do to relax, I was able to learn some other very good ways you can blow off steam and bond with your spouse at the same time.

CHASE AND MARK
Teachers Who Do It Old School

Chase and Mark have been together for twenty-four years, and married for eighteen, and they have one very tall and charming son. Chase is also tall and lithe, with curious, round, blue eyes. She has an alternately reflective and then suddenly spontaneous way of expressing herself in conversation that kept me on the edge of my chair during most of the interview, never knowing what to expect. Mark is a salty Irishman with a raspy voice and a no-nonsense demeanor who says what's on his mind.

It was clear that Mark had agreed to the interview to please his wife.

Within minutes of meeting me Mark told me he meant no offense, but he wasn't all that excited about talking about his marriage. "It's like talking about it will put a curse on it," he said. This wasn't the first time I'd gotten this response to a request for an interview, usually by the husbands. It reminded me of the old comedy axiom that when you explain a joke, you ruin it. Some people feel the same way about their long-term marriages.

For them it had a similar fragility, which if analyzed or

reflected upon might pop like a soap bubble. In fact, when I started this project several people warned me, "You know, the minute you hold up your marriage as an example of anything is the day it falls apart." Fortunately my curiosity outweighed their warnings.

Mark and Chase are natural performers who met as cast members in a stage production of *Tony 'n' Tina's Wedding*. Today Mark is a high school AP English teacher and Chase teaches improvisational comedy at the famous Groundlings School in Los Angeles. Their home has a warm, New England feel to it.

Within minutes Chase and Mark were finishing each other's sentences, recounting at a rapid-fire pace disarmingly honest stories about their life together. They took great delight in telling me the inside scoop on who the other one was and how they make it work as a couple. Before we dove into the topic of relaxation, Mark wanted me to understand something that he had to figure out for himself before he ever even approached relaxation in his marriage. In a David-Mamet-esque rant he said that in order to find peace for himself and their life together, he explained that he had had to let go of his image of marriage because hanging on to that image meant that "the truth of the moment is going to bother me. And then really everything will bother me because it's not the image I have in my mind. How can you put that kind of burden on another person? I don't want that kind of burden on me."

I noticed my head nodding, like I was witnessing a kind of sermon. I stopped short of yelling "Amen!" Mark went on, "So now I tell myself, you are going to sit here and bear it and try not to dump it on her. I've got to deal with what is. I can tell her what I'm thinking and feeling, but I can't make her do something about it—"

"That's the hard part," Chase said, "because you just want to make them fucking change. And you can't. That's my biggest struggle."

As tough as I believe these adjustments have been for Chase and

Mark to make, I found the candor and authenticity with which they talk about it wonderfully comforting. Their obvious sense of humor about the task of accepting each other gave me hope that next time I feel like I'm choking from my need for Tod to be some other way, I will remember these two, and pause to consider that the one who has to change is me and my attitude. Now, back to relaxation.

A GOOD STORY, A DRY COCKTAIL, AND SOME CHANTING

Because of the snap-crackle-pop way that Chase and Mark are with each other, at first I didn't get the sense that "relax together" is anywhere near the top of their to-do list, if it makes a list at all. Surprisingly, they value it very much. They shared with me a few ways they prioritize relaxing together, which are simple and very doable, if you have a similarly predictable lifestyle.

Their first one is to read aloud to each other in bed.

"Often it's me asking Mark to read from *The New Yorker*," Chase said, "which he reads every night, usually a profile. It's how I get him to connect with me, because he's such a bookworm. But it's also nice to just snuggle and actually listen to his voice. It's soothing." This relaxation ritual has the added bonus for Chase of also making her feel connected to Mark. Which in case I haven't been clear enough about this, is the underlying intention of creating relaxation, whether you do it separately or together. Relaxing slows you down and lowers your defenses, which allows you to feel more connected to each other, the way Chase does with Mark when he reads to her. In addition to making you feel more at peace, relaxing creates the space for you and your spouse to enjoy each other more.

Their next favorite way to relax together is with their nightly evening ritual of cocktails and dinner—"Just doing that Donna Reed kind of thing," as Chase put it. "I'm not a cook, but I make sure there's food, even if it's takeout. We always have dinner and a cocktail together. This may be boring to other people, but it definitely relaxes us."

Listening to her describe this lifestyle, it didn't sound boring, just foreign. Tod and I never know from one night to the next who will be home for dinner, so it would be tough to have this daily ritual.

Chase and Mark threw out one more, dare I say unexpected, calming activity that they engage in regularly, regardless of their schedules. They both said the most effective tool for relaxation they use, either together or separately, is Buddhist chanting. Chase has been a committed Nichiren Buddhist for twenty years, and when they met, Mark was also a Nichiren practitioner. They both swear by the practice for keeping them peaceful, positive, and, once again, connected.

Nichiren was a thirteenth-century Japanese Buddhist priest. The main idea of Nichiren Buddhism is that all people, regardless of race, gender, or social standing, have an innate Buddha nature and are capable of attaining enlightenment in this lifetime. Nichiren Buddhism includes several major schools and many sub-schools, all of which focus on chanting "Nam Myōhō Renge Kyō," which can be roughly translated as "Devotion to the Mystic Law of the Lotus Sutra." All adherents of all forms of Nichiren Buddhism believe it to be a powerful and transformational chant.[2]

I asked Chase what her Nichiren practice means to her and what makes it so effective in her marriage. "It's about each person doing their own 'human revolution,'" she said. "We chant for 'absolute happiness' or to bring forth the highest life condition—or our innate Buddhahood. We are chanting to be in the world and show proof in our daily lives, to challenge any obstacle. It's a great practice because it forces you to summon determination and hope—it's not outside yourself—you just fuse with the mystic law."

When I pressed her to tell me specifically how chanting affects her marriage, Chase paused and then sat forward in her chair. "Practicing together is great but, more importantly, chanting for my family's happiness is the key thing for me. If they chant, great. But it's not about them. It's about me and it's not going to sound right or generous or whatever, but I chant for my own happiness, which creates happiness for my family in the 'If momma ain't happy ain't nobody happy' sense." She took a breath and leaned back. Catching Mark's eye, she quickly added, "Chanting with Mark is great, though!"

The two of them have practiced different kinds of Buddhism at various times in their marriage. Nichiren Buddhism is notably different from Zen Buddhism. Chase and Mark see Zen Buddhism as being about acceptance and creating peace. The practice itself involves zazen, which is a way of sitting and silently monitoring the breath. It is believed that Buddha achieved enlightenment when he was in seated meditation, so in a Zen meditation practice you return to seated meditation again and again.

But Nichiren Buddhism and chanting are like "the roar of a lion," said Chase, "where the intention is to effect change for the greater good—it's radical. It's out there—an almost embarrassingly sincere and rah-rah type of experience. Chanting is not just about acceptance," she said, "it's about creating change for the better."

Chase's commitment to her practice has grown so much that she now hosts a chanting group every morning at 6:45 for anyone interested. Mark also chants for an hour a day, which, although not essential, makes Chase happy. She laughed while eagerly telling me a story about a period when Mark had stopped chanting and she panicked.

"I was like, 'We can't have a happy marriage if we're not both chanting!' So I went to talk to an old Japanese sensei and she said, 'Oh no, you can marry monkey and be happy if you chant!'"

"That's true," Mark said, laughing. "Because sometimes I'm like, OK, this is where Chase is being a monkey."

"Your happiness does not depend on the other person," Chase added.

"I actually pause and say to myself now, 'Stop trying to get her to be *that*.' That's fucking stupid. That's one thing the practice helps me to do."

"Yep," Chase said. "Chant to be happy. Chant to be happy, regardless of what he does."

Later, I repeated this last thought to myself. *Chant to be happy, regardless of what he does.* Was this actually possible? I'd heard a variation of this way of thinking before, not in connection with chanting but with retaining separateness within a marriage. I suspect that this works, but so far I'm not very good at doing it. This must be what makes daily chanting so effective. I mean, in addition to the mystical power of repeating "Nam Myōhō Renge Kyō" for an hour, starting your day with sixty minutes where you visualize what you want must focus your mind in a way that makes it harder to get thrown off by anyone else throughout the day.

When answering the question about relaxation, the importance of tending to your own needs in marriage came up not only with Chase and Mark and their chanting practice, but also with other couples. Obviously, chanting isn't the only way to do it, but husband and wives in successful long-term couples all seem to figure this out over the years and find different ways to achieve it. From what I can see, in order to not take on the pain and suffering of the people closest to you, you often need those big guns such as Buddha, God, or salted caramel ice cream.

Without otherworldly support, this "loving detachment," as it is called in the Twelve Step program of Alcoholics Anonymous, seems nearly impossible. How can I not be affected by Tod's moods? Wouldn't that make me a cold, unfeeling woman, a latter-day Mary Tyler Moore type of character she played in *Ordinary People?* Apparently the answer is no. According to quite a few couples, not having your happiness dependent on your spouse's actually frees you to breathe more deeply and be more compassionate, like being able to reach your hand out to a drowning man without fearing you will tumble into the swell yourself. With discipline and some support, you can actually learn to, figuratively speaking, watch your spouse running frantically from room to room in a self-constructed house of hopelessness without feeling you have to move in with him or her.

One consistent message I heard from all the longtime couples on the subject of relaxation that gave me pause is that like happiness, being relaxed is a state of being we can actually bring to the marriage, rather than expecting the marriage to deliver it to us.

And frankly, folks, relaxing together doesn't have to be that deep.

CLAIRE ROTHMAN AND ED HILL
A Little Retail Relaxation

Claire Rothman and Ed Hill are both in their eighties and have been together for thirty years. They have put in their time being intense about life and now very much appreciate relaxing and letting themselves enjoy life. It's easy to pick Claire out of a crowd with her wildly colorful outfits, fabulous hand-crafted jewelry, and one long thin braid adorned with a feather peeking out of her stylishly cropped silver hair. Although she has mellowed over time, you can feel vestiges of the powerhouse she used to be back when she served as general manager and vice president of the Los Angeles Forum from January 1975 to May of 1995. Ed has twinkly azure-blue eyes, a warm smile, a soft-spoken sensitivity, and a highly inquisitive nature that made him one of the most sought-after Beverly Hills ophthalmologists back in the day. He's also an artist whose sensuous sculptures are displayed throughout their home.

When we met, Claire and Ed sat very close together holding hands. It's a second marriage for both of them, which is one reason they didn't rush to the altar, marrying only three years ago. They do, however, rush to just about every cultural event in Los Angeles, New York, San Francisco, and London. Age has not slowed them down. Whether it's a museum, a concert, or a play, these two have a genuine shared passion for the arts.

What makes them giggle like teenagers, though, is talking about buying clothes.

"We love going to the shops together. I'll try things on and, well, no one has better taste than Ed," Claire told me, squeezing his hand.

"We have a lot of fun together," Ed said. "Shopping helps us forget all the intense stuff in our lives. It relaxes us."

Touch is also very important to these two lovebirds. They both feel strongly that being affectionate with each other, something that Claire credits Ed with teaching her, also creates a connection that instantly relaxes them.

DID SOMEONE SAY TAE KWON DO?

Johanna and David, the couple who made the surprise move to Chicago and then back to LA, have found their own way to relax. In the last few years they have been studying martial arts, like Sherman

Oaks ninja warriors. Johanna told me about the blue belts they both recently earned together in both tae kwon do and hapkido. David was looking to fill the void after giving up his main passion, sailing. He sold his boat soon after their daughter Sadie was born. "He felt it was too dangerous for the baby, and he couldn't fathom wanting to spend whole days away from us to go sailing by himself," Johanna told me. Fortuitously enough, in a silent auction at their daughter's preschool Johanna had won two weeks of lessons (and a uniform!) at a martial arts studio.

Within weeks she persuaded David to join her, so he bought a two-week pass and a uniform, too. They have been going to classes ever since and it's become something they look forward to doing together.

"No matter how crappy my mood is when I walk in there," Johanna told me, "I always feel better when I leave."

Hearing her, I envision the perfect romantic evening where, after their fabulous class at which her husband artfully and yet forcefully throws her on the mat a few times, he then whisks her away to a candlelit dinner where they talk about the philosophical, historical, and psychological impact of martial arts on the human spirit. I asked Johanna to share with me the juicy passion of a dojo-ing couple for a vicarious thrill.

"We usually just go home since we have to relieve the sitter."

Oh, right, *real life*. Which is important to remember (yet again) when exploring options for relaxation together. It doesn't have to be the most magical and transformative relaxation ever. What's more important is making the effort to do something that helps you breathe deeper and slow down with each other.

HUG IT OUT

One surprisingly low-impact relaxation technique that is so obvious it sounds like a joke is something called "hugging until you relax." It's a genuine exercise that was introduced by David Schnarch in his book *Passionate Marriage*. Schnarch breaks it down very simply. "Stand on your own two feet. Put your arms around your partner. Focus on *your-self.* Quiet yourself down—way down."[3]

Schnarch goes on to analyze how hugging between couples is a reflection of how they relate to each other in nonphysical ways, and how learning to do it effectively can help in a lot of areas of your relationship. His detailed analysis is complex—trying to follow it all was making me tense. My mind cleared as soon as I read that a good hug can also lead to some good sex. You already know in great detail what a fan I am of couples having sex, so this basic by-product of Schnarch's hugging exercise makes it an excellent one to add to your list of relaxation techniques.

But what if it's been a long day and you're bone-tired and don't feel like having sex or even a deep, meaningful hug, or shopping, or chanting, or schlepping to a tae kwon do class. There is one other highly effective way to relax together that even the most tightly scheduled and exhausted can find the time and energy to do: laughing.

Dr. Annette Goodheart (1935–2011) had a successful career as an artist, but after three years of therapy with her husband to try to salvage their marriage, she became involved "in a peer counseling organization that focused on catharsis." This is where she was introduced to the cathartic value of laughter. According to Goodheart, "I made more progress and changed my life more spectacularly than I had in my previous three years of conventional therapy."[4] She laid out her basic belief clearly in her book, *Laughter Therapy:* "Laughter itself is a delightful form of whole body relaxation. It gives our diaphragm much-needed exercise that contributes to our inner well-being."[5] When it comes to promoting relaxation, Goodheart wrote, "One of the most extraordinary things about laughter is that it is impossible to laugh and not have one's awareness in the present. It is a totally present activity. It is impossible to laugh and think about what you need to get at the grocery store or pick up at the cleaners or what someone said to you earlier at the office."[6]

Goodheart was not the first expert to extol the far-reaching benefits of laughter. In 1979, the acclaimed writer, editor, and political activist Norman Cousins brought the idea front and center in his book, Anatomy of an Illness. In it Cousins wrote about how he cured himself of ankylosing spondylitis, a painful form of arthritis for which there is no known cure, with laughter. He is probably most known for referring to laughter as "internal jogging," claiming that "ten minutes of genuine laughter had an anesthetic effect and would give me at least two hours of pain-free sleep."[7]

The interest in humor and laughter is still strong. Almost thirty years after the publication of Cousins's book, in 2014 the cognitive neuroscientist Scott Weems published Ha! The Science of When We Laugh and Why, dedicated to the investigation of humor and "it's most common symptom—laughter."[8]

In an article for Psychology Today, Weems tells his readers, "Comedy is like mental exercise, and just as physical exercise strengthens the body, comedy pumps up the mind."[9] Most important for couples, he adds, "Compared to those in dysfunctional marriages, couples in strong ones also say that they value and appreciate their partner's humor more. Indeed, studies examining long-term couples—those who have remained together for forty-five years or more—have found that laughing together is essential for marital success."[10]

I know from experience that after a long day where I've been chasing kids and Tod's been holed up at work, the two of us living parallel and disconnected lives, laughing about a New Yorker cartoon together or sitting on the couch laughing at some crazy shenanigans that Stephen Colbert was getting away with definitely connected us. Exactly as Weems says, by sharing a laugh. This experience not only creates all those positive physical effects on your body, it can also provide hints, however momentary, of what else you might be able to share.

Swirling all the positive effects of laughter in my brain, that it oxygenates the blood in the same way working out does, improves the immune system, and on its simplest level relaxes us, made me reflect for a minute on the relationship between relaxation, comedians, and couples.

The more I learned about the positive power of laughter to create human connection, the more my own suspicion was confirmed that laughter is what we all need. I love the idea that comedians find ways to relax themselves—by practicing TM, going to the gym, or listening to music, whatever it takes, so they can be fully present to make people laugh, which then relaxes those people and makes them more present and connected to whoever they're with, a friend, a date, or a spouse. No apps, no smartphones, no electronic interfacing needed. By use of the transitive property, which I haven't talked about since high school algebra, comedians, and the work that they do, create connection between people, including married people, and this is why I celebrate them. It's an even bigger gift to couples, because as the therapist Jan Jorden told me, "Shared laughter is the closest point between two people other than an orgasm."

As far as creating relaxation in your marriage is concerned, if you retain nothing else from this chapter, except maybe that last statement, remember that how you relax is not important, it only matters that you find ways to do it. Maybe some days it's not about laughter—maybe having a good cry is the order of the day. Or chanting, or dancing around the living room naked with a feather boa. Anything that allows you to breathe deeply and shake off the stresses of the day will be a great service to you and your marriage.

TIPS FOR CREATING RELAXATION

- Make relaxation a daily habit. Create calming rituals in your day. Share a bottle of wine, sit down together for a meal. Slow down, and free yourself of distractions. Carving out the space and time to slow down and take some deep breaths will help you be more present not only in your marriage but also in your life.

- Be creative about where and how you relax together. Relaxation shouldn't be complicated. Snuggle up and read out loud to each other, take a walk around the block holding hands, go shopping if that makes you both happy. Explore a physical discipline or practice, ideally together. Bonus points for ones that involve deep breathing or total focus, such as yoga, martial arts, playing musical instruments or singing, and chanting.

- Don't wait for "perfect relaxation." Sometimes just being affectionate for a minute on the couch or passing each other in the hallway can be soothing and create connection.

- Give your spouse a hug for at least a minute or two. It is scientifically proven to relax you and make you feel bonded—almost literally—to your spouse.

- Laugh together—a running theme throughout this book. Laughing together creates an immediate connection. Share a video or a cartoon that makes you laugh, or find a comedian you both like and make a point to go see them live. Laughing immediately relaxes you and laughing together creates a shared experience that opens your heart.

9

Watch Your Wardrobe

} How You Look Matters {

The kinkiest thing I ever did was when my husband asked me
to dress up for him, as a nurse, because that's his fantasy, that
we have health care.

—WENDY LIEBMAN, comedian, married eleven years

A woman who looked to be about thirty, wearing no makeup, a flannel
shirt, faded jeans, and Birkenstocks walked onstage. She said nothing.

"Single," a voice from the audience yelled out.

"From the Northeast," said a second voice.

"Angry daughter of a Republican," guessed another.

"More comfortable with animals than people," a fourth one shouted.

This woman was not getting heckled at a show, she was participat-
ing in one of my favorite exercises for a comedy class, one I do with all
my students at every level. As soon as everyone has checked in, before
they've had a chance to chat with each other, I bring them up individually and invite their classmates to shout out adjectives describing the
person they see. I set up some boundaries to protect people's feelings.
You can't yell out anything a Seth MacFarlane character might say.

When you're a comic, audiences make decisions about you before you even step up to the microphone. What you choose to wear affects those perceptions. Obviously, what you have on is not the only part of your physical appearance that people take in when they see you, but unlike being seven feet tall, or having a nose like Jimmy Durante's, or any other physical feature you are born with, how you present yourself, your clothing choices, hair, shoes, these are all choices you make that tell us something about you. Whether we want to acknowledge it or not, our physical presence communicates a part of who we are. How we choose to dress is part of the picture we paint onstage. So wardrobe choices matter for us as performers.

Clearly, these choices affect nonperformers, too, or the fashion industry with its impossibly skinny women and the people who clothe them would have to go away forever. That would be unbearably sad.

The exercise confirms something we've all heard, but not often in regard to our appearance: a picture tells a thousand words. Often my students have no idea the impression their "picture" is making. Some of the descriptions have included "hidden sexiness," or "smarter than he looks," "tired," "defeated," which can be a little overwhelming to hear from strangers. Nevertheless this feedback is invaluable to people who are using their physical presence in their art.

A lot of the comedian Sarah Silverman's early success was due to the contradiction between her looking like a fifteen-year-old girl and saying outrageous, X-rated things, a contrast she intentionally created to get laughs. Although she's changed her image to become a lot more glamorous in recent years, she sometimes will still put on a hoodie and a ponytail for performances.

What's startling about this exercise is how shockingly accurate the responses to the person onstage often are. Comments that may sound flippant at first, like "hates cats," or "left home at a young age," can be bull's-eyes. In fact, the woman onstage at the beginning of this chapter was raised in Connecticut and, when the exercise was over, revealed that she worked as a dog walker and did, in fact, prefer the company of animals over humans. Of course, this impression was not just a function of her wardrobe, but what she was wearing played a significant part in shaping the assumptions people made about her. Whether you are aware of it or not, how you hold your body, your facial expressions, and your grooming also all say something about you. Everyone who sees you takes all of this in—strangers, classmates, audience members in a club, and, no surprise here, spouses.

But wait a minute, I can hear you yelling defiantly: a marriage is not a performance! A marriage is a deep, soulful connection to a life partner! We shouldn't have to worry about how we present ourselves to our spouses. In our home life is where we can let it all hang out. This is a politically correct, postfeminist, and romantically sound idea. In theory. Unfortunately, it just doesn't work that well in a real marriage for the long haul. In a marriage, as onstage, when it comes to our self-care, attention must be paid.

I must admit that I absolutely resist this rule of comedy in my marriage. I, too, would love to believe that home is where the sweatpants are. In fact, my instincts are to wear a college T-shirt and jeans every day for the rest of my life. There are two problems with this jeans and T-shirt uniform. First, for most of us who are over forty and have had children, it is harder to pull off without looking lumpy. Second, it's a slippery slope heading to the aforementioned sweatpants. Sweatpants are to clothing what Nutella is to food. Yes, they function as pants, just like Nutella is edible. Yet, each of them, either worn or eaten to the exclusion of all other choices, can depress the shit out of you. And your mate.

The comic Karen Bergreen (from chapter 4, "Know Your Audience") brought up an interesting point about looking nice early in my research that turned out to hit the nail on the head for a lot of couples. "The issue of physical appearance is consistent with my audiences and my husband," she said. "It's about effort. Audiences want to see me make an effort for them, and so does my husband. If I did this more consistently, I am sure both my act and my marriage would benefit from this." Making an effort in your appearance is important for a lot of couples.

David Hunt, husband of Patricia Heaton, expressed himself passionately about this when we talked. "Our entire marriage Patty's been dolled up for everybody else, for twenty years, and never dresses for me. If she dresses up it's for the business or for her girlfriends, but it's never for her husband." He seemed genuinely hurt.

Just a few months before I spoke with David, I had heard almost the exact sentiment expressed to me by the very funny comic Sam Brown, a dear friend who was losing his short battle with pancreatic cancer. His wife had plans to go out, so I went to their house to spend time with him in case he needed anything. After the door shut behind her he leaned in to me and said, "You have no idea what it's like for me to watch her get dressed up and go out with her girlfriends when she never gets dressed up for me."

"Yeah, that must be tough," I said. But what I was thinking is that Sam's wife is a very attractive woman, who always makes sure she's put together. I'd seen her clicking around their kitchen in kitten heels making him smoothies. I suspected he was feeling sensitive about any time she spent away from him, knowing his days were numbered, so any attention not paid to him was understandably upsetting. But hearing David express a similar sentiment—having hurt feelings seeing his wife dress up for everyone but him—so soon afterward gave me pause to reconsider what I thought was Sam's illness talking. That these were two very different men at vastly different stages in their lives made their sentiments hard for me to dismiss. I wondered if I was guilty of this with Tod. Did I take more care dressing for pitch meetings, lunch dates, and my ladies' night out than I do when it's just the two of us? I couldn't say for sure.

The other interesting facet that these two men brought to the surface was that their disappointment wasn't limited only to the physical or the visual of, say, not seeing their wives in high heels and push-up bras more. No, as I found with every discussion about wardrobe that I had with couples, either separately or together, the conversation always gravitated to a deeper place than the clothing choices themselves. In long-term marriages it's not just your spouse's physical appearance that matters; it is also the effort you make just for them that can make them feel loved. Or not.

I asked David to tell me more about his experiences with Patty in this area. "When you were dating, your wife's intention was about attracting you, but the moment after you get married, that goes away. You feel not valued. If it happens over a long period of time it's hurtful. That's how you start to create distance [in the marriage]."

Fortunately, Patricia was in the room so I was able to get her reaction, which she was eager to share. "Part of it is, there are some women that enjoy doing the kinky dress-up thing, but I've always been sort of Catholic. For me it feels creepy and stupid. It's not my nature. It's not who I am. I'm more of a sweatshirt gal. But it's true that I do dress up for showbiz stuff." She threw a contrite look to David. Then another thought came to her. "I also think women work all day with the kids and do all this stuff and then they're supposed to do yet another thing, it gets to be too much. Women are caretakers and it bleeds over into the bedroom and they feel like they have to be caretakers there, too."

The three of us looked at each other for a moment. Patricia wasn't wrong, but I think we were all wondering how we got from making the effort to look nice for each other in a marriage to women feeling like oppressed caretakers.

David broke the tension. "That's a bigger conversation," he said, and laughed.

A bigger conversation. Yes.

Exactly what I discovered about the subject of wardrobe in marriage. When I first focused on my stand-up rule to "pay attention to wardrobe" as being relevant to marriage, I thought this would end up as a throw-away chapter. I figured I'd toss out the wardrobe question to couples and some of the wives would share a few ideas about shopping while the husbands nodded and checked their smartphones, just like they would if their wives dragged them to any store other than Victoria's Secret. I was wrong. My supposition was that this would be a superficial issue, but what was revealed to me is that a spouse's physicality, how they groom and dress themselves, has deeper meaning in many marriages. It functions on a visual level, sure, but in many cases it can also touch on many other issues and feelings, including but not limited to the following:

- Feeling like you're not being seen by your spouse
- A measure of the effort the other person is willing to make just for you
- A desire to control the other person
- Openness to your spouse's suggestions
- Something requiring acceptance
- Maintaining a sense of humor

Leaving the house in a ripped T-shirt and flip-flops on date night can actually hurt your spouse's feelings. Who knew?

In talking to long-term couples, I found that a discussion about wardrobe included not just how you present yourself to the world, but also grooming, and even complementary lifestyle habits like not chomping on cookies while lying on the 400-thread-count sheets on the bed, please. Or not wearing the skins of dead animals or, God forbid, their fur, thank you very much. These actions can also affect the level of happiness a couple shares.

In the previous chapter we talked about not letting your contentment be dependent on your spouse. But if what the other person wears offends you—whether it's leather jackets or a "work in the front, party in the back" mullet—you have to be able to share these feelings with the person you look at every day, sometimes twice a day.

For many couples, holding a "this is what I like you to wear" conversation is very effective. In Sarah and David Aftergood's case, Sarah made sure she created this kind of communication before they married.

SARAH AND DAVID AFTERGOOD
A Look That Didn't Kill

Sarah and David have been together for thirty-five years. They met on a blind date set up by one of Sarah's brothers. Today, David is a well-respected endocrinologist, and a soft-spoken man of very few words. Sarah, a mother of three and also a grandmother of three, is a vivacious, enthusiastic woman who loves to be surrounded by lots of colorful art and people. When I visited them at their home, there was a full-size reproduction of a Native American teepee set up in their living room.

"The grandkids love it," Sarah told me with a broad smile, "and now we do too!"

When they met in 1977 Sarah and David's fathers both worked in the garment industry. David's father manufactured men's Hawaiian shirts, the kind with the print on the inside, which was "very fashionable at the time," Sarah said. David was a new resident at UCLA and showed up to a date wearing one of these shirts. It did not impress his future wife. Neither did his mop of frizzy brown hair. She quickly got him two Lacoste T-shirts, and had him get a haircut, because, as she said, "I like a man preppy." More than thirty years later, she still makes his wardrobe decisions. "Say how often you go to a store," Sarah told her husband.

"Quite rarely," David obliged.

"I buy all his clothes," she said, smiling.

"Basically I gave her that part of the relationship. She's my dresser," David said.

"The first time we met he was so schleppy looking," Sarah explained, "but I knew he had potential. But those shirts . . . I swear, on our second date we went shopping."

"She has certain taste in clothing and the way people dress and I was happy to accommodate that," he said, in the rational tone you would expect of a successful doctor.

Although this arrangement would not work for everyone, it works for David and Sarah. Interestingly, when I asked David what he feels about Sarah's wardrobe choices, he paused and said, "I don't usually have criticism of Sarah's clothes."

Sarah laughed nervously and added, "I don't think he sees what I'm wearing unless there's a thread hanging." She was joking, but there was a painful undercurrent in her words of not feeling seen by her husband, and also that when he does notice, it's to point out a flaw.

I commented on how tough this must be for her, which led us to a brief discussion about David's work as an endocrinologist. How he is paid to detect the tiniest hormonal anomalies, and that after three decades doing this work, finding the flaw has become reflexive for him. The aberration, what is wrong with the picture, this is where his eye goes first. Sarah is not blind to the challenges of living with a man whose mind has been conditioned this way. She shrugged in a "What can you do?" way and quickly added, "He's very good at what he does."

Sarah's joke about what her husband sees and doesn't see in her clothing choices stayed with me as I drove home. Her staccato laugh immediately after her comment, and the quick blinking of her eyes felt like she was trying to flick away how not funny it actually felt. If I were Sarah I would long to be looked at by my husband with more nuance and passion than how he looks at an X-ray. But maybe I was projecting something onto her that she stopped worrying about decades ago.

Betsy Stern also makes a lot of clothing choices for her husband of twenty-three years, Mark Stern, but it isn't only about giving Mark a makeover. Given her expertise as a former stylist who now runs her own interior design firm, Burnham Design, when it comes to having your wife dress you for success, Mark couldn't be in better hands. Which is great for him because as a television producer in image-conscious Hollywood, it also makes good business sense.

BETSY AND MARK STERN
Living, Loving, Dressing

Betsy and Mark Stern have been married for twenty-three years. They met as undergrads, took a short break, and have been together ever since. Mark is fit, with darting brown eyes and short-cropped hair. He has a wiry intelligence that makes his raucous laugh a surprise. Betsy, also brown-eyed, has a more reserved and careful way of speaking. You get the sense that everything about her is thought through with an eye on being tasteful. Sitting on a big soft couch covered in a soothing fabric, my arm resting on the exact right throw pillow and looking across at Betsy in her tailored pants and T-shirt with just the right cut to flatter her figure, I started to fantasize about what it would be like to be her. But then her disarming honesty about adjusting to Mark's less demonstrative family early on, and about missing her daughter who is a college freshman 3,000 miles away, reminded me that no matter how chic one may be, no one goes through life unscathed.

Lucky for Mark, Betsy is ready, willing, and more than able to keep him looking fashion forward from head to toe. It's a job she apparently takes seriously, because when I asked Mark if there is pressure living with someone so tuned in to style he quickly said, "Yes, there is."

"I've let a lot of that go in our marriage," Betsy cut in.

"Really?" Mark responded, in a way that made me feel like only minutes before she'd asked him, "Are you really going to wear that?"

"Yes, I have," Betsy said, and pointed to his leg. "Look at the shoe and sock that I'm seeing right now. It's so upsetting. But you know, I love him."

"Despite his sneakers," Mark joked. "Actually what we do a lot now is, I just ask her point-blank, can you pick out what I'm going to wear?"

"And I'm happy to do it," Betsy said.

Mark elaborated. "It can be a real imposition, but it makes her feel good to help me."

Betsy smiled. "Here's the funny thing about that. Yes, I want the control. I'm lucky that I have an easygoing husband, so he doesn't stress about it. If I lay something out, he just puts it on. Happily."

When I asked if this is a reciprocal relationship, meaning if Mark put a few items out on the bed for her to wear, would that work? They both did the snort-laugh.

"That would be funny," Mark said.

"Oh my God!" Betsy said, louder than I'd heard her before.

"There's no way I would put it on. It doesn't work both ways, but we know that about each other."

Since the mood was light and everyone was being so direct, I asked Mark what it feels like to be a grown man and have someone lay out his clothes.

"Well," he replied, not backing down from the question at all, "I get a lot of positive feedback from people, so I've learned to just go with it. For the most part. It's hard for me because Betsy will hand me a shirt and I'll say, 'I'm never going to wear that,' and then it turns out to be my favorite shirt. So I've learned to let that instinct go, too, where if it's different and weird and I don't get it, I try to still give it a chance."

Was he only talking about shirts or might this just be the key to the success of their twenty-three-year marriage? This seems like a terrific attitude to have about any suggestion your spouse makes. And I'm glad Betsy used the word "control" first, because I was certainly thinking it and didn't want to risk being insulting. As I mentioned earlier, control can play a role in dressing and resisting dressing each other and is something to be aware of.

So it's great to be open to trying suggestions from your spouse, as Mark discovered. You can always take something off and never wear it again. But you might discover that an item you never would have put on becomes a favorite that you run home to change in to.

The image-wardrobe-grooming conversation isn't only about control. In fact it's a great opportunity for that other marriage "c" word— my favorite for couples—collaboration. And in case you thought it's only women who dress their husbands, I have some news for you.

DANNY AND MICHELLE GREENBERG
She (Also) Wears the Pants in the Family

Danny Greenberg is the listening challenged husband we met in chapter 2. He may not be good aurally, but he certainly pays attention to visuals. "He loves me to dress conservatively," his wife, Michelle, told me. "If I wore a button-down white shirt, tweed pants, and a blazer, he'd be thrilled."

"Only to work events," Danny responded. "My image is conservative, so I prefer her to be consistent with me."

Michelle laughed. "I'm pretty conservative, but if I'm wearing a shirt and my bra is sticking out even a little, he'll say something. He loves it the most when we go to functions and every girl is in a dress, and I'm in slacks."

"You look good in slacks," Danny said. Michelle smiled knowingly. "I found this great pair of tweed pants, very conservative, New England pants, and he loved them, so I bought two and I wear them to every function. It makes him very happy."

Michelle's openness to dressing in a way that makes her husband happy was an accommodation a lot of couples talked about to a greater or lesser degree. Either one or both people were willing to groom themselves or dress in a way that pleased their spouse. Whether it's the woman who wears short skirts for her husband, even though she hates her legs, or the man who leaves his sandals home on date night, each one cared enough to wear what their mate liked.

I noticed that my own reaction to hearing about these concessions was always the same: nervous laughter. "That's so great!" I'd say, a little too enthusiastically, followed by a barky-sounding guffaw. It took me a while to figure out why I was having that reaction. Then it hit me: it all just sounded way too—here's that word again—vulnerable. There is something so open about asking what your spouse likes, having them tell you honestly, and then doing it. It made me think about the fact that Tod loves it when I wear boots. So in our time together, when I feel like it, I wear them. When *I* feel like it. Not when he feels like it. Talking to these couples, I had to ask myself if there isn't a part of me that's afraid that if I wear what Tod wants me to when he wants me to, wouldn't that be lame? Or at the very least, antifeminist? A political dodge—talk about lame! The truth is that by being responsive to what Tod likes I would be saying, "I love you so much that I am willing to alter my appearance for you."

As much as I resist it, in couple after happy couple it was exactly this level of vulnerability and openness that I saw working. They open themselves up to each other even when it feels dumb and scary and nearly impossible to do.

> Maybe your spouse doesn't care what you wear, but maybe he or she does, so take the time to ask them and to give them a chance to have enough influence to make them happy. It costs so little to do this, and the potential payoff of feeling connected to each other in this intimate way is worth it.

Sometimes the way you show your love for your better half has nothing to do with making or not making clothing choices for each other. Sometimes the real expression of your heart when it comes to image and wardrobe is accepting that your mate is never going to give a hoot about his or her appearance and finding a way to laugh about it. This is the highly effective approach that Rae Dubow, a public speaking coach, takes with her husband of twenty-five years, the writer and critic David L. Ulin.

DAVID AND RAE
Clothes Do Not Make Her Man

David Ulin and Rae Dubow met as undergraduates and have been together for thirty-two years. They have two teenage children. David is a staff writer for the *Los Angeles Times* and author of several books, including *The Lost Art of Reading*. He has dark hair, dark eyes, and a relaxed presence. He feels comfortable with himself, confident without being cocky. A "No, I didn't invent an app, but I've done something worthwhile with my life," kind of man. His eyes light up whenever Rae talks. Rae is a former actress who now has a business coaching people for public speaking engagements. She has lovely gray-green eyes and an unexpected girlish quality when she smiles. Or maybe it just felt girlish because she showed me a picture of herself the year she met David, when she was twenty, and her smile hadn't changed. Her manner is slightly more reserved than David's. Of the two, she feels like the one who keeps the trains running on time in the family. These two have a warmth and ease together that makes you want to snuggle up on the couch with them. Although they have a lot in common, like a deep appreciation of the life of the mind and a love of great art and music, an interest in physical appearance is not something they share.

Rae's resignation about David's lack of interest in what he looks like made me laugh more than once. "I've dressed the same way since I was twelve," David told me.

"Exactly," Rae responded.

"It's a big deal. It's one of those acceptance things for me," Rae said. David readjusted himself on the couch and added, "I don't care about my own wardrobe. I guess I care about your wardrobe."

Rae was struck by this comment. "What are you talking about?" she asked.

"I mean that I like the way you look in certain clothes," David explained. "For myself I don't care. I just want to be comfortable."

"That's true," Rae said, taking a sip of tea. David has no problem complimenting Rae, but it's not reciprocal. "There's nothing good to say about the way David dresses," she said. I couldn't tell if we were having a good-natured discussion or if Rae was genuinely upset.

Until David leapt to his feet and said, "You never say to me, 'David, you look great in that promotional T-shirt! In that Common Sense T-shirt!'" Then they both laughed hard. David the anti-dresser is clearly an inside joke they have shared for thirty years.

When they stopped laughing, Rae, now loosened up, was motivated to tell me more about the sacrifices she's made for David's lack of vanity. "He had a ponytail until seven years ago."

"Yep," David said, "and until 2000 I was the guy with the long gray beard."

Rae laughed. "Ugh. When I met him in college all my friends said, 'He's disgusting, why are you going out with him? He's dirty; you can do so much better. Look at the way he dresses.'" I looked over at David and he was smiling ear to ear, the sly cat who married the hot canary. Rae smiled back. "And you still dress exactly the same way," she said, slapping his thigh and then turning back to me. "Like I said, it's an acceptance thing. I mean, I love him. What's not to love? I mean now that the long gray beard is gone."

You can and should make requests of your mate, but there comes a time—and it's different for every couple when that is—that if you keep being met with resistance, and you want to be happy together, you have to, as Rae said, make it an "acceptance thing." Decide that your love for your spouse is bigger than how they dress or how they wear their hair and focus on all the parts you love about them. Their sexy voice, their graceful hands, or the way they care for your children. Or, hopefully best of all, the way they make you laugh.

Jan Gordon and Derek Chow, together for thirty-three years, are another couple who are on different pages when it comes to fashion, and yet they have found a way to make it work. Jan is a sporty mother of three who doesn't have the time or interest to doll up for her man. Derek is fine with this, although he does have one criterion for Jan's clothing.

"Her clothes have to come off quickly and easily."

Well, all right then!

There's one other dynamic that can exist in a couple's wardrobe arena that is tougher to bring to the surface, but worth mentioning. It's something that happens when it seems like one person doesn't care but really, they do. I wouldn't have thought about it if it hadn't happened with us.

With the exception of Tod's love of boots, neither of us tends to say much about what the other is wearing. However, on one particularly exhausted Saturday night when our boys were still very young, I donned a peasant skirt with an elastic waist in used-to-be forest green with a stretched out T-shirt and flip-flops. It wasn't that I didn't want to make an effort for our date night, it's that I didn't want to make an effort for myself. I had tried a few other outfits on before landing on the homeless beachside peasant attire, but either the other outfits didn't fit or they had kid puke on them. So I gave up. I wasn't actually in a depression (although if someone is consistently and uncharacteristically wearing torn, dirty clothing and not bothering to wash his or her hair it's a possibility to consider). I just didn't have the strength to keep working my way through my clothes, so I grabbed the few items that live permanently at the bottom of my closet.

"Sweetheart, really?" Tod asked as I headed to the car.

"What?" I answered, glancing down, looking for a stain or a moth hole. All clear. I looked up. "What?"

"Nothing. It's fine."

Long story short, two weeks later a woman showed up at the door carrying a large purse and a stack of magazines. "She's going to help you organize your closet," Tod said, pushing the boys out the back door. Tod was concerned that my extended postpartum head had gotten the better of me and hired someone to help. I certainly can't ever claim I don't feel seen by my husband.

"There's no reason for you to leave the house that way. Ever," he told me after she left. "Was she great?" he asked. "Um, I guess so," still reeling a little that he thought I was in such dire straits that we needed to hire someone to help me get it together. But the truth is, I would never have done something like that for myself, and it was worthwhile. She championed my getting rid of clothes I hadn't worn in years and also helped me accept my body after carrying two children in four and a half years. I believed Tod when he said he was more concerned for me than offended by me—but hiring this woman also made it clear that he was not giving up on me, even if I had. He held out higher hopes for me than my apparent resignation to wearing ill-fitting, faded, faux prairie-girl outfits for the rest of our lives together.

WHEN LOOKING BAD REFLECTS FEELING BAD

To be clear, none of this matters in the face of illness. If you are going to cancer treatments, no one who loves you is going to give a shit if you are in soft, stretchy gear. I am talking about making the effort to keep ourselves looking our best, or at least not our worst, for each other. So if you feel yourself or your partner slipping into some kind of new self-destructive resignation, often accompanied by gallons of ice cream, bottles of scotch, and cartons of cigarettes, bring it up and talk about it.

Tod actually has a theory about image and long-term couples that he surprised me with recently. "When you meet someone and you are attracted to him or her," he told me, "there's that thing that drew your eyes to them, the way they present themselves is part of that, but then, we get older. How do you retain whatever it was about that style that initially attracted your mate and allow it to mature appropriately without obliterating it?"

A heady question I would have loved to take on when Tod first asked, but I was too distracted by the idea that apparently I was supposed to "mature appropriately." I had never done this at any time in any area of my life, but there's a first time for everything, and if my wardrobe was where it was going to happen first, I was game. It's good he brought in a professional to help me with this because other than buying some Ann Taylor separates and ditching my gold platform thrift store sandals, I was clueless how to realize this vision. After I got over the shock of the expectation that I should mature, I had to give it up to Tod for his take that when it comes to your looks you need to mature in a way that still keeps your mate hot for you.

If, like the rest of us mortals, physical appearance is something you both value,[1] there is no definitive answer to Tod's question, but I did uncover a solid suggestion. Which, in truth, is the answer to this entire issue of wardrobe and grooming in a long-term relationship. The only way to be responsive and happy with each other about it at any age is to have the curiosity and the courage to ask the other person what they like and don't like. Not just that hackneyed question, "Do these jeans make me look fat?"(which every sane person knows only has one right answer), but genuine questions such as, "What do you like to see me wear?" Then, spouses need to be willing, despite how vulnerable it feels, to keep looking good for each other. Or find a way to laugh about it.

TIPS FOR DRESSING FOR (MARITAL) SUCCESS

- Make an effort just for your spouse. We all have occasions when we have to dress nicely, for work or weddings or special celebrations with friends. But once in a while, women, throw on the boots or the push-up bra! Men, take off the sandals or the college Converses and put on something other than jeans, and go paint the town red.

- Don't assume you know what your spouse likes you to wear. Take the time to ask them the question directly. When you get the answer, give it a try. Even if it sounds unflattering. You may be surprised, and whatever it is, it's not permanent. You can always never wear it again.

- Matters of appearance are not limited to clothing. Be open to suggestions from your spouse about beards, haircuts, manicures, man-purses.

- Let the spouse who likes to shop do it. Have a conversation about what you both like and then let the person who enjoys retail therapy have a field day.

- Let your look mature as you do. If, unlike me, you plan on maturing as you age, your look should also evolve. Get to the essence of what attracted your partner to you and do your best to retain whatever that is. Check in with each other periodically to see if tastes have changed for either of you.

- Pay attention to your own physical appearance, too. Just like the comic who needs to be aware of his or her presence and to be comfortable enough with it to use to their advantage, you also have to stay in touch with your body and how you present yourself so you can be your most confident. Plus, people who are confident have more sex—you don't need a scientific study to prove that!—and sex is good for your marriage.

10

Stay Current

> WITH JOKES AND MARRIAGE,
> STAY UP TO DATE

My wife loves me, wants to trust me, but she thinks I'm fooling around on her in my own home, while we're *in* it. The thing she asks me most is "Where're you going?" I get up to get a cookie, "Where are you going?," just roll over in bed, "Where are you going?" Two o'clock in the morning getting out of bed in my underwear she'll pop up out of a dead sleep, "Where are you going?" Where am I going? To have sex with a midget I stored in the medicine cabinet, where do you think I'm going?"

—TOM PAPA, comedian, married fourteen years

"I have a favorite joke," Laura House, a comedian and writer for twenty years, told me recently over coffee. "It goes something like this: 'I have a friend who is so upset about the remake of the Willy Wonka movie, but I was like, what's the problem? It's not like they tape over the original. You can still watch the original.' I can't do that bit anymore because who 'tapes over' things? And also, they shot that remake nine years ago. No one would get this joke. As a comic, it's kind of a drag because no matter how much you love a joke, you have to stay current. There are things that have left the zeitgeist and you have to know this. No one wants to hear jokes that riff on Monica Lewinsky's dress any more. You gotta give that one up."

I was glad Laura brought this up—staying current, that is, not Monica Lewinsky's dress. I was looking for a way to differentiate the importance of staying current from knowing your audience (discussed in chapter 4). Laura's insistence that comedians be in the present moment with their material gave me the distinction I needed.

Clearly she is passionate about this topic, because she had more to say about it: "I have this middle-aged buddy who has been married for, like, eleven years. The guy wears a ring, and then he gets up onstage and does dating material. Or the comic who says, 'I have a six-year-old' and you know the guy's kid is in college, but they tell me, 'Yeah, but I love that six-year-old bit!' Or the comic who has his own television show but when he does his act he's like, 'Yep, just scrapin' money together for the Taco Bell.' Um, really? 'Cause I think your show went into syndication, so you probably don't have to do too much scraping by anymore," she said, and then laughed.

As a comedian, you have to respect your audience enough to write jokes that are in touch with what is happening right now, both in the club and in the world. People can log in to VH1.com to see outdated material at home in their underwear. When they get dressed and leave the house and are paying to see you live, they expect the lion's share of the jokes to be up-to-date.

Marriage needs updates, too. Spouses can also stay home in their underwear, bury their heads in their laptops or their smartphone or their television and not hear anything new about each other either. Don't let this happen. Expect at least as much from your spouse as you do from a headliner. Yes, you need to know them in the ways we discussed earlier, you need to know their history, what matters to them, what their aspirations are, what they care about on a soulful level, all of the elements that make up their character. But staying current involves staying on top of what is going on with them on a daily basis. You can know all of that deeper stuff about your spouse and still get to a place in your marriage where you don't know what they do all day.

As a comic, you might be able to get away with one or two oldies but goodies, but if all you are bringing is the old stuff, pretty soon the audience will tune you out and start to read the two-dollar-appetizer menu with enthusiasm. By the same token, you can coast for a little while in a marriage, without sharing specifics about your feelings and your life with each other, but if it goes on for too long pretty soon you are looking across from each other at dinner wishing there was an appetizer menu at home to peruse because you're so disconnected you can't find anything to talk about. Then it can start to feel like you'll never get that connection back.

We're all busy, so it's not hard to imagine how this can happen even with someone you love. But if you don't keep your husband or wife current with what's going on, not only will you feel disconnected, but also it becomes hard to fully understand or appreciate what your spouse is talking about when you finally do check in with each other. When this happens, you're not only robbing your marriage of shared laughter, you're also limiting all the other shared feelings of compassion, empathy, and even joy.

The marriage and family counselor Dr. Donna Emmanuel strongly advises people to stay current with their spouse. Ignorance, within a marriage, is not bliss.

According to her, staying engaged with each other and each other's lives outside the home isn't just a precaution against disconnection; it also goes a long way toward protecting monogamy. Not sharing the ups and downs of whatever you are spending most of your time doing when you are not together is a setup for some adoring coworker (or fellow grad student or barista) to bat his or her eyes and hang on every adrenaline-stoked word of your mate, until pretty soon they're texting each other, meeting for drinks after hours. And ripping each other's clothes off in a mad passionate embrace. She didn't actually say that last part, that's just where my mind goes. Not all cases of losing touch in a marriage end this way, but you can understand how it could happen.

Dr. Emmanuel, who has been a couples counselor for over twenty years and has been married for fifteen, referred me to the work of John Gottman, a psychology professor at the University of Washington. Gottman has written many books on couples, including a best seller (with Nan Silver), *The Seven Principles for Making Marriage Work*, and seems to be the go-to person for thorough research and deep understanding of how couples work. Through his research on marital stability Gottman has found that happy couples have "rituals of togetherness" that they observe on a daily basis.[1]

Emmanuel explained that Gottman's prescription for these twice-daily check-ins with your partner, one in the morning and one in the evening, is that they "are often very quick—not long, drawn-out soulful talks." She explained in more detail:

> The key to daily checking in with each other is that this is not just a conversation about "what," but also includes a genuine interest in how the other person is feeling about the "what." When I see couples who only ask about the "what," that's an indicator that the relationship is not in a good place. They're just reporting what they're doing, with no emotional tone at all. The difference between the tone of voice in a neutral "what" conversation and a caring, feeling implication of "And how do you feel about the 'what?'" is subtle, but very distinct. Neutral conversations are not truly neutral—they're actually negative, because the participants are ignoring or disregarding the emotional aspect of the "what." When couples are happy together, they're genuinely interested in and want to stay current with how their partner is doing. Every day. About everything. These days, people use texting, instant messaging, and voice mail to stay current with each other throughout the day. Sometimes what people talk about seems small, petty,

or insignificant. But what's important is that they're both saying: "Hey, nobody else on this planet but me really cares about how you feel about this seemingly petty detail of your life today. It may be small—the actual event or complaint—but no matter how small it is, I care about you. I want to know what you feel about your life events. I'm the person you can turn to, to complain, rejoice, moan, whatever. I care about you and I want to know you." Real people don't always say it in these words. They don't necessarily ask the second part. They know that when they ask "What?" they really mean "What *and* how do you feel about it?" They say it in their attitude—and by maintaining the daily ritual.

DOES TEXTING COUNT?

Funny thing about the seeming "pettiness" of texting. I take it for granted in my marriage now. Tod is a film editor, mostly for television. He sits in dark rooms with directors and producers, often for hours on end. On some jobs the mood is relaxed, he's working by himself, at his own pace. We text back and forth easily, and I don't give it much thought. But then he'll be on a job where he is working within six inches of a director for eight hours, fully focused. The thought of him interrupting his work to say something like, "Um, excuse me, Mr. Director, just need to text my wife back about what happened at the bus stop," makes me want to throw my smartphone out the window, get a rotary phone, and never text again. So on those jobs, unless there's an emergency, we go on texting lockdown. I find I do miss those little connections.

Bonnie and Russ Tamblyn are not big texters. Although they have always made staying current with each other a priority, they prefer to use a more long-standing ritual to do it, an exercise Bonnie learned in her training as a council facilitator with the Ojai Foundation. Grounded in Native American culture, the ritual is called "taking council."

BONNIE AND RUSS
Reaching Back to American Indian Ritual

Bonnie started this council practice for the family in the period when she and Russ were raising their teenage daughter. The three of them would sit down together, light a candle, and set an intention to speak from the heart and listen with an open mind. Now that their daughter is married and out of the house, Bonnie and Russ still maintain this practice.

"The energetic field between two people who sit together and have a conversation, the loving connection, is palpable," Bonnie told me. Their willingness to stay current and honest with each other using this "council" technique certainly makes their relationship feel like a genuine love fest.

Maybe engaging in a Native American "council" ritual is not your style and texting messages throughout the day is about as interesting to you as swatting flies. Not a problem, because there are many ways to skin the staying-current cat. Allow me to contradict a New Age axiom, "It's about the journey, not the destination," because when it comes to staying current with each other, as with relaxation, it doesn't matter what method you use to make it happen, you just want to make sure it does. Coming up are some simple and effective ways to help you connect consistently.

ASK QUESTIONS

A comic who senses that their audience is not with them needs to have the presence of mind and courage to ask directly, "Are you following this?" or "Are you with me?" It's the same within a marriage. You can and should ask your spouse these same questions in any given conversation. If the response you get is affirmative, like, "Yes, honey, I'm totally with you and I know what you are going through," kudos to you. But if the answer is any version of "No, not really," take the time to fill each other in. Comics don't care what's going on with you deeply—we just want to know that you've gotten enough of the setup information to get the joke and laugh: so, unlike the comic performing for an audience whose only interest is making them laugh, staying current in a marriage is a two-way street. You each need to be curious about the other person.

What I heard from a lot of couples, and something I know a little about from my own experience, is that there are times when one or both people resist asking these questions of each other. Either we think we already know the answer, or we're afraid of what we might hear if we ask, or we're afraid of our reaction to what we hear. The two last fears sound very similar, but there is one major difference. Although we can't control what we hear, we can absolutely control our reaction to it. So go ahead and ask the questions. Then take a deep breath and listen. Give yourself and your marriage the gift of sitting with the information. If it's too much to handle on your own—too much emotion, too high stakes, too vulnerable, too shocking—whatever the case, go get help. (See chapter 13, "Get Help to Get Better.") As our experienced marriage counselor Donna Emmanuel cautioned earlier, ignorance in long-term relationships does not create bliss. Have faith that you'll be fine, no matter what the answer is. And as far as assuming we already know what our spouse is thinking, take the advice of the Morocco-born Michele Bohbot, married to her husband, Marc, for over thirty-five years: "We are all always growing, so you can't assume you know everything about a person. You don't." Mais oui!

WE'RE CURRENT, BUT WE'RE MISERABLE. NOW WHAT?

There is always the possibility that finding out what is going on with your spouse means that he or she might reveal that they are unhappy. And that in order to become happy, aspects of your life together are going to have to change. It doesn't necessarily mean *you* have to change, but it may require making some adjustments to your life. Like the husband who decided to become a pastor after having been an actor. Although he didn't ask his wife to change per se, there's no doubt that making his transition from thespian to religious leader meant big changes in their lifestyle as a couple. But she fully embraced them and has found now she even enjoys their new life centered around a religious community.

Not everyone is excited about being called to action like this, so I have compassion for being gun-shy about asking and then really listening to the answer to how your spouse is feeling about life. But not doing it is a little bit like ignoring a dull, aching, throbbing in your tooth and then finally getting to the dentist and finding out the tooth is dead and has to be extracted. Please stay on top of the aches and throbbing in your marriage. You don't to end up with spouse extraction. Ba dum bum!

What about when the news is good? People like sharing good news with each other, so make sure to milk the good news for every drop of joy by taking the time to celebrate together not just your shared victories, like anniversaries, but your individual ones too! There is one possible reservation around sharing the details of a banner day that I heard a few couples mention, which is that sometimes hearing all the juicy details about a spouse's life outside the home—particularly when one of you is home with children, or in a job you're not excited about—can make you feel competitive with them. Or sometimes even jealous.

BEWARE THE GREEN-EYED MONSTER

I know when we think about jealousy in marriage, we usually think about an interloper—the threat to the marriage that an affair poses. But there is another kind of jealousy that people who are competitive by nature have to watch out for in a marriage: being envious of your spouse's success outside the home.

One couple I met tells each other outright when they are feeling envious of the other one, so the feeling doesn't sit inside them, creating resentment. They say it aloud to each other and give the other person a chance to acknowledge how the first person feels. Not only does it create a bonding moment for them where they share some real honesty, but it also allows them to figure out together how to make the person feel better, which may be as simple as explaining that whatever the other one is imagining to be so fabulous has its trade-offs, or devising some kind of game plan to help the envious person realize whatever goals he or she feels they are not meeting. "Sometimes just saying it out loud makes me feel better. Or hearing myself say it, it sounds so petty or whiny it even makes me laugh," one wife of seventeen years told me. "Feelings change all the time, and getting them out allows them to move along quickly." Also, talking through these feelings (or any feelings, frankly) with your spouse can remind you that you're a team building a life together. Knowing in their hearts that a marriage is a team is the most effective and common way that all of the couples I spoke with face this issue of competition with each other if and when it comes up.

Herbert and Zelmyra Fisher, the longest-married couple on record, eighty-six years married when Herbert died in 2011, believed above all else that being married meant being a team. When asked what is the most important thing to remember at the end of the day as a couple, they said, "Marriage is not a contest—never keep a score. God has put the two of you together on the same team to win."[2]

If you are prone to jealousy and you want to be happily married, you have to figure out how to manage this, because—and forgive me for being crass—jealousy is one fluid, nondiscriminating bitch. Not only can it come between you and your spouse, around issues of achievement or in thinking someone has the hots for your mate or vice versa, but once jealousy is out of the bag, you can even find yourself envious of a marriage you're not even in.

If you find yourself feeling jealous, take the energy you're using to obsess about how good you think someone else has it and do a little soul searching. Ask yourself what exactly it is about their life that is making you envious and make it your goal to create that for yourself. Rather than letting it paralyze you or make you bitter, use your jealousy for information about how you can improve your life and, in this case, your marriage. Like the way a couple is kind to each other and affectionate? Treat your spouse with kindness and affection. There is no shame in noticing qualities you like in someone else, or a goal they have attained, and challenging yourself to create what you admire in others.

One last word on jealousy: you may want to take a little time to find out if what you are feeling jealous about is real. Remember Patricia Heaton's experience of being envious of a couple she saw at the PTA meeting and learning that she was making erroneous assumptions. You can't just look at another couple, or have a brief interaction with them at a party and decide they are perfect and your marriage is missing the boat, a sinking ship, or whatever maritime analogy you like.

For new comics, hanging out in a comedy club can also create anxiety. Comics knocking back shots and talking about all the amazing opportunities coming their way, the agents that are going to sign them, all the meetings they're taking and the "deals" they have in the works is tough. Overhearing all this chatter can naturally make you start evaluating your own progress. I always remind aspiring comics that it's possible that none of it is true—perhaps they are followers of "The Secret," or some other life philosophy that believes that if you keep saying it you will manifest what you want. Or maybe they are exaggerating. Either way, it's none of your concern. The only work you have to concern yourself with is your own. You can admire another performer's jokes and allow their perseverance to inspire you to work harder, and to write better, funnier material, but you have to be vigilant about not letting someone else's success, in your mind, reflect badly on you. This is also true when it comes to being in a community of couples. You have to know yourself, because if you don't have the mental discipline to tease the inspiration out of whoever evokes competitive or jealous feelings, then it really is best to do what my father always told me when I was sure my sister had more French toast than me: Keep your eyes on your own plate.

TOM AND KERRI
Comrades First, Comedians Second

Tom Cotter and Kerri Louise were both comedians when they met nineteen years ago. Tom is a fair-haired, blue-eyed jokesmith who doesn't miss an opportunity to land a precise one-liner onstage or off. Kerri, on the other hand, is an attractive, dark-eyed brunette who, unlike her husband, tends to speak in high-energy rants. Their styles differ, but they share a refreshing take-no-prisoners directness. And neither of them is afraid to work hard, which is good, since they are raising three boys ages six to eleven. They moved from Boston to New York City to pursue stand-up when they had only been dating a short while. It took some years for them to actually tie the knot, breaking up a few times on the way to the altar. But even before the rice was thrown, these two had a sincere understanding that they were a team.

"When we first came to New York from Boston," Kerri told me, "the phone would ring off the hook for Tom. It was difficult. I'd answer the phone and I could hear the booker trying to end the conversation with me as fast as they could. It was terrible. So we got different phone lines to deal with it. I wasn't jealous—"

"Sure. We're never up for the same role," Tom interrupted. (Easy for Tom to joke now, but he admitted to being upset when, in 2003, Kerri moved further along in the competition than he did on the NBC show *Last Comic Standing.* Then, in 2012, Tom got even greater public acclaim as runner-up on the seventh season of *America's Got Talent.*)

"Right," Kerri continued, smiling. "The bottom line is that the money is going to come to the same household."

"Our goal is a healthy retirement," Tom added, "and not living in a tiki hut. It's a shared mission."

Ping-Ponging jokes back and forth the way these two do, it's easy to miss the value of what they are saying for the health of a long-term marriage. The most obvious asset is that they have a great sense of humor about themselves and each other. But they're also self-aware and not afraid to speak honestly with each other about how they feel. How else would that additional phone line have happened? A small gesture, but it says a lot about how they interact. Kerri didn't like how fielding Tom's calls made her feel. They talked about it and took a simple action to make her (and, by extension, their marriage) work better.

At the end of our interview, Tom made another comment about how he sees their marriage that I also found telling about their success as a couple. "The way I look at our marriage and our work, it's like this: maybe comedy won't be the bus that drives us to the end zone, but you're still the person I want to be with, " he said, looking over at Kerri. They share an understanding that what they do professionally is distinct from their commitment to being together. Like any marriage, it helps that they have common interests and passion for the same work, but at the heart of it, their work is not the tie that binds. I believe that this combination of fully embracing that they are a team and also knowing that their relationship transcends whatever transitory success (or failure, for that matter) each of them will experience professionally in a long life together has enabled Tom and Kerri to keep enjoying each other for almost two decades.

Hearing the reference to teamwork as often as I did over this last year, I couldn't help but think about it in terms of my marriage. Tod and I still laugh a lot together, which we all know is high on my list for a good marriage, so I don't struggle with envying other couples much, although sometimes I wish I had their master bedrooms and bathtubs, especially the ones with feet on the bottom. Thinking other couples do it better is not my marital albatross, but since I'd already worked for many years as a comic when we got together, my "teamwork" muscle was pretty flaccid. I can't only blame this on my competitive nature and on "show business"—many of us in varying fields are not set up in life to be the kind of team players that healthy marriages demand.

Whether you're a lawyer trying to make partner, an intern at medical school hoping for residency, an academic looking for tenure—heck, even a violinist fighting for first chair in an orchestra—these are life goals that require extreme focus and personal ambition.

Today, driving yourself individually to win is as American as having 836 TV channels. And the focus starts very young. My seven-year-old already wants more "Pokemon points" than his friends. Thousands of messages program us to push for the highest grades, to win at sports—heck, even the Girl Scouts gives rewards to the girl who sells the most boxes of Thin Mints. Then we grow up a little and fall in love and marry, and after a lifetime of fighting for what we want and being told no one is going to look out for you but you, and if you want something done right, do it yourself, and a bunch of other phrases Americans are weaned on, you are expected to drop this way of thinking and become part of a loving, caring, supportive team.

Huh?

You can understand why, for many of us, there might be an adjustment period for surrendering to the "we" of marriage. We've been aggressively being "I's" a lot longer.

I decided to talk to some long-term couples specifically about this issue, of individuals coming to a marriage with many expectations for themselves both inside and outside the home. I love that Zelmyra Fisher stayed married to Herbert for eighty-six years, but she also married in 1924, when women had very few expectations for their lives other than to be a wife and mother. I never met Zelmyra, but I doubt that she lay awake at night tortured by the thought that she was wasting her political science degree doing endless loads of laundry and reading *Are You My Mother?* sixty-four evenings in a row. Much has been written about the postfeminist generations and the freedoms we were given as women, and thank God for Gloria Steinem, but with this came much greater expectations of ourselves, our lives, and, yes, our marriages.

Ideally, according to the lifestyle portrayed in glossy magazines, you are each pursuing your goals with mutual support and love together and then you come home and share your uniquely challenging and rewarding days over organic free-range roast chicken and steamed quinoa with kale while sipping single-malt scotch before nursing a single-source decaf espresso and nibbling on vanilla-infused macarons. But even if you did live in the pages of *Dwell* magazine and this scenario were real, at some point, over the decades, it could feel like one team member is doing better than the other, because, in fact, one of them is. That's when reminding yourself that your marriage is a team effort is so important.

Sometimes even believing you are a team player in your marriage is not enough to allow you to waltz through the day. Especially when, say, one person gets to travel, staying in cinnamon-scented hotel rooms, while the other one smells dirty gym shorts from the kids' soccer practice stuffed in the crevices of the back seat while stuck driving hungry children home in rush-hour traffic. Which is exactly what happened to Jan Gordon and Derek Chow. They have been together happily for thirty-three years, despite some major sacrificing on Jan's part.

JAN AND DEREK
Leaning Out

Jan and Derek met as undergraduates on a foreign-exchange program in France in 1982. Jan has a no-frills presence: with straight, dark-blond hair, she wears no makeup and prefers outfits that allow her to run from place to place quickly. Her personality is tough to pin down: gregarious yet no-nonsense one minute, then thoughtful and highly sensitive the next. A film school graduate and former tennis player, Jan is a latter-day Renaissance woman—if Renaissance women also raised three children and ran each one's life "like a small corporation," according to Derek. It's one of their ongoing jokes, that Jan is the CEO of three small companies.

Jan gave me a candid explanation of how they got to the place in their lives, despite her two degrees and years of work, where their roles break down so traditionally.

"When I realized that Derek was going to make more money than I could ever make, I took over the home life. My grandmother, who just turned one hundred last week, always said 'There is only room for one star in a family,' and no doubt, I always thought that 'star' would be me. Derek and I were on a similar career path for a while. He was making his way up the finance ladder, while I was a television producer for a decade. I also had my MFA from USC film school. We always dreamed that once we had a family, we'd both keep up our careers, switching on and off whenever we felt like it. And then reality set in."

After they had their first child, it became clear that someone was going to have to raise him. Since Derek's career was further along, the smart choice seemed to be to have Jan leave her job and be home full-time. "I still thought we'd switch at some point," she told me. "That Derek would become Mr. Mom, and I'd get back to my TV and film career. But his career really took off, financially and otherwise, in my child-bearing years, and it became rather obvious, once again, that I would be the one to defer my personal goals for the greater good of our family."

The greatest misconception about comedians and comedy writers in relationships is that we need to be partnered with hysterically funny people. No thanks. Don't need the competition! I love that my partner, Lori, gets me and laughs at (most of) my jokes. Don't get me wrong, Lori has a great sense of humor, but I love that she is a great and willing audience for me. Can't have too many people fighting for the mic in a long-term relationship! I guess it's working because we've been together eighteen years.

—CAROL LEIFER, comedian and writer

I needed to ask Jan, despite the support and comfortable lifestyle that Derek's work affords them, if there is ever a time that she feels envious of his career success. "Always!" she cackled. "Do I feel like I've sacrificed my personal and professional dreams to raise my family? Absolutely! If I could have figured out (still trying) how to mix my professional life with raising my family (as Derek travels every week), I would have, but I didn't want my kids raised by a nanny. As far as the future goes, it ain't over 'til the fat lady sings! I am starting to get nervous and feeling the pressure to get back into something of serious interest soon, because when my kids graduate from high school, I'm going to want to do something. I am editing documentaries on occasion for people and sitting on the selection committee at the Boulder International Film Festival as a start. Hopefully, I'll be able to pick up the pace as my kids graduate one by one."

I loved Jan's "It ain't over 'til the fat lady sings!" attitude toward her future. It sounds like version 2.0 of her grandmother's advice that there is room for just one star in a marriage. I would add, and Jan's words support this, there is only room for one star *at a time* in a marriage. This revision takes into consideration the matter of timing (see chapter 5). I would argue that, in order to have a happy, connected marriage, letting the other spouse be the star is not a lifetime sentence. Although it is very hard for both spouses to be going full throttle on careers at the same time, particularly if there are children, I have seen how a couple can thrive with simultaneous full-throttle pursuit of career: when they own and run a business together.

WORKING TOGETHER WORKS WELL

If the couple doesn't kill each other, or tank the business from fighting too much, joint entrepreneurs who are equally passionate about their work seem to work very well. I wanted to know more about the positive effect that working together has on a couple, so I asked the marriage counselor Michael Latimer (the source of the idea of time-outs for grown-ups) if he had any observations about shared work for long-term happiness.

"Shared passion, in this case a business, leads to a deeper connection because it leads to a deeper attachment," he told me. "Often I find that when couples share a passion, be it books, movies, sports, exercise, a business, and so on, and they talk about or participate in this passion almost daily, whatever little conflicts they have that might create distance between them often seem inconsequential in comparison to the joy they experience sharing that passion."

His next comment was very interesting to me since it incorporated so much of what I had already found to be true. "The more couples share, especially the more experiences they share outside the home, the closer they seem to feel, maybe because they're sharing an experience of the bigger world together. This is not to say that creating a home and family do not create connection. Of course, it absolutely does, but the degree of that connection is dependent upon many factors. Yet when couples have more to talk about than the kids, it no doubt provides more novelty and mental stimulation. This can give them a shared foundation, a source of conversation and connection, and probably spikes brain chemicals that lead to romantic love (dopamine) and attachment (oxytocin). Couples who work together usually have a common goal that connects them outside of the home. Plus, working together may also provide the couple an opportunity to admire each other and to see strengths in one another that they might not otherwise see."

REAL MEN STAY HOME

Most definitely, not only women make career sacrifices for the family. In my hipster neighborhood in Los Angeles, there are more men with beards carrying babies in slings than possibly anywhere in the world. Much has already been reported about how men are staying home while women become the family breadwinners, but I was surprised to hear about this shift from my son's seemingly laid-back surfing coach over lunch with his son. "Up until recently, I worked for the Israeli government as a weapons consultant, before the family moved to the U.S. What can I tell you?" he added, smiling and wiping pizza grease off his four-year-old's chin. "I never thought my life would look like this, but my wife makes more money. She has the big career." He took a sip of his beer and then tousled his son's mop of brown hair. "And I love him," he said.

So far in our discussion of family "stars" and "supporting actors" we have been hearing from younger couples, where husbands and wives are often overwhelmed with the dual jobs of building two careers and families. What about marriages where people have already raised a family or climbed up whatever financial ladder they chose? With the care and feeding of children and pets far behind them, with no further need for a nagging, relentless drive, they laugh effortlessly together all the time, right? I had to find out for myself.

MIDLIFE MARRIAGE

The couples in this section are people who met later in life, with no distractions of caring for children and when both had established careers. Despite their relative freedom from obligations, they still have to make an effort to pay attention to their marriages to make them happy ones. For some, this comes easier than others. For instance, Claire Rothman and Ed Hill, the art enthusiasts who love to shop (see chapter 8), were established in their careers when they met thirty years ago. She was the general manager and vice president of the Los Angeles Forum, a high-status, high-profile position, whereas Ed's work as an ophthalmologist didn't have quite the glamour of his new girlfriend's career. Many people would point this out to Ed when they heard of his new romance. But Ed never felt threatened by Claire. "We have a running joke," he told me. "Particularly if she was at the Forum or in a group, she 'works the room,' it's automatic with her, and I really am content to stand in a corner and watch her."

Claire spelled out one of the secrets of their success for me simply. "We were fortunate in that we came together with full careers and grown children. I had my career, and Ed also had an active career and meetings and things to go to early in our relationship," she said, "so we had a juxtaposition of that. Then I could stand back and let him get the accolades. I never felt that he didn't pay attention to me. I think that's why it worked."

I never felt he didn't pay attention to me. I love this almost childlike and yet insightful reflection. If you and your spouse lead busy lives, you have to find the time to pay attention to each other. It's that simple. Kids or no kids, stardom or no stardom, this is "staying current" at its most basic level.

Deborah and Stephen Goldblatt, who have been married for thirty-five years, learned how important paying attention to each other is at a time when both were doing well in their professions. Deborah would argue they were doing *too well,* since juggling two booming careers was what almost sank their marriage.

DEBORAH AND STEPHEN GOLDBLATT
Attention Must Be Paid

Stephen is an Oscar-nominated cinematographer (*The Help; Lethal Weapon; Closer,* directed by Mike Nichols), but when he and Deborah first met he was a lowly cameraman from London and Deborah had a production company for independent European productions coming to LA that didn't have a studio or accountant or anyone to set them up. According to Deborah, "These productions would come in with literally suitcases of cash and I would set up the whole thing. From beginning to end. With crews and equipment companies, film labs, whatever they needed. Stephen was one of the cameramen that came in with a French company. We were doing a commercial for Dubonnet, the aperitif."

Stephen laughed. "There was an actress who looked like Miss Piggy, and they mistakenly thought I could make her look like Catherine Deneuve. Which I couldn't."

"Not true," Deborah corrected him. "Stephen made her look completely amazing. The sets, the ideas, were just more than I had ever experimented with in American television."

"Which doesn't mean much," David quipped.

"It does," Deborah said. "It means everything."

Certainly in this case it did, because it is clear from the way she looks at David when she says it is on this job that she fell in love him, despite the fact that he lived in London and was divorced with two children. According to Deborah, it wasn't just the long-distance relationship and family obligations that nearly wrecked them, it was about both their careers going full tilt at the same time.

She described this precarious time, obviously having spent a lot of time working it through in her mind. "We both dive into scary big projects with everything we've got," she began. "Too much of big and scary at the same time creates a lot of separation and distance between us and results in dangerous consequences. We were on the brink of ending it all when I was successfully selling *LA 411*.[3] I suspected we weren't doing well as a couple because of my success, but it was much more about both of our successes. Stephen was doing a big movie and we were earning more money than we had ever dreamed of. Home by that time was in Northern California, but he was living in a rented house working in LA. Needless to say, an affair ensued and things got ugly. We chose to stay together with the help of good marital therapy and to shape-shift our relationship into a loving, committed one with one big career between us: his. We are still learning through therapy how to better ask for attention from one another, be mindful of our timing when asking for that attention, be clearer about one another's needs rather than giving each other mixed messages like "I'll be fine if you can't be there" when we are really wanting something else. It's a practice in reciprocity—and using the right language and the right timing to communicate it."

So much that Deborah says here is worth highlighting. First is the dangerous disconnection that can happen when one or both spouses are overwhelmed with work. This leaves you pretty vulnerable to seeking—and finding—intimate connections outside the marriage because you don't have time together to have them with your spouse. The second is their mutual decision that there be just one career in their marriage at that time. This is what needed to be done for the sake of the marriage. Given the nature of Stephen's work, that it involved (and still involves) a lot of travel, Deborah had to be the more flexible spouse, which ultimately meant surrendering her career for the time being. This was a choice she was willing to make. The third is their dedication to working with a therapist to learn how to ask for the attention they need, and also how to time these requests. As ever, timing plays a key role in creating a happy marriage.

> Speaking of timing, I heard an anecdote about the acclaimed actors Jessica Tandy and Hume Cronyn, who were married for fifty-two years. Apparently their secret tool was hats. Each had a hat they would wear when they needed some space or time alone. The couple knew that when one of them had the hat on, that person needed time to think. When the hat came off, he or she was ready to talk again.

I'd given a lot of thought to timing in long-term relationships, but hearing Deborah's assertion that the key to the success of their marriage was her learning to ask for attention from Stephen, and precisely how to do it, was a new piece of the successful marriage puzzle for me.

Given how resistant I am to making myself vulnerable, I could not imagine saying to Tod any version of "Please pay attention to me." That's about as appealing as doing a six-month press tour, naked, without tweezers. And yet, if it ever becomes a question of risking "neediness" with Tod, or risking losing my marriage because I am too afraid to ask, I can see now that I must, as Lady Macbeth says, screw my courage to the sticking point, and ask.

For our final couple in this chapter, Jan Gordon's grandmother's "one star" theory falls completely off the rails. In the case of Jerry Stiller and Anne Meara, referring to either one of them as "stars" wasn't just a figure of speech, it was actually true. Which, sixty years on, doesn't appear to have been a problem for either one of them.

JERRY STILLER AND ANNE MEARA
Teaming Up Onstage and Off

Jerry Stiller and Anne Meara were one of the most successful husband and wife comedy teams of the twentieth century. Back when they met Anne was a young, feisty Irish actress from Rockville Center, Long Island, with a quick wit, a big smile, and a mane of red hair. Jerry was a shortish, Jewish, eccentric twenty-something from New York's Lower East Side. Stiller and Meara quickly became a team and together they wrote and performed candid, very funny sketches about their life together. They appeared on the *Ed Sullivan Show* over thirty-five times and played every significant venue in the country. During the 1970s they also wrote and performed a hugely successful radio campaign for Blue Nun Wine. From 1977 to 1978 they had their own five-minute sketch show, *Take Five with Stiller and Meara*. Throughout their marriage they have also worked separately as actors. Anne's credits reach back to *Rhoda*, *Sex and the City*, and up to *Law & Order: SVU*. Jerry is most known for his role as Frank Costanza on *Seinfeld*. He also had a long run as Arthur Spooner on *King of Queens*. In 2010, they appeared together on *The Daily Show with Jon Stewart*.

Due to illness, Anne was unavailable for the interview, but their daughter Amy, an actress and comedian, offered to sit down with me and her father in their rambling apartment on New York City's West Side to fill in any details that Jerry, now in his eighties, might not have at his fingertips. I must report, he remembered almost everything.

Given my admiration for both of these enormously talented people, and since I already knew all their credits, I wanted to hear about how they made their marriage work. How they overcame their struggles getting started and if they ever found themselves competing with each other. Jerry immediately recalled the early years, when he and Anne were hungry, out-of-work actors. To help me understand he told me a story he clearly relishes, the one about their first date.

Jerry had invited Anne out to a diner after they first met at an audition. Anne ordered coffee and, he hoped, nothing more, since he wanted to be chivalrous but was broke. Anne did stop at coffee, but went even further into starving-actor territory, asking him to grab his silverware off the table and stick it in his pockets. "My roommates keep losing ours," she said, wrapping hers in a napkin and throwing it in her bag. As far as competing with each other, according to Jerry, there just wasn't any place for it.

"People saw the two of us together, so there was no reason to compete. People would stop and say, 'Oooh, she's tall and beautiful and good-looking with nice red hair and he's a little Jewish boy, so what's she doing with a guy like him?' That's always what went through people's minds. We'd be on the street and people would yell out, 'She's the funny one,' because she was the funny one. She always made something funny. I was smart enough to appreciate what was going on, I wasn't getting competitive, there was nothing to get competitive about. No one knew who the heck we were. So when they said, 'She's the funny one,' so what? What was really upsetting to me was when my father saw the act with my mother and he came up to me and said, 'She's the funny one.' That put a rock in my head."

They rarely argued, if ever. "We were so poor we never could fight. We needed each other. We were broke and we had no work. The only connection we had was to each other. If one of us had a job, that was good." The story of their six-decade relationship is one of two comic geniuses fitting together, as Amy described it, "like puzzle pieces." Jerry's face lit up hearing this analogy and he blurted out, in his signature staccato way, "That's it! That's exactly right. It's just like you were floating out there in space, no rhyme nor reason. Nobody knew you, there were no agents or managers, all you had was what you could come up with together."

NEED IS GOOD

In the original *Wall Street*, when it comes to business, Gordon Gekko asserts "greed is good." Apparently when it comes to long-term marriage, need is good. Despite my fear of it, needing each other is not something that should send you heading for the hills, the nearest airport, or even a bar. In good marriages, people own it, embrace it, and dare I say it, lean in to it. Not to take anything away from your movement, Ms. Sheryl Sandberg, but I like it so much better in this context.

I wondered whether there were any specific challenges that came up for them from working together and being married. Jerry thought for a minute and then gave me a measured answer, speaking slowly to make sure that what he was saying landed. "We were not like ordinary people. We felt so lucky to have a job, to know that we had something, that we never thought about what it was like to be married and working. It was the only thing we knew. It really blended in some ways because we both knew we wanted to be in the theater, in front of an audience, and nobody was hiring us. So then we started working together, then we decided we definitely wanted a child, so we planned it." (They had two children; the first is Amy and the second is the movie actor and director Ben Stiller.)

To illustrate how "not ordinary" their family life was, Amy recalled the challenges of figuring out what was going on between her parents in their living room on any given night. "They would be going over their sketches and their writing. One of them was the 'I Hate You, You Hate Me' sketch," Amy recalled. "They were rehearsing and they were really getting into it and as a toddler I walked in and asked, 'Mommy, Daddy fight?' and they said, 'No, Mommy, Daddy rehearse.' Then another time I heard them and I came in and said, 'Mommy, Daddy rehearse?' and they said, 'No, Mommy, Daddy fight.'" Jerry laughed. "It's true. They never knew what the hell was going on there in that room. They were victimized by two parents who wanted to be comedians."

"Yeah, it was awful, Dad," Amy said, taking his hand.

Witnessing the Stiller family, or at least two members of the four, presents a strong argument for a marriage in which each person shines brightly, knowing better than to compete with each other, and fully accepting how much they need each other.

Dealing with the challenges of staying current has led us to look at dueling careers, great expectations of ourselves, the sheer pace of how we live, all of it pertinent to life as a couple in the twenty-first century. This chapter would not have been written fifty years ago—there would have been no need. But for all the reasons I have identified, the ideas brought to the surface about how and why to stay connected to each other are some of the most important for the health of your marriage. Once again, be brave, ask questions of each other, listen to the answers, be honest in your responses. Don't pretend you are not feeling what you are feeling. Rather, acknowledge it and use it as a chance to create more intimacy with your spouse.

One couple I interviewed (who chose to remain anonymous) has a name for their jealous feelings: Ed. They tell each other, "Ed was loud today," and "Ed told me . . .," and so on. Then they laugh, which as we already know makes them feel connected. Then they go and have sex. Well, not always, but we already know that once people start laughing together, anything is possible.

TIPS FOR REMAINING UP TO DATE IN MARRIAGE

- Stay current with your spouse. Check in with each other and ask questions. Make the effort to know not only about their day but also how they feel about it. In a marriage, ignorance is not bliss.

- Feelings of envy might surface in a long marriage. When they do, consider telling your spouse how you are feeling so you can strategize about how to improve your life. Pursue your own goals so you are not so focused on your spouse. Always remember that you are part of a team. Knowing this in your heart makes it easier to let feelings of jealousy pass.

- If you find yourself envying other couples, make sure you know the truth about them—otherwise you could be making assumptions that aren't true. If you do find real qualities you admire in someone else's marriage, try to create them in your own.

- When both of you come to a marriage with high expectations for career success and family, recognize that unless you are in business together, it's tough for there to be room for more than one "star" in a marriage at the same time. Remind yourself of the importance of timing in every aspect of your marriage and trust that there will be opportunities in the future for each of you to shine. In the meantime, figure out together ways to keep the "non-star" in touch with his or her personal goals, to head off resentment. Festering resentment is not good for marriage.

- Marital partners expect to be paid attention to by their spouse. It's not always obvious to our partners when we need it, so pluck up the courage to ask for it. Asking for what we need, even if it sounds childish or feels embarrassing, is essential if you both want to get what you need and have a happy marriage.

11

Stick with the Winners

COMPLAINING IS EASY;
SPEND TIME WITH PEOPLE
WHO DON'T

You have got to stop listening to your girlfriends about your relationships—especially that girlfriend that ain't got nobody.

—LESTER BARRIE, comedian, *Star Search* winner
best comedian, 1993

There was a certain type of conversation that I could hear on any night of the week at any comedy club bar from LA to New York City, from 1990 to 1997, and it can probably still be heard. It went something like this:

"It's just so hard to get work."

"I know, right?"

"And then when you do get work, it's at these crappy clubs, where the blender starts whirring right when you're about to say the punch line!"

"I know, right, just when I'm about to get the punch line, *whrrrrrr!!!*"

"Such a drag. And the driving everywhere, and my insurance expired so now I'm always a nervous wreck about being pulled over."

"Bummer. Written anything new lately? I haven't. I don't have anything to say. [*Checks watch.*] I gotta go. If I don't get home soon my cats will pee on everything."

"I hate when cats pee on everything. That's why I don't have cats. I hate pets, they're awful. They just die eventually."

Something like this was said in hundreds of conversations I may or may not have participated in. One thing I know for sure is that, as seductive as commiserating together can be, I didn't ask these people for their phone numbers so we could hang out more. This kind of sad-sack energy was not going to get me where I wanted to go, and even if I wasn't going to be famous, I wanted to at least enjoy being a comic.

What I find so interesting as a married woman today is that it is completely possible to overhear this same kind of exchange on any park bench between wives or at a sports bar between husbands or any combination of married friends talking. I don't begrudge humans their need to relax and vent about married life. But making it a habit and not making friends with happily married people is a good way to stay unhappy. What I am saying here, basically, is don't call your bitter, divorced brother for marital advice. As I first heard in a Twelve Step recovery room, stick with the winners.

"Sticking with the winners" is probably not a piece of advice you expected to read in a book about marriage. I'm not saying stick with the rich and powerful. In this context, wealth and status are irrelevant. I am talking about winners in relationships. People who after years together still seem to genuinely enjoy their spouse. They're honest with each other, listen to each other, they're affectionate, happy for the other's successes, give each other hugs when the going gets rough, and even when it's not, respect each other, and have all the qualities that you wish for in your own marriage.

I acknowledge that in the wrong context, "Stick with the winners" could sound tacky and mercenary, like something a coach with a buzz cut would yell in a sweaty locker room to motivate some underachievers. But I promise, it's more universal than that. It has solid roots: it's a slogan often used in Alcoholics Anonymous to help people stay sober, instructing newcomers to seek out happy, sober people for their own survival. Broken down to its essence, "Stick with the winners" is a highly effective saying to take to heart in helping you reach a lot of your goals, from sobriety to a fulfilling career and even to a happy marriage.

I understand the temptation of finding people who can relate to you to complain about your life to; "Misery loves company" is not just an expression. Certainly, in terms of stand-up comedy, it can be very comforting to have other aspiring entertainers as friends to share war stories with about a bad audience, an agent who doesn't return your calls, and so on. As a comic you are your own band, if you will, so it can be a particularly lonely profession. You work alone, you travel a lone, and until you find a waitress or bartender to marry you, you pretty much live alone. (I'm kidding about the waitress part, although it's not unusual for a comic to hook up with someone who works in a comedy club.) Because of this loneliness factor, stand-ups are particularly vulnerable to negative commiseration. You just want to talk to someone who understands how maddeningly hard it can be. Despite entertaining crowds that might number in the hundreds, you can still start to feel very isolated from human connection.

Plus, and I'm sure some scholar of human behavior knows why this is, the first thing that often comes out of people's mouths after being alone for a significant amount of time isn't usually all the joy they are experiencing. What people often feel desperate to share is the bad news, maybe because it's a better story, or maybe because it's part of being human to want someone to witness our pain.

SAY SOMETHING POSITIVE!

In marriage, too, it makes sense to be aware of the impulse to leap to share bad news. Sometimes at the end of a long day, the first thing we want to blurt out when we see each other is a list of all the bad we had to contend with: the parking ticket, the hour on hold with the gas company, how our coworker is trying to steal our account. But there is something to be said for greeting each other with some positive thoughts and then easing into the disappointments. In fact, maybe if we could discipline ourselves to share the good of the day first, by the time we got to the misery, it wouldn't seem so miserable anymore!

What can happen with comics is, you want to share your pain, your friend wants to share his pain, and pretty soon, it's a pain fest where everything is dire and no one is looking for a way out of their abyss of awfulness. But I have discovered that not everyone is interested in jumping into this cycle of despair! There are people able to see their life through a different lens, and whether you're a comic or a spouse, these are the people you want to seek out. You may have to look a little harder, but you can find people who are happy with their lives. Or if not happy in the moment, able to look at what is making them unhappy in a positive way, like, this is bad, but how can I learn from it? Exactly the way the comedian Wendy Liebman talked about not quitting after a bad night (in chapter 7).

Find these people and nurture your connection to them. Just as I would advise anyone pursuing stand-up to find people who are still jazzed about their work, who continue to be excited about the construction and rhythm of a great joke, and who maintain a positive attitude toward seeking and creating work for themselves. I encourage you as a spouse to take the same approach to your friendships.

Surrounding yourself with hopeful, positive, committed people, whether you've made the unconventional choice to live the life of an artist or the highly conventional and yet no less challenging choice of staying married for the long haul, is a terrific way to create support for yourself to go the distance.

SOCIAL CONTAGION

I didn't know this advice had scientific evidence to support it until I read an article in the *New York Times* with the title "Are Your Friends

Making You Fat?," by Clive Thompson.[1] Since I'd love to be able to blame my friends for not being able to button my jeans instead of blaming the softball-sized muffins I insist on eating with abandon, I devoured the article. Although the title was a great hook, it turned out the article was about a lot more than weight gain or loss.

In his *New York Times* article, Thompson described the work of two social scientists, Nicholas Christakis and James Fowler, who conducted a comprehensive study on the effects of the phenomenon of "social contagion." The inspiration for Thompson's catchy title was from the researchers' findings in the study of obese people. Christakis and Fowler spent several years analyzing data from the Framingham Heart Study, a famous study that spanned fifty years and tracked the health profiles of over 15,000 people. Christakis and Fowler's study revealed that obese people "broke out in clusters." According to them, people in groups are highly influenced by each other. The Framingham data, when analyzed by Christakis and Fowler, revealed that the subjects became obese together, remained the same size, or in some cases even droppped weight as a group. And this was not a coincidence. According to Thompson's article, "When a Framingham resident became obese, his or her friends were 57 percent more likely to become obese, too."

Christakis and Fowler's next observations were what made me think about these ideas in terms of long marriages. Thompson also reported in the *New York Times* that Christakis and Fowler found multiple examples of "contagious behavior." The researchers also discovered that "smoking . . . also appeared to spread socially—in fact, a friend taking up smoking increased your chance of lighting up by 36 percent, and if you had a three-degrees-removed friend who started smoking, you were still 11 percent more likely to do the same than if that friend had not started smoking. Drinking spread socially, as did happiness and even loneliness."[2]

There it was in black and white. Our friends, and the way they think and behave, have a significant effect on how we think and behave. If this is true for practices such as weight loss and smoking, and emotions such as happiness and loneliness, couldn't it also be true for creating and maintaining long-term relationships that are happy and fun?

With very few exceptions, the long-term happily married couples I met with, whether they had a conscious understanding of "social contagion" or not, had their own instincts about the importance of surrounding themselves with other contented, committed couples. One woman, married over eighteen years, told me with resolve, "I have two friends I call when I am feeling anxious about my husband, and both are happily married. If I call my divorced friends, they are just going to tell me how awful men are and how marriage is a sham and I should get out now."

Some of the married people I met with had also formed "clusters" of long-term married friends. Russ and Bonnie Tamblyn were part of a circle of four couples, one of which is Ralph and Joanne from chapter 1. They have all been friends for over forty years. Russ and Bonnie, Donna and Paul, Joanne and Ralph, and Ingrid and Harvey have all shared more than half their lives together, supporting each other through everything from their own weddings (two of them married later in life), the births of six children (one tragically stillborn), the discovery of one love child, career transitions, successes, retirement, decades of birthdays, the weddings of each other's children, the births of grandchildren, the passing of their own parents, and all the day-to-day minutiae of life in between. When Joanne and Ralph endured the death of their first baby, Donna held her friend throughout her grief. A year later Donna danced at the birth of their son, and of their daughter after that. When Donna was overwhelmed with photography gigs she couldn't miss, Ingrid picked up her daughter from elementary school. When Ralph knew he wasn't ready to retire from teaching at the LA Music Academy and performing as a drummer, Paul and Harvey supported him in getting a small studio in Los Angeles while his wife, Joanne, oversaw the design and construction of their dream house in Mendocino.

I talked to Joanne and Donna separately about the value of

decades-long friendship, where they can talk freely about their thirty-plus year marriages. Not only did Joanne offer insight regarding one of the pitfalls of long-term marriage, but there was so much love in her voice when she talked about Donna, it left no doubt how much she values having a friend in the same boat to laugh with.

"I've found in long-term marriage that you hit a turning point. The comfort level grows and the sexual attraction thing recedes to the background. What emerges is a feeling of being taken for granted. Part of this is good, because you know each other so well. I like having a girlfriend who understands this. For instance, I know Ralph enjoys it when I look nice, so I make the effort. Then I'll go someplace with Donna and I'll say, 'You look so nice, Donna,' and she'll say, 'So do you! Nice that we both have each other to notice. Paul didn't say one fucking thing!' Then I'll say, 'I know, neither did Ralph, but he will when I get home. As I'm getting ready to go to bed.' And we laugh. We laugh over that all the time."

That's right, they laugh about it. They don't suck down a bottle of gin and drunk-dial the gym teacher at the kids' school and ask him what he is wearing. They don't wallow for hours in how bad it all is and whine about how marriage isn't all it's cracked up to be and fall into a rabbit hole of marital despair.

When I met with Donna later, I told her that Joanne had told me this story. She laughed heartily. "We're family. Of course I'll listen and not worry for a second because I know for a fact Ralph thinks she's the most beautiful woman in the world."

This story illustrates another benefit of having long-term couple friendships: other couples not only may be faced with the same ups and downs of marriage, but they also know you and your spouse well. They can be your reality check. It is so important to have someone to laugh with over minor infractions, instead of using them as evidence that you should leave.

This scene would be quite different for Joanne with someone who didn't have the same commitment to long-term marriage. Like me twenty years ago. I had no understanding of why or how you stay past the sexually charged adrenaline of those first few months of knowing someone, let alone years. "He doesn't notice you? You should get out!" is probably what I would have said to Joanne. And then hung up the phone alone in my studio apartment and watched Letterman until I nodded off.

That attitude pretty much describes my romantic life from my twenties through my mid-thirties. As I've already alluded to, if you pissed me off, I left. I'm not proud of this; on the contrary, I am specifically saying that present-day happily married me wouldn't be friends with me at that age and stage of life today. I might admire her spirit, and on some days her freedom, but then I'd visit her at her studio apartment with the futon on the floor, her empty refrigerator and bare walls, hear the deafening quiet of her singleness, give her a hug, wish her well, and look forward to getting home to my family. On my way out I might take a few minutes to suggest that if she could stop being so trigger-happy with her anger and have the courage to reveal even a teensy bit of vulnerability to a person, and be a little more forgiving, she might get what she wanted, which was someone cool to share her life. Then I'd go home and be grateful to have figured out some of this and also to have some like-minded married friends to call.

The "clusters" of couples I encountered often had other aspects of their lives in common, in addition to being married for a while. Some worked together, or belonged to the same temple or church, or they shared a passion for a particular sport or art form. In another long-standing group of couples I met, the husbands have all known each other for forty-eight years, since being roommates together at law school. They break from the framework of the Framingham Study "cluster" model slightly in that they currently live in four different cities around the country. But distance doesn't keep these couples from staying very involved with each other's lives. Barbara, the most recent member of the group, having married into it in 1992, is probably the most impressed with their closeness. "There is such value in having eight pals who are the same age, have similar life experiences, seven of whom have known each other for forty-eight years, all of whom have children and grandchildren and all of whom have hilarious memories together and will continue to add to them. There's just an incomparable shorthand born of history and an appreciation for exactly where we all are."

> We all know laughter is healing. When we laugh in a group the healing is exponential.
>
> —WENDY LIEBMAN

When six of these friends were vacationing together in Arizona, I was lucky enough to get together with them in a restaurant for a conversation. It didn't take much provoking for them to start debating the value of humor in long-term marriage, the conversation triggering decades-old memories. I could feel the joyful rapport that time has given these couples. On the drive home afterward, Barbara's words echoed in my mind: *Incomparable shorthand . . . appreciation for exactly where we all are . . .* It sounded so ideal and comforting, and also like something Tod and I don't have with another couple. We married late in life, at least late in mine. In our experience so far, finding a couple in which I like the wife, Tod likes the husband, and it's reciprocated by the other couple has not been easy.

I felt inspired by this tribe of happy long-term couples, but also found myself wishing I'd gone to law school. Not because I wanted to practice law, but so I would have had some fabulous roommates and be able to have dinner with them and their husbands forty-eight years later. I didn't have the best luck with roommates in college—my first one in a suite of three was not a fan of Jews, an obvious limitation. I liked our third roommate a lot, but she stayed in the New Hampshire area after school and we lost touch. Most of the other people I lived with during my college years were actors and directors who, like me, lived as stones gathering no moss after graduation, and no phone numbers. Facebook, as much as it can be a distracting curse for a writer, has been great for reconnecting. It's heartwarming to see people's lives twenty or even thirty years later, but Facebook friends do not "a cluster" make.

I do have some long-standing comedy friends whom I hold dear, although since having children, I don't see them as often. When we do see each other, that feeling of being kindred spirits hasn't gone away. Maybe "clustering" isn't my thing. But sitting with that group of law school grads I had to wonder, is this a bad omen for my future with Tod?

I called my friend Jill, whom I met three years ago. She's been married twelve years. I told her my stress du jour.

She was incredulous. "Who has friends for forty-eight years? That's ridiculous. Andrew and I don't have friends like that. Couple friends are very hard, everyone liking each other equally? And then there's the kids, I mean, it's like trying to find a pair of cashmere gloves for eighty percent off that doesn't have six fingers. Relax, you're fine."

I took a breath and smiled. There it was, proof that all you really need is one friend who appreciates the value of unadulterated cashmere on sale.

Jill's unqualified response helped me fine-tune my application of the social contagion theory to marriage. No study defines "a friendship cluster" as four couples who have been friends for at least forty-five years. But as married people, it absolutely helps to have a few good friends committed to staying married. The bottom line: you need just one friend or two with whom you can drop the facade and talk from your heart. Not to have a bitch fest, but a friendship for honest conversations, one where you both feel safe enough to let your guard down, take a deep breath, and support each other.

The final reason for having a few true-blue, happily married friends is one that most people won't say to you. It's so you can be unapologetic about your own happiness. Most of us have worked long and hard to have the privilege of working long and hard in happy marriages. We don't want to always have to downplay and make like it's not a big deal. Sometimes you want to be able to express sincerely how much you love your spouse and how happy you are to have this great person to spend your life with. It's nice to have a friend or two to share this with, without feeling braggy, self-conscious, or guilty.

MICHELE AND MARC BOHBOT

Optimism, Realism, and Luck

The Morocco-born Michele Bohbot, a mother of seven and grand-mother of ten, has been married to her husband and business part-ner, Marc Bohbot, for thirty-five years. She has no problem expressing her feelings about the importance of surrounding herself with posi-tive, happy couples. A friend of mine told me about the Bohbots, in-sisting that their romantic vibe after three-plus decades together was worth writing about. When Michele came to the door of her impressive home (even by Beverly Hills standards!), I instantly under-stood why I had been sent there. With her tightly pulled back black ponytail and petite body that appeared to have been dipped in black cotton spandex, it was hard for me to take my eyes off of her. She extended a cleanly manicured hand in an *enchantée* way, her blue eyes sparkling.

"I am so happy to meet you," she said, ushering me in to a sitting room where tea on a silver tray was waiting for us. She gestured for me to sit and I did, skeptical of how much truth would be revealed in such a grand setting. As soon as she began talking, my doubts van-ished. Maybe I'm a sucker for a koi pond, but Michele's positivity didn't feel like a pose. There is a lightness about her, a strength and authenticity.

"Zis ees my husband, Marc," she said, with more than a hint of her native French accent, looking across the room to where a tall, lean man with a shock of white hair had walked in. He smiled and nodded. "Nice to meet you," he said, and poured himself a cup of tea.

The only detail I knew about this couple before we met was that they were the co-owners of a multi-million-dollar clothing business called Bisou Bisou. When we first began speaking and they were so positive about their life, I assumed it was the opulence they enjoyed that made them so content. Who wouldn't be smiling with such abundance—a huge family and having built a successful business, not to mention all that cash? But as we talked, I realized that it wasn't the wealth that had created the positivity; it was the unflagging positivity that had created the wealth.

As soon as Marc and Michele met in France, in 1978, when he was twenty-five and she was nineteen, they knew they were going to spend the rest of their lives together. Yet all this time later it is a mystery even to them that their instincts were so good at such a young age.

"It's luck," Marc said, running a hand through his silver hair. "What else can it be?" After spending a few hours with these two determined people, I wasn't convinced. Their meeting was luck, but almost everything since has resulted from a lot of other qualities, like drive, commitment, loyalty, and love. For me, the luck is that they shared these qualities. Because over the past four decades, the road wasn't exactly paved with lucky stones.

They arrived in Los Angeles seven years after their first visit to the United States, on their honeymoon. As ambitious entrepreneurs, they were determined to replicate in this country the success they had in Paris in clothing design and manufacturing. Without speaking English, or having contacts in Los Angeles, their first business did not go well.

"It was a total failure," Marc told me.

"Total," Michele echoed. In fact, Marc was ready to leave the country, but Michele was determined to make it, so she marched her seven-month-pregnant self into a bank and got a loan to start another business, the one that ultimately paid for the koi pond in front of their house.

Although Michele is very proud of the business they created together, her face becomes even more alive when she talks about their long marriage, one in which there is still "mystery," and "discovery," two aspects of a relationship she believes are the most important for happiness. For the full effect of Michele's insights, read them in your most elegant French accent:

> The major secret is to try always to discover the other one. You have to be aware that nothing is forever. You cannot take any-

thing for granted. The person that you live with must not only be your priority but must be the person you admire most, the person you want to discover, because we all change. Sometimes we think we know that person, but we don't even know ourselves, so how can we know them? So you have to always look at marriage with a fresh perspective. Each one must make an effort to talk to the other one, to surprise him and to flirt, to discover him or her. My thoughts are always moving and transforming themselves, and they are better, and the same is true for my husband also. You want to evolve. We continue to learn from each other, really. One person pulls the other one. We move together side by side, no one in front of the other. The most important thing for the couple is the mystery! To always be discovering each other, because we are always changing!

UH-OH, FLIRTING NOT MY THING

I've never been good at flirting, even when I was single. I've always seen flirting as a big waste of time. Why flirt? If you want something, just ask for it directly. Also, I'm a sucker for it when men do it. To this day, when someone flirts with me, I don't seem to get that it's just a game. I take it literally and feel like I should respond sincerely, "I'm married, and . . . you're great, but I just can't and I'm so sorry, I know how hard rejection is and believe me if I was single . . ." I'm formulating these thoughts in my head, working up the courage to tell it like it is, and meanwhile the person has left the room, or bar, or playdate and is texting his girlfriend or playing Candy Crush. Flirting has just never worked for me. But maybe I could try it on Tod. "Hey, honey, you're all sweaty after your long run. I'd like to get sweaty, too. If you know what I mean." No, God help me . . .

One place where there is no mystery in Michele's marriage is her opinion on "sticking with the winners."

"You have to have married friends because then as women you understand each other. It is also important to have people the same age who also have healthy marriages. People who are divorced don't want to be next to us, I disturb them." I find this hard to believe, so I ask her to say more about that.

"They don't believe it's true. For example, we know a couple that is really not happy but they are still together, and they really believe that Marc and I, we are faking it when we kiss. They can't imagine that we can be happy. They cannot see beauty. They don't believe that they can get inspired. They are dead people, in their marriage." Michele quickly added, "When you are happy, you should be around people alive in their marriage so your relationship can grow healthy, without thinking of the negativity of others. If you want your happiness to grow, you have to release all the toxic people out of your life. It's hard to say, but it's true. They don't understand you. At the end of the day you are making them more miserable than they are. As for yourself, you feel not very good because you are not talking the same language, you cannot be yourself. When you are with people who are happily married, you are talking about other things, having fun, and no comparison, no jealousy, no misery."

I love the clarity of this mini-rant. I also love that Michelle is un-apologetic about getting the toxic people out of your life. It took me years to even know there was such a thing as a "toxic person."

I may not have had the discernment (or the courage, frankly) to clean the toxic people out of my life when I was single, but having a family has lowered my tolerance for misery so I had to become vigilant about this. Harsh as it sounds, it is not crazy to take stock of the people in your life and make sure they have the same vision for a happy marriage that you want. And, added perk, once you get all the dead wood out of your life, think of all the extra energy you'll have to create "mystery" and "discovery," or at least do a little flirting with your spouse!

TIPS FOR STICKING WITH WINNERS

- Positivity is contagious. Find happily married couples to spend time with. Discover for yourself if they really are happy by spending time with them. In the beginning, try more listening and observing than talking.

- Stay in touch with long-standing couple friends. They will offer a unique touchstone for your life, and remind you of the good times when you need it.

- Find a nurturing outlet: Seek out at least one long-term married person with whom you can have honest conversations about the frustrations, and joys, of your marriage.

- Try to clean out the "toxic people" from your life, or at least limit your time with them. These are people who consistently love to wallow in whatever problem they are having instead of actively looking for ways to improve their lives. It can be very draining to listen to them, and since they are committed to complaining, any positive suggestions you make are going to fall on deaf ears, and it's a waste of your precious time. Time you could be using batting your eyes mysteriously at your spouse!

Have Patience

GREAT MARRIAGES, LIKE GREAT COMEDY CAREERS, TAKE TIME

Being a good husband is like being a stand-up comic. You need ten years before you can call yourself a beginner.

—JERRY SEINFELD

I've got a wife of sixty-one years, thirty of which have been fabulous.[1]

—PAUL MAZURSKY

Think of the comics who make you laugh out loud—Louis C.K., Chris Rock, Amy Schumer, Conan O'Brien, Chelsea Handler, Patton Oswalt, Margaret Cho, Tig Notaro, Jim Gaffigan, and more. These people did not become brilliant comics overnight. All of them have been honing their craft for many, many years and have kept performing long after they needed to work just to pay the bills.

Needing to gain confidence, trusting that you can tell the truth, your truth, not what you think an audience wants to hear, and having your anger propel you to speak is a spot-on recipe for what is often referred to as "finding your voice." The process of finding your voice as a comic has a lot in common with the process of creating a great marriage. They both take hard work, commitment, and patience. There are no shortcuts or magic fairy dust to get you there more quickly.

I remember doing "bringer" shows—shows where you are given stage time at a decent club in exchange for promising to bring in an audience—with Chelsea Handler when she was in her early twenties. It was a little like watching a baby bird learning to fly—an often inebriated, crass bird that looked a lot like Brigette Bardot—but one who was obviously testing its wings. It was always clear that Chelsea was going to take off, but she definitely fell out of the nest a few times before it happened.

Never without a drink in her hand onstage, early on in the set, after talking about a number of mishaps, she'd throw out, "And there's a pretty good chance I'm an alcoholic." This brazen honesty would always get a laugh. She also did a bit about her father: "My dad wonders why I don't bring home any men and then he asks me if I am a lessssbbbbiiiaaannn [pointing to her lady parts] and I'm, like, 'No, Dad, I am not a lessssbbbiannn . . . I fuck guys all the time.'" Not the most brilliant joke ever, and it didn't always get laughs, but it doesn't matter. She was working out her whole persona. She was planting the seeds of her take-no-prisoners brashness, which would go on to be her most identifying, and crowd-pleasing, characteristic. This was more than fifteen years ago. Chelsea never stopped working in all that time. I would run into her over the years and she was always going on the road doing shows. She put in the time to gain the confidence she seemingly effortlessly displays today, anchoring her television show, selling out huge venues, and writing best-selling books.

"Finding your voice" might sound like a phrase you would hear at writers' workshops or spiritual retreats, but it is so valuable for comedy that I want to take a few minutes to define what it means and how relevant it is to being part of a long-term, healthy couple.

Sometimes when a comic is starting out, one or more established comedians inspire them. Not surprisingly, the jokes these freshman comics write, their intonation, and even their mannerisms can remind you a lot of those established performers. Being inspired to the point of imitation is a pretty natural part of many new careers. Also, if new comics are hanging out in clubs they may try to write their own versions of jokes they hear their comedy idols doing. This is not even necessarily a conscious decision, but facing an audience is terrifying. If you see that a certain topic or a certain style is working for someone else, it's understandable that you might be influenced and reassured, thinking, "Well, at least I'll be talking about stuff audiences want to hear." This is the opposite of finding your own voice, but it is does seem to be a common step along the road.

Finding your own voice means resisting the temptation to mimic someone you admire and turning your attention inward. Rather than focusing on what everyone else is doing and saying, it means taking the time to dig a little to figure out what you care about, what you want to say, and how you want to say it.

Naturally charismatic and smart beginning comics can use their mimicry of other comics' work to sustain them for a while. But if they are truly impassioned about being a comedian, and are not using stand-up as a stepping-stone to something else, they will quickly tire of doing some version of what they think a comedian should be. They will become restless and dissatisfied. Out of that discomfort (and probably some anger), his or her own truth will emerge. It is at this point that a comic begins to find his or her voice.

This part of the development process of a comedian, according to Mark Lonow, a comedy coach for over twenty-five years and the co-owner of the Improv comedy club chain, is absolutely essential for their success. He also happens to be married to JoAnne Astrow (a former comic and co-owner with him of Astrow-Lonow Management) for forty-five years.

In a recent conversation Lonow told me, "The most important thing is to find who you are as a comedian, your specific point of view, because then anything you say can be funny, it doesn't even have to be in joke structure." Then he stopped talking. He made this point so strongly, I figured we were done. He surprised me by continuing. "My biggest challenge as a coach was when people weren't willing to do the work to find this, when they didn't get this concept. They either didn't have the patience to figure out the germ of who they were and build on it, or the focus, or they wouldn't listen to feedback." Even years after he stopped teaching I can hear his frustration.

Lonow's comments made the parallels between finding your voice as a comic and finding your voice in a marriage so clear. In both cases, this process seems to be essential for success. With very few exceptions this discovery process doesn't happen overnight either onstage or in a marriage. For most of us it takes some time to figure out who we are and then a little more time to find the courage to express it, even if it's only to an audience of one, your spouse.

> Listening and hearing have to be learned, and also involve self-development. You have to learn how to be confident in yourself. If something really hurts your feelings, you can't not say it because you're embarrassed about expressing how you feel. I didn't know that forty years ago. The biggest shock to most people is how much work it takes. They think love should solve it all. And it doesn't because you have to find where your anger is. Sometimes it's your anger that makes you stand up and find the truth.
>
> —GERI HURLEY, married forty-two years

In marriage, revealing only what you think your spouse wants to see about you is like the comic who only writes material they think an audience wants to hear. It's simply not sustainable over time. And apparently, I am not the first person to observe this. As far back as 1938, a forward-thinking sociologist, Willard W. Waller, found, "Courting couples are generally blissful, optimistic lovers who, in order to sustain their romance, draw attention to their desirable qualities, suppress thoughts and behaviors that might weaken their romance, and try to see the best in the other person. After they are married, however, spouses may no longer be as motivated to 'put their best foot forward' to impress their marriage partners; moreover, *the intimacy of marriage makes sustaining such idealized images difficult*" (emphasis added).[2]

To have a sustainable career as a comic, or a long marriage, you have to find the courage to be your most authentic self. And as for the emerging comic, the only way you'll achieve this in marriage is by taking the risk of revealing your true opinions and feelings.

> The one benefit of being married a long time: if she's eating garlic, I can eat garlic.
>
> —LEW SCHNEIDER, comedian, married thirty-three years

Here's a lightweight example of what I am talking about. Tod likes to go camping. When he and I met, I never wanted him or anyone else to think of me as a princess. I'm a Jewish woman who spent some formative years in Connecticut, not feeling very comfortable about "my people." Nothing was more horrifying to me during those years than the thought of being labeled a JAP, a Jewish American Princess. Toward this end, I didn't wear makeup until I was thirty and wore the same clothes for two decades, lest anyone think I had an attachment to the material world. What better way to claim non-JAP status than by embracing camping? What says "I'm earthy and cool and don't need four hundred–count Egyptian cotton sheets" more than squatting in the woods? So despite the fact that I didn't have any camping equipment, own a sleeping bag, or even like s'mores, I talked animatedly with Tod about camping.

Most important, though, I always managed to get out of doing any actual camping with him. I got pregnant six months after we married, and who goes camping with a newborn? Then I got pregnant again. Then I had the second baby.

"Going camping with two kids under five? That's just too much," I said when Tod brought up the idea one morning. For a while the whole idea got tabled, until we got the Spring 2014 *Sunset Magazine*

Camping Guide. The fact is, our boys are probably old enough now to chop the firewood themselves, or at least carry it. But the thought of sleeping on the ground, twigs and stones jutting into my spine, and boiling water for coffee over a fire where an ember might pop out and sear one of my aging corneas—not so fun.

"I'm sorry, Tod. I love you," I said, peering over his magazine, "but I don't want to go camping. Even the idea of it makes me feel itchy." I took a breath. "And while I'm being honest, I don't even really care about constellations. I'm more of an ocean person. I'm sorry I misrepresented myself," I said, lowering my head.

I wish I could tell you Tod didn't care, that he laughed it off and told me I was awesome with a joke, like, "And I was so looking forward to getting you in a sleeping bag and having you search for the big dipper!" No, that's not how it went down. Tod was (and probably still is) genuinely disappointed. He told me that staring up at stars in the Joshua Tree National Park is one of his big passions that he was looking forward to sharing with his wife.

Ugh.

It took us both a few days to digest my big reveal. At one point, feeling guilty, I blurted out, "Don't be that upset! After all, I birthed you two sons, backup campers who will be much more fun than me. It will be special father-son bonding!"

I just couldn't see faking enjoyment in something for the next thirty years. But then I had another thought. Now that the cat was out of the sleeping bag, I could give it a try, with very low expectations. There is a good chance that by nightfall I'll be zipped up in the tent with a lantern and reading. But the fact is, once I told the truth and lowered everyone's expectations, I felt a little more game. But additionally, my telling the truth freed Tod to get his camping fix elsewhere, with people who really love it.

Many husbands and wives I spoke with talked about this challenge of finding the courage to reveal the truth of who they are over the years. It's not going to happen instantly, but at some point you have to stop behaving like your idea of how a married person acts and be yourself, otherwise you're going to start to resent keeping up a facade to make your spouse happy. If you don't, pretty soon your marriage will start to feel like a resentment-filled volcano waiting to blow. (Note: Running out of images to describe built-up resentment in marriage.)

THE "VOICE" OF THE MARRIAGE

As with other comedy tools applied to marriage, a couple's process of "finding your voice" is slightly more complicated than it is for a comic. In marriage, finding your voice is twofold: it often involves finding your individual voice, and also finding your voice as a couple. Finding the way to be together with the most ease and happiness. This ease, then, becomes the voice of the couple, or as they used to say in the late sixties, the couple finds their groove.

In stand-up, there are rare exceptions where a comedian hits the stage out of the gate with an irrepressible, distinct point of view and delivery and their only task is to keep strengthening it.

Maria Bamford is one of these rare exceptions: a comedian with complete originality from day one. She's the quirky, blond comic you may recognize from various Christmas season Target commercials. We both performed at the Aspen Comedy Festival in 2002, but I knew her from coffee-house comedy shows in LA for many years before. From the first time Maria came onstage her point of view and whole presentation was completely unique. Then, as now, with her raspy voice, her spot-on impressions, and her unabashed exploration of the darkest topics, there is only one Maria Bamford.

Very few couples also experience this phenomenon of total ease and authenticity with themselves and as a couple out of the gate. Of the over fifty couples I interviewed in depth, and the hundreds I have quizzed at every coffee shop, cocktail party, and school function I have been to over the last two years, I met just one couple for whom this was true. It was the second marriage for both—the Grammy-winning composer Mike Stoller and his wife, Corky Hale, the esteemed harpist, clothing designer, cook, cabaret performer, and political activist.

MIKE STOLLER AND CORKY HALE
Love at First Album Cover

Mike Stoller, half of the Grammy-winning hit machine Leiber and Stoller, and his wife, Corky Hale, have been together for forty-five years. According to both they were completely in sync in every way from the moment they met and have maintained this perfect communication for over forty years.

Mike was first introduced to Corky through her music on an album his first wife brought home from her job as bookkeeper for a local jazz company. "It was an album with Kitty White singing and Corky Hale on harp," he said, "and I fell in love with the playing of the harp and then there was picture of her on the back and I thought, 'Oh my God, how is it possible? This couldn't be worse timing. There she is, and I just got married!'"

Eleven years later, after his first marriage ended, Corky walked into Jerry Leiber's office to record a demo. Jerry introduced her to Mike: "This is my partner."

"It was real love at first sight," Corky said. "We talked and talked, and remember, he'd known my work for eleven years, and then I walked into his office, so he asked me out to dinner." Two years later they married.

"There's an old Yiddish word, *bashert*," Corky told me. "It means destiny, 'meant to be.' Our meeting was really *bashert*." She repeated this slowly for emphasis. "It. Was. Meant. To. Be."

Corky is a loquacious and unapologetic spitfire of a woman. She has very strong opinions on why she and Mike have such a happy marriage. In truth, they were so over the top that my first instinct was to not believe them. But as a relative newcomer to marriage with my thirteen years compared to her forty-five, I felt I should at least consider her ideas. Plus, listening to Corky's monologue about marriage was darn entertaining. Here are some of the highlights.

"People are always asking me, 'Why have you had such a happy marriage?' Let me tell you the reasons why. I start off first with *money*. A lot of people break up because of money. Number one, we have never one minute's problem with this because I've always had money."

She paused to take a sip of water and must have seen the surprised look on my face. Although many of my interviewees may have thought this, no one before Ms. Hale had had the audacity to say this out loud. Mike just smiled. Corky went on to explain her money-causing-the-most-fights-in-marriage theory. She stood up and paced in front of me.

"For instance, we have friends that were married twenty-five years and they broke up two years ago and the wife said, 'I'm sick of it. I saw a pair of earrings that I wanted and he said, 'No, no, I just bought a new car for my kid,' and she said, 'You care more about your children from a previous marriage than you do about me!' So, if the wife has money, that eliminates that, and I think that helps."

She continued. "Number two: *Adultery*. We're always together. Every night. I know where he is during the day, he knows where I am. At night time, he doesn't really have a lot of guys he hangs out with. We're both basketball freaks. We go to games together. I once took a tour playing harp for Judy Collins. She wanted me, so Mike said, 'Take it. I'll come to Philadelphia with you.' We're always together. I sat in New York City last year for a month, while he had a show on Broadway."

Mike, still smiling, interjected, "It was called *The People in the Picture*."

"Right. So now we've got money and adultery. Next is children," Corky continued. "We don't fight about children. It's just beyond us. What are we going to fight about? Because he gives his child more money than me? I don't care about that. You know what people fight about with kids? What school you're going to send them to? Why?"

It seemed to be a rhetorical question, but she paused, so I did an "I don't know" shrug anyway. But really I was thinking, because they disagree? I was too self-conscious to say it, though. I didn't want to expose myself as someone who disagrees with her husband. Also, her ideas were coming at me so fast, I was still thinking about the money and infidelity theories and I noticed I was starting to sweat. After all, I am not independently wealthy, nor do I spend every second with Tod. And we have two school-age children and I would absolutely fight with him about where they should go to school if we had different ideas. I started casting lines out to Corky for some indication that despite these marks against us, there was hope we might be able to hang in there for forty-five years too.

"You must fight about something though, right?"

"Not really," Corky said.

"No," Mike confirmed. I scanned my notes for another question. Corky filled the pause.

"Number one, our tastes are very similar," she said.

I looked up. Similar taste? Bingo! Tod and I have that. But can I hang my hat on mutual disdain for labels on clothes, cluttered office space, and weak coffee?

"We wake up at seven, seven-thirty every morning," she continued, "and then we lie in bed and talk for about half an hour about lots of things. We have dinner together every night."

Hmm, we get up at six or six-thirty every morning, say hello, and race around each other in a silently choreographed dance that includes making coffee (first things first), cooking breakfast, making lunches, and occasionally reading shocking headlines from the newspaper to each other. We have dinner together two to three nights a week, tops.

Interviewing these two I found myself of two minds. Number one—Thank you, Corky!—I was very happy that they had met and had found such crazy happiness together. Number two, despite the fact that I know better, I was killing myself with comparison. Even knowing what a fruitless endeavor this is, I couldn't stop myself. As with every couple I met, I was there to be inspired, and yet with each recollection of their undying and zero-conflict love for each other and Corky's recitation of marital pitfalls I felt I'd never be able to dodge, I was getting increasingly anxious.

Determined to shake myself out of it and grab some unique nugget of wisdom from these lucky paramours, something perhaps they learned about being a "we" after forty-five years together, I went in with my big closer.

"Would you say you're better at being married today than you were when you started forty-five years ago?"

"No," Corky replied.

"No," Mike added quickly, smiling anew.

"We were happy from the first day we met," Corky said, matter-of-factly.

And that, my friends, was that.

Mike walked me out to my car, the embodiment of affable. As I drove away, still slightly unnerved, I made the mature choice to reframe their interview in my mind. I decided to see sitting and talking with Corky and Mike in their stunning white living room with floor-to-ceiling windows overlooking Los Angeles as something slightly fantastical, like having tea with unicorns. Very happy unicorns. They were the exception to the rule about finding your voice as a couple. They didn't struggle to find their voice, they had it from day one. Although I couldn't help but notice that it is mostly Ms. Hale's. And that Mr. Stoller could not be more content than when he is listening to it.

The rest of us non-unicorns, though, go through a process over time of revealing more of ourselves and figuring out how best to communicate with the other. Fortunately, right after this interview, I had dinner with real-life mammals who confirmed these ideas for me. I was sitting with a bunch of friends we catch up with several times throughout the year when the conversation turned to work. I mentioned my book—I was now writing specifically about the idea of finding your voice as a couple.

My friend Becca, who I don't talk to regularly but who has been married over ten years and is always genuinely interested in the subject of marriage, asked, "What does finding your voice as a comic have to do with being married? What's the 'voice' that you and Tod have found?" she pressed.

No one had turned the question on me yet, so it took me a minute to answer. My mind flashed to our most recent therapy visit.

"Well, for us, we have moved from brutally honest to honesty with kindness," I said.

"Interesting," she said, licking a tiny espresso spoon. "And that's something you figured out together?"

"Yes, over time. Which is what I'm saying. That figuring out what works as a couple, your most effective, authentic, and loving communicating style, your 'voice' [Yes, I made air quotes with my fingers] doesn't happen overnight."

"No, of course not. Like I don't say the first thing that pops into my head anymore either."

"That's a good one," I said. Making a mental note. I have become a marital-tip sponge.

"It's helped *a lot*," she said. "You just don't always need to say that first thought. Sometimes it's good to breathe first. Think it through a little, let the dust settle."

> Real love amounts to withholding the truth, even when you're offered the perfect opportunity to hurt someone's feelings.
> —DAVID SEDARIS, *Dress Your Family in Corduroy and Denim*

It is interesting that in Becca and her husband's case, finding their voice as a couple meant *not* giving voice to every thought that comes into her mind. I'd heard this before, but until Becca brought it up, I hadn't thought about it in terms of finding your voice as a couple. Resisting the impulse to name-call or let other hurtful thoughts fly that you can't take back is important for maintaining a happy marriage, as we've already talked about. This self-editing also falls under my definition of finding your voice as a couple.

But how about some examples of finding your voice that actually involve talking? For me and Tod, the next step after learning to bite back the most honest response we could think of was to temper our thoughts with kindness. Tod and I share a fierce passion for honesty. Brutal honesty is a highly effective way to communicate if you are, say, in a battle and the enemy is fast approaching, or if you are a crime scene investigator, or in any profession where brutality is valued. Not so much in marriage.

Even though it felt to us like we were being helpful by telling it like it is, most of the time it was just plain hurtful and unnecessary. The outside world will kick you in the teeth often enough; you don't need to do that to your spouse, even when it's tempting to get them to "wake up," or however we justify it. Tod and I have learned this through painful trial and error. Today, we do our best to shortstop our impulses to be brutally honest. The "voice" of our marriage is that we continue to be honest with each other, but we also aim for kindness.

Tracy Vilar and Eric Daniels, who talked about learning to listen better in chapter 2, have also fine-tuned their voice as a couple over time. Consequently, they are much more comfortable in their marriage today than they were fourteen years ago. Tracy is indebted to Eric for showing her how to stay calm, even when she feels strongly about something.

Since she was only twenty when they met, part of being able to ward off the emotional storms that would overtake her was a function of maturing, but in addition to growing up, in the interest of protecting her marriage, Tracy also had to figure out how to express herself in a gentle way. She learned that when stress levels were running high, she needed to take her voice down a notch so she could actually be heard. A fiery young woman raised in a household with a highly volatile mother, gentle expression was not her gift. With Eric's influence, though, the two of them have found their way to more sane and loving conversations. Eric has helped Tracy calm down.

"Because I am so much like my mom," she told me, "not a listener, a reactor, she's always already off on her own thing. When I saw how calm Eric was, I was, like, How are you so calm? My dad is like that. After a while I just started to talk like Eric. We'd have calm conversa-

tions where we can work something out. Now when I am saying something that's a problem, I start out being more vulnerable. I tell him my
deeper feeling about it. It totally changes the conversation. He always
makes me feel better about something. He'll remind me, 'Tracy, you
know how you get.' I used to never tell him my deeper feelings because
I didn't want to get hurt. I'm coming from my parents' relationship, or
a friend hurting me, and then I remember, 'Oh, yeah, he's not going to
do that to me.' It took a while to get to that."

Tracy's words articulate exactly the value of reflecting on your own
behavior, and hanging in there for the long haul with your mate. After
years together, Tracy trusts that she can be open with Eric without fear
of getting trampled or being abandoned. Proof positive that good marriages grow and strengthen over time. It's one of the perks that is helpful to remember when jumping ship out of frustration seems like a
good idea.

If, after many years together, you don't feel that trust, you might
want to get to the bottom of it with the help of a professional. We talk
about that in the chapter 13.

YOU ARE NOT IN YOUR PARENTS' MARRIAGE!

Tracy realized two important things. One, that she is not in her parents' marriage, and two, that getting to the peaceful communication
she and Eric enjoy today, even despite their strong foundation as
friends, takes years to achieve. Whatever marriage your parents had,
good or bad, understanding that you are not destined to re-create it in
your own is very liberating. It might not be easy to break free from your
role models for a marriage, but with effort and guidance you can create
a different marriage for yourself.

Tracy's recognition that their communication didn't improve
overnight, despite their having been friends for years, is a great argument for being patient, not only with your spouse but with yourself.
Unless you're Corky and Mike or another unicorn-esque couple,

there's a learning curve to marriage. Go easy on yourselves. Don't have unrealistic expectations for finding your groove. Trust that if your hearts are in the right place. You'll get there.

In case you are afraid that slow-growing intimacy, the idea of finding your voice as a mature and loving couple, sounds like it will suck all the thrill of new love and passion out the window, the happiness expert Sonja Lyubomirsky also had some interesting discoveries about this. She and her colleague, Katherine Jacobs Bao, found that "rushing intimacy in a relationship can produce high levels of positive emotions. However, these types of relationships are quite unstable."[3] Lyubomirsky appreciates the slow, steady deepening of a relationship over time rather than the mind-blowing adrenaline rush that we sometimes think is missing from long-term relationships. Bao and Lyubomirsky point to a study in which researchers determined that high levels of romance and passion and affection often led to high levels of divorce.[4]

It was good to find researchers confirming what I'd heard a million times about marriage: it's a marathon, not a sprint.

In the marathon of marriage, even in my relatively short thirteen years, I've already learned the lesson of hanging in there well beyond what feels good. My challenge with staying married is consistent, and has been made abundantly clear in these pages: it's about being willing to make myself vulnerable. It may be different for you. Your challenge may be that you don't want to work that hard, or share your stuff, or have to collaborate with another person all the time. But if you want to be happily married, as Shelley Bonis taught us, do it anyway—show up for your marriage. But be forewarned: unlike a marathon, unfortunately with marriage there's no finish line where people applaud you for your efforts. That's why there are anniversary parties. Or other expressions of joy for hanging in there. Make sure you celebrate each year as a milestone worth popping a champagne cork for—or in our case, driving downtown to eat five-star food in a hole-in-the-wall full of bearded men and tattooed women half our age who know it's not a party without grilled brussels sprouts and chunks of bacon.

My favorite story of a couple finding their voice over four decades was told to me by Geraldine Hurley and her husband, Maurice.

GERALDINE (AKA GERI) AND MAURICE (AKA MAURY)
Standing Up to Your Man

The Hurleys have been married for forty-two years. Their first date was on a Friday night, and by Sunday Maury knew he wanted to marry her. Six weeks later she agreed to it. Geri is a petite, reserved, African-American woman. She dresses impeccably and has a compelling stillness in conversation. Her husband is a lanky Irishman with big eyes, big hands, and a big voice. During both of our meetings, Maury reminded me of a tall human Saint Bernard. Geri is much more catlike: elegant, thoughtful, with perfect diction.

Geri never thought she would marry, so she didn't give it much consideration before meeting Maury. When she found herself living with him as his wife in Minnesota six months after their first meeting, she was pretty shocked. Maury was writing and directing films for the Carmichael-Lynch ad agency for their biggest client, Arctic Cat Snowmobiles. The only thing Geri was sure she had to do was be perfect. Set perfect meals on the table at six every night, look perfect, with lipstick on, and be ready to hear about her husband's day.

"But I didn't want any of that bullshit!" Maury said, striking the dinner table with a hand the size of a salad plate. "That's a bunch of malarkey, that's what that is. Fuhgettabout my day, what did you do today? That's what I wanted to know. I didn't want any of that 'perfect' bullshit."

"No, he didn't," Geri said evenly.

"I called her mother, I was putting her on the next plane. I said, 'You gotta get outta here, I don't want this, this isn't interesting, no way, no how.' And her mother said, because she was a very wise woman, 'Well listen, it's eleven-thirty P.M. there; no one is getting on a plane tonight. People say a lot of things when they're newly married. Why don't you get some sleep and you call me in the morning and tell me what you want to do.'"

"So we talked that night," Geri said. "A lot. And we decided I needed to go get a job. So I did."

It was Minnesota in 1972. She got a job in PR at a Dairy Queen. "You should have seen Geri with all these Svens and Hilgas, it was fantastic!" Maury recalled. "And Geri was awesome, because she always is, everywhere she's ever worked, they always love her."

Geri described for me the impact that getting a job had on their early marriage. "It gave me a life of my own. I only knew his friends, which weren't many beyond work. After I started working, I now had friends to go out with when he worked late. I'm more social and gregarious, and in meeting people we were invited to dinner parties where we met more new people. Our social calendar was very busy."

Geri and Maury's description of finding their individual voices and working out how to be happily married is one of the most vivid examples I encountered. Their marriage is also a great example of how humor can be used both positively to confirm connection and negatively to deflect from the deeper issues. Geri and Maury revealed to me early in our conversation that they had some kinks to work out in their communication in the early years of being together. "When we first married I would say, 'Listen to me, listen to me,'" Geri said, "and I knew he wasn't listening to me and he knew he wasn't listening to me, so I would break down crying. And then the argument is over."

"I made her cry," Maury interjected, matter-of-factly.

"He isn't sorry he made me cry," Geri continued, picking up on his deadpan inflection. "He's just glad that we aren't arguing about what we are arguing about because he wants to avoid it. It took me a long time to be able to say, 'I'm crying because I'm angry.' Then I learned how to stay angry enough where I wouldn't cry. So forty years later, when he is not listening I can call him on it. But he's also become a better listener. He can hear me now. I can express what needs to be said and know that I'm heard so that when we get off on these tangents, I know he's being emotionally lazy."

Maury was eager to add his take on what he called the arc of their relationship. "Now when we see that happening, we laugh about it, it's not like, now you caught me and I'm mad. It's like 'Hah, you caught me!'"

"The humor reinforces that I got him," Geri explained. "Then I can laugh because I'm reinforced that I got him. His laughter is a 'tell' that he knows I'm right. But thirty or forty years ago I didn't know that." It took Geri years to gain the confidence to express herself honestly to Maury, which has been good for both of them.

"If something really hurts your feelings, you can't avoid it because you're embarrassed about expressing how you feel. I had to learn how not to break down, and face him with whatever I am thinking. As I've done that more frequently he doesn't hide as much, and now I know if I walk in and say I want to talk about this, he can either stop and put his work down, or he'll say 'Can we talk about this later?' And I don't feel like I've been put off. But it's taken *a lot* of growing up for me to not take it all personally."

Yet again the best communication is a function of timing! Geri understands, "It's not that he never wants to talk about it, just not now."

Sensing that the interview was wrapping up, Geri had a few more words of wisdom she wanted to be sure she shared with me.

"The biggest shock to most people is how much work it takes, because love should solve it all." Marriage for her has been a process of learning to stand up for herself. She learned that when you are angry about something or disappointed in your spouse, "You can't just throw up your hands and say, 'Oh, well, what am I gonna do?' No! You have to fight back. 'You are not going to walk over me, motherfucker, I don't care who you are! I am going to be heard!'"

Maury nodded, widening his eyes as if to say, yep, she's not kidding. There was something very moving about this small, proper woman being moved to profanity to land this point. This couple has done their homework together to create what I can only describe as a marriage of substance. Admirable not only for its ease, which clearly they now have, but also for how much they have taught each other in this lifetime.

Almost all couples said they are less volatile with each other as a result of time together. The ones who met later in life, after previous marriages, seem to start out more mellow, usually having thrashed around unsuccessfully in a previous marriage. In first-time marriages, fights happen much more frequently in the beginning, when couples have less time under their belts, and feel much more threatening. Married people together a long time confessed to finding character traits in each other that, however annoying they were in the early years, they have come to accept with time, which keeps everyone calmer and happier.

Once you get acceptance down, ideally the next step is being able to laugh about each other's quirks. Not in a mean way, which can lead to hurt feelings, but as a form of surrender to each other's humanity and the marriage. We're all odd in some way, and being able to laugh at ourselves and each other is such a relief, a welcome acknowledgment that neither of us is going to be perfect so we may as well ease up. Mark and Chase, those refreshingly candid chanting Buddhists whom we met in chapter 8, are very happy to have arrived at this much calmer state after seventeen years together. Listening to them talk about how they found their way as a couple is a wonderful example of the gift of time.

"We both make each other laugh at our shit," Mark told me.

Chase took a deep breath, nodded her head, and sighed, saying a thoughtful "Yeah."

Mark wasn't finished. "I used to take her responses a lot harder than I do now. I just told myself, buddy, you have got to start laughing at yourself more with her. All I ever wanted to do was please Chase and when she made fun of me, or teased me it was like, 'Oh I'm disappointing her,' see? Then I decided, so fucking what? Get over it and laugh at yourself. That's made my life a lot easier, instead of taking offense at everything she says. 'So you don't like my fucking shoes, live with it.'"

"He's really sensitive," Chase interjected quietly.

"You don't like the way I hold my hands?" he continued. "Deal with it!"

"Sometimes the way he held his hands used to bug me," Chase confessed. "But I'm over it."

"Good," Mark said, running his hands through his hair like he was physically trying to push the bad thoughts behind him. He let his hands fall back down into his lap.

"What can I say? I'm crazy about her."

I asked them if they thought they were better at being married today than when they started.

"We know each other better, so there's just less to worry about," Chase said. "Like, for a while Mark was really into serial killers, he even wrote a play about it. When we first met there was this documentary I was watching and a serial killer was being interviewed and I thought, 'Oh my God, he reminds me of Mark. Fuck, Mark's going to kill me. Maybe there're bodies somewhere.' I really did think that. So far I haven't found them. But if I wind up dead, you'll know what happened."

I'm not sure which is the bigger bonus of long-term marriage, being able to laugh at yourself, as Mark learned, or staying together long enough that you stop suspecting your spouse of having strange, hidden idiosyncrasies, like being a serial killer.

Mark and Chase were not the only couple to mention learning to take yourself and each other less seriously in marriage. Candice Chopra, married to Gotham for twenty-two years, since their sophomore year in college, agreed. "When you're young, you just take things so seriously. Things that bothered me [in my early twenties] wouldn't bother me now."

We have just stumbled on one aspect of marriage that, unlike stand-up comedy, becomes easier over time: the anxiety level around showing up for it. From my first comedy set to the one I did last week, I have never stopped being nervous beforehand. Most performers will tell you, if they're not a little bit nervous before a show it's a bad sign. For many, a little nervousness is part of the adrenaline cocktail that fuels you as a performer. Marriage, on the other hand, should not be this way. Eventually the butterflies of anticipation and wondering-if-he-or-she-really-loves-me torture should be replaced with peace of mind and the deep knowledge that you love someone and are in turn loved back. Unlike stand-up, a long-term marriage should not be anxiety provoking.

As Geri Hurley said, timing is also something that gets better the longer you are together. Because you know each other better, you can read each other's moods more easily and figure out when to bring up something and when not to. You also learn, like David and Alysia, that when you have something important to tell your spouse, it may be better to sit down and say it outright than try to create the perfect moment. They are glad they no longer try for that version of perfection.

"There was a good ten years of trying to manipulate information," Alysia said.

David explained further. "One time, Alysia had been working and had been out of town, and we were really missing each other and we had been talking about how grateful we were to be back in town together. This was before we had our daughter. Then I found out I got a job out of town. I was terrified to tell her because I thought, 'Oh she's going to be so upset—'"

"I ended up finding out through my agent," Alysia interjected.

"I purposely didn't tell her for two days because I was trying to figure out the timing, and while I was busy doing that, her agent spilled it."

"He said, 'I'm so excited about David's job!' 'Excuse me?' I said." Alysia smiled, reflecting on all the hoops they used to jump through until they finally made the decision to just be honest with each other.

This anecdote made me also think about the importance of staying current with each other. Over time, David and Alysia learned that if waiting for the perfect moment to reveal something means you risk being out of sync, it's best to spill the information and deal with the fallout ASAP.

Couples who have the fortitude to stay married for a long time also get to enjoy a perk that comedians relish as a tool for making audiences laugh: the callback. This is when a comic makes a joke about something at the start of their set and then, later on, makes a reference to it, often in a different context. Audiences love this because it feels like you're getting a gift for paying attention. It also makes you feel very smart for catching it, and makes you feel connected to the performer, like getting a wink across a crowded room.

The callback has the same effect in long marriages. So many couples talked about the value to them of inside jokes, the knowing glance, the phrase they don't even have to finish that will make the other person laugh reminding them of a shared experience. There is something so light and fun about these shared moments. Callbacks between spouses feel like the whipped cream frosting on the many-layered cake of marriage.

As a comedian, having patience and going the distance in your career is rewarding on many levels: it gives you more ease on stage; creates better rapport with your audience; provides you with more time-tested material, more confidence, more laughs, more opportunities to do what you love and an overall better time when you're doing it. A good marriage shares a lot of these benefits and then some. Long-term couples report the same growth in confidence and rapport with each other, more laughs and an overall better time. But they also acknowledge gaining more trust in each other, learning to listen better, connecting more easily, being more comfortable with vulnerability, and—wait for it!—more intimate sex! And we know how I feel about the importance of good sex for keeping a marriage happy.

Pete and Lisa Cook have been married for sixteen years. Pete shared the great insight about marrying a person "in character." He and his wife Lisa had a priceless exchange about long-term monogamy and intimacy.

Lisa: It's gotten better over time.
Pete: Thank you.
Lisa: Because—
Pete: I practice.
Lisa: There's more trust. I feel more of a connection with him now than I did sixteen years ago when we got married. Thank God.
Pete: How do musicians get better? They use the same instrument, they get to know it intimately, and they practice all the time, and suddenly they say, "Oh, that's how you make that sing."

Building on Pete's musical analogy, with time and attention, couples can not only make each other sing, but also dance and laugh.

Here's to becoming virtuosos in our marriages. May our voices, both individually and collectively, be as clear as trumpets, our bodies as responsive to each other as the strings on a cello, and our laughter as light and fluid as melodies played on a piccolo. And may we all have the patience to stay in them despite the sharps, flats, broken strings, sweaty mouthpieces, narcissistic conductors, annoying mothers-in-law, flirty bosses, sagging body parts, reappearing ex-girlfriends, curious ex-boyfriends, bad investments, and all the rest of the chaos of a long life lived together.

TIPS FOR HAVING PATIENCE

- Understand that, like for a comedian, finding your authentic voice in your marriage can take time. It's risky to expose yourself fully to another person, so be gentle with each other. For most couples, it also takes time to figure out "the voice" of the marriage, which is to say, a way of communicating with the greatest sensitivity and ease.

- As the years together expand, so should the level of trust between you and your spouse. If, ten years in, you still feel as anxious and doubtful about your husband or wife's love and commitment to you, you need to explore this anxiety. Seek out the help of a therapist or a spiritual advisor to discover what is causing this dis-ease in your heart.

- In staying with the same partner for years, you learn how best to respond to each other, so, naturally, you get better at it. You learn how to listen better and how to adapt to each other effectively. You are better able to lighten up in times of stress and not take every minor infraction as a signal that it's time to leave.

- Staying together over time means you'll be able to witness each other growing up, which means becoming less reactive and less volatile. Be patient. Gaining both the confidence to fully express yourself with your spouse and confidence in your stability as a couple can take time.

- Timing, one of the most important tools for long-term marriage (see chapter 5), gets easier! The better you know each other, the better your timing will be. You'll also have more ease around timing how you share news with each other, since hopefully the marriage will feel less tentative as the years add up.

- Knowing each other physically and emotionally, a by-product of putting in the years together, will make your sex sexier. Like any musician, the better you know your instrument, the better you'll be at playing it.

13

Get Help to Get Better

{ BEFORE YOU WALK AWAY, }
{ CALL A PROFESSIONAL }

There isn't a therapist more expensive than a divorce costs.

—STEPHEN GOLDBLATT

Allow me to state the obvious: stand-up comedy is a very competitive business. Some nights you can wait hours for seven minutes of stage time and then get bumped by Chris Rock. You finally get on at midnight after he has made the audience convulse with laughter for an hour, but it's your shot, it's what you love to do, so you get on the stage and hit 'em with your best stuff. Walking out there you know the bar has been set very high by the guy before you and you might just tank. But maybe that joke you've been tinkering with will land in a way it hasn't before. Maybe it will be a sympathetic crowd that knows it's tough to follow a legend, or maybe none of what you thought would happen does. That's the crapshoot of live performance and you love it. The only thing you know for sure is that you belong on that stage. So you pull courage up from your toes, passing Rock as he heads offstage, and give it your best.

Married people are similarly challenged. Not because you never know when Chris Rock will walk in and be funnier than you, but because you must also have the same rock-solid belief in your marriage that a comic has about his place onstage. When it comes to your marriage you have to believe you deserve a happy one. And in the same way that a comic gets the help he or she needs from friends, or a coach, and then fights for the opportunities to improve, there may be times when you must also fight to create and preserve a happy marriage by being willing to use whatever resources you can. Practically speaking, what this means is that, as we heard from Geri Hurley in the previous chapter, in marriage you do not get to throw up your hands and say, "Oh, well, what am I going to do?" when either one or both of you is not happy. Whether you're telling jokes to crickets or getting into bed nightly with someone you are not sure you love or loves you anymore, you owe it to yourself to get help before you give up.

For comedians looking for help, sometimes your peers are the first stop. In *How to Succeed in Business without Really Crying*, the best-selling author and comedian Carol Leifer talks specifically about the value of asking for and getting help from her fellow comedians over the years. "I always asked other comics to watch my act, to get a realistic gauge on my progress, and lend an objective eye to stage problems I was trying to fix." There is no shame in this game.[1]

In the introduction I mentioned that in addition to telling me that stand-up comedy is the hardest thing to do in the world, people also love to tell me that being funny is not something that can be taught.

"You're either funny or you're not," is how they usually put it.

I understand why a person might feel this way, but experience has shown me otherwise. I agree that you can't teach charisma, that magnetic quality that some people are born with that keeps your eyes constantly drawn to them, but a teacher, or an intuitive and generous friend, can guide people to their own idiosyncratic truths, which, if revealed in their most raw and unedited state, are often very funny. Especially if they are also taught some recognizable, proven comedy formulas to give their material structure, such as escalation, where the comedian takes a situation or problem and escalates it to its most extreme conclusion. Louis C.K.'s take on women dating men is a great example of this:

"How do women still go out with guys? When you consider the fact that there is no greater threat to women than men. We're the number one threat to women, globally and historically, we're the number one cause of injury and mayhem to women. We're the worst thing that ever happens to them. You know what our number one threat is? Heart disease."[2]

Another comedy standard is "the rule of three," also known as the "comic triple." This is probably the most commonplace of all comedy rules because it's used in everything from advertising (sometimes with only pictures) to traditional storytelling. It occurs when the writer establishes a pattern, creating a certain expectation, and then defies it. For example, "Whenever I'm feeling nervous I take a deep breath, say my mantra, and torture a small animal." You see how the third one breaks the expected pattern? That's the structure of the rule of three, and it's one of the more foolproof ones.

Then there is the popular device of "listing," used when a comedian rolls out seemingly endless adjectives or examples of the original premise, often at a rapidfire pace, the final one being the most absurd. At a certain point you can't help but laugh, if not from the items in the list itself, then from the comedian's compulsive mind spewing an inexhaustible list (hence the name) of preoccupations or images.

Given these simple comedy rules, and the chance to write and perform them in prescribed exercises either with a teacher, a coach, or a patient friend, even people with limited comic instincts can get better at making people laugh.

My personal experience, as a teacher and coach who has been working with comics for over twenty years, is that if you give people who are passionate about making people laugh and are interested in learning some tools a safe space in which to use them (one free of critics and hecklers) they will develop confidence. The more confident they become, the more courage they will have to reveal what they really think and feel about a subject. This authentic point of view is where they will find what is uniquely funny about them, their "voice." Do their ideas need to be shaped? Of course. Do they need to be crafted into jokes so the audience knows when to laugh? Absolutely. But the ideas flow and the associations become more fluid in a private and safe space.

Giving people some tools for better communication and an unthreatening space in which to practice them is also *exactly* the kind of support that can help a struggling marriage. We know that long-term couples can go through hard times. But like the fledgling comic, many couples have not been given tools needed to help them get through bad times. Or they might have been given tools, perhaps by their parents—if not directly, then through watching Mom and Dad duke it out—that don't work for them in their marriage, as we heard from Tracy and Eric in chapter 12.

Much data has been tossed around concerning the incidence of divorce in America, depending on the year, but regardless of the statistic, you probably don't want to be one of them. But you may need a few more skills and tools to avoid this fate than you currently have. Since so many people are products of marriages that did not work out, there's a good chance that some of the tools we were taught by our parents are faulty. Or maybe we inherited great tools of communication from our parents, but we never had to use them before because our previous relationships ended before things got complicated. But that doesn't mean that with the proper guidance, we can't learn how to be better, more contented married people. Like the floundering comic who can genuinely benefit from input from a more seasoned professional or a teacher, married couples can also flourish with the right support.

The tricky part for a couple, as opposed to a single comic, is getting both people in the marriage to want to go to counseling at the same time. Sometimes one is ready before the other, then when the other person finally surrenders the first might have a change of heart—more evidence for the importance of timing! But if both people become willing to go for help, to making a commitment to change whatever is getting in the way of their enjoying each other, that's when some real work can begin.

THE BRASS TACKS OF GETTING HELP

When Tod and I feel like we're about to come to blows, going to see a neutral and educated third party has helped. When I say educated, I mean a licensed couples and marriage therapist. And there are many other sources of help. I talked to several couples who have received successful guidance from members of the clergy or other religious or spiritual advisors. (Apparently, having Deepak Chopra as your father-in-law is very helpful!) At their best, these supporters and guides create a safe space for a couple to express themselves and offer tools to take home. At their worst, they fall asleep while you are talking. Seriously, in researching this chapter I met a couple to whom this actually happened, which ultimately had its own therapeutic benefit because it gave them something to laugh about together.

For Tod and me, finding the right therapist wasn't easy. One humorless, doughy woman we saw instructed us to "unpack" some of our layers of resentment and anxiety. This wasn't a bad idea, but her presence was so dour that we both clammed up and stared at our hands. It turned out that the most effective part of seeing her was the relief we felt at not having to be around her a second longer after each session ended. But maybe that was all part of her master plan, because our discomfort being around her became something we, like the couple with the narcoleptic therapist, shared and laughed about, which in itself had a healing effect. She was the third out of the four therapists we've seen in the fifteen years we've been together.

FIND A THERAPIST
You May Have to Kiss a Few Frogs

Tod and I went to a therapist together even before we married because, well, typical of me, I don't remember. I would guess it had to do with wishing Tod was more like me. Because of course that's what you want in a marriage: two hyperemotional, hypersensitive commitmentphobes! I do remember thinking that our needing to go to therapy before we married was a bad sign.

Or maybe it was my mother who thought that. I don't know exactly who said it, but I can still hear the critical voice in my head: "If you're going to therapy *before* you're even married, what's going to happen when you really have problems?"

My answer to this question today? We'll solve them together with the tools we learned in therapy.

Last year we landed on our fourth and hopefully final therapist. He's a soft-spoken man who has the smarts and sensitivity to get who we are, and who is articulate and compassionate enough to find a way to move us toward each other. One of the most effective aspects of these therapy sessions is that much of the time he offers up a third interpretation of our disagreements. This response has helped us see that there is always another view to a situation apart from our two opposing ones. Hearing this other point of view gives me clarity: if there's a third way, chances are there are even more ways to see it. These sessions enable us to at least *consider* the possibility that each of our stances isn't the final word on anything. Opening our eyes to a third way of interpreting a conflict has helped pry open our stubborn minds. What this has meant for us practically is that now Tod isn't always wrong and I'm not always "crazy." Hearing a third perspective for one hour a week has made us more open to listening to each other in between sessions.

Courtney Kemp Agboh and her husband, Brian Agboh, had great success with therapy early in their marriage. They are a dual-career couple who met in their twenties. Courtney has a bicoastal life as the co-creator (with the rapper 50 Cent) and executive producer of the show *Power*, and Brian is an entertainment lawyer.

COURTNEY KEMP AGBOH AND BRIAN AGBOH
Help in the Nick of Time

Courtney and Brian met as undergraduates and had been together for eleven years and married for four when, she said, "The whole thing fell apart. We were looking for separate apartments. He went home to New Jersey to collect his thoughts, and I spent that weekend preparing myself to be single, which meant drinking a lot of wine." Courtney assumed that they were done, but when Brian came back they went out to dinner and, "weirdly," decided to give counseling a try. Brian had his own therapist at the time who recommended a woman named Lisa, "whose red hair and Midwestern accent somehow put us both at ease," Courtney told me. Lisa was empathetic, generous, and understanding, which is not how either of them were feeling at the time.

Courtney described for me their first few sessions. "We wasted little time feeling Lisa out. Instead we began airing our frustrations in earnest, actually, honestly telling each other about our long-held resentments, truths which we were previously too polite or too afraid to air. It was a brutal and painful escalation, which finally culminated in me turning to Brian and saying 'Fuck you.' This was not the norm for Courtney. She and Brian both grew up in loud, angry homes, so they made—and still make—a point of not talking to each other that way.

"This was a watershed moment between us, the end of our first marriage and the beginning of the second," she said.

Throughout my research I noticed that people in second and third marriages seemed genuinely happy and calmer and have a real gratitude for each other. It's like they got all the bad behavior out in their first marriages, realized what a mistake that was, and came to the second one more prepared to collaborate. They often know on a cellular level what doesn't work and usually come out of a divorce never wanting to go through that pain again. This turns out to be a good thing for the next spouse.

I talked with a few couples who felt like they had lived through several marriages together within their one marriage, even though the players hadn't changed. Sometimes, as with Courtney and Brian, the "first" marriage actually has to come to a breaking point for the next marriage, the healthier, more honest, more connected one, to begin.

LORI AND DAVID ROUSSO
Three Marriages in One

Lori and David met in 1959 and married in 1964. Sitting in their living room, I saw a group of family pictures poised on every flat surface—including a black-and-white one of them walking down the aisle that looks like a movie still—it struck me that they've been together longer than I have been alive. Lori wears her red hair closely cropped, with small eyeglasses that magnify her clear, blue eyes. Whenever she speaks, she looks you right in the eyes. This woman shies away from nothing. I notice that David, a tall man with a shock of white hair, is not quite so direct in conversation. Where Lori cuts to the chase, David is more diplomatic, frequently pausing to think before he speaks, appearing to weigh how his thoughts will be interpreted.

David was the one who introduced this idea of having one partner in life, but several marriages. "Lori and I are at least on our third marriage to each other, and possibly our fourth. It's not just the [passage of] time; it's the evolution of your character, what interests you, what motivates you, what you respond to. Being a grandparent with young grandkids is clearly a different phase. You're sort of in Act Three of your life."

The transition from phase to phase isn't always effortless, though, as Lori and David discovered. Aging was a motivator for them to seek help. "You know you are getting older," Lori said. "You don't have lots and lots of time left. I'm so glad that we had enough insight to know that when we were in trouble we needed to work on it."

When we met, David had recently had some serious health issues that required multiple surgeries and raised the possibility of permanent paralysis. Lori described for me how the ordeal unfolded, and then added, "It's been a very serious few years."

"Yes, it has," David confirmed, looking away for a second, but then quickly back with a smile and a glint in his eye, giving a glimpse of the charisma that even near paralysis couldn't kill. Not surprisingly when

I checked in with Lori six months later, she told me, "After years of physical therapy, the walker was thrown away, as was one of the canes. He walks with one most of the time and occasionally will walk with just the strength of his legs. He is doing amazingly well, very motivated, laughs a lot now, and has definitely come out of the hole."

Although they felt fortunate to get the help they needed from a particularly effective therapist, they also relied heavily on maintaining their sense of humor.

In fact, Lori felt so strongly about the need for levity in the home while acting as David's caregiver that she decided to bring a puppy into the house. As if on cue, a large brown poodle who looked to me like a small man in a fur suit ran up to her and started licking her cheeks.

"Doesn't he look like Will Ferrell?" Lori blurted out, laughing as the dog slathered her with kisses.

"No, he's like Kramer!" David shouted over her. "Kramer, from *Seinfeld!*"

"Wasn't it hard taking a puppy when your husband was . . . paralyzed?" I asked them.

"Well, I had to do something," Lori answered. "Otherwise, what? You sit around crying all day? He makes us laugh."

"Excuse me a second," David said, hoisting his body up out of his chair with great force and steadying himself before exiting to the back of the house. Lori, who in our time together was disarmingly candid about her feelings during David's health crisis, told me plainly, "I wouldn't have made it without the dog, without something to laugh about. And we started seeing that very good counselor. We've had to face very real stuff together through this. But we're doing it. Both of us. And we're honest in a way we never were before. I mean, it was that or . . ." She shrugged, and looked away. "I just wasn't willing to let that happen."

Before meeting David and Lori, I wouldn't have considered getting a puppy, in addition to counseling, as a way to keep laughter in your marriage. Although I had heard about couples who think having a baby will bring them together. As a parent of two young children, I can see how this might backfire. Babies mostly shred the freedom and spontaneity you enjoyed as a childless couple. Sure, they are crazy cute, and yes, a child is something you and your spouse create together, but adding an infant to a strained marriage is just not a good bet for bringing more happiness to your marriage. A 2014 study of 5,000 couples by the Open University in the UK found, "For both men and women, those who did not have children ranked the quality of their relationship more highly than those who did. They also did significantly more to 'maintain' their relationship, such as taking time to go out together or talk, than those with children."[3]

These are the conclusions of just one study, but anecdotally, I can tell you from all the couples I spoke to that once children are born, fighting for a little time to yourself individually and as a couple is a big source of tension. One divorced father of twin five-year-olds said, "When we were together it was all about, 'You take them now, you take them now,' then you divorce and it becomes, 'You can't take them, you can't take them, I want them!'"

When you are raising small children, when you are tired a lot and wondering what happened to your life so that it feels like now all you do is clean diapers and dishes, it can be all too easy to start blaming your spouse and the family you created together as the reason why you are so unhappy. The frustration with this phase of parenthood is genuine, but in addition, often the real source of your unhappiness is a lack of perspective, a failure to remember that wherever you are is temporary, and in a relatively short time, it will change. There's also the sobering realization that as much as you thought you could and would have it all, you can't, at least not all at once. This is a legitimate disappointment. It's not something to blame on a spouse—it's life.

Winnie Holzman and Paul Dooley were poised for the blame game even before they had their baby.

WINNIE AND PAUL
Blaming Is for Amateurs

Because both Winnie and Paul have a background in sketch comedy, they came into their marriage keenly aware of the deadly trap of looking outside yourself for someone to blame when something doesn't work. Beginner comedians can be known to do this. When their jokes don't go over, they'll make it the fault of the audience.

"Blaming the audience as a performer, let's face it, it's an amateur thing to do," Winnie told me. "When you start to really become an interesting artist is when you stop doing that."

Paul connected this point to marriage, adding, "And when you stop doing that in your marriage is also when your marriage gets interesting. The most successful comics in the world have bombed."

Winnie jumped in. "Oh, yes, failure has to be allowed, especially in show business, you just totally have to be able to fail. And I also absolutely feel this is true in a marriage, too. You have to be able to—to some extent—to fuck it up. Have moments where you are not your best self. Then you just have to own it and not blame the other person for it."

Exactly. You have to be able to "fuck up" in marriage and not feel that it will be the end of everything. But you also have to take responsibility for the mistake. This is key. If one or both spouses' behavior becomes consistently hurtful with no self-awareness about it, you must find some help from one of the options we've already discussed: a therapist, clergy member, a father-in-law who's a guru, or even a wise friend, but some kind of intervention is necessary. And getting this kind of help so you can have a happy, lasting marriage doesn't have to bankrupt you, even in a major city.

THERAPY ON A BUDGET

Private marriage counseling can be expensive, but it doesn't mean you can't do it. Several couples I met with have found low-cost, sliding-scale therapists to work with for as low as $5 per session. Eleven years ago, when I was pregnant with my first child, I visited the Saban Community Clinic in Los Angeles to find a therapist. I wasn't making enough money to afford the going rate in Los Angeles, at that time somewhere between $160 and $200 per hour. We weren't having marital issues at this time, but I was having impending-motherhood issues. It was completely shocking to me that I actually had gotten pregnant.

Since I was over thirty-eight when we started trying, I assumed it would take years for me to conceive, if it happened at all. In fact, it took just two weeks. I was in the throes of trying to sell a TV show based on a live show I had been performing for a year, ending with a run at the Aspen Comedy Festival. Suddenly I was pregnant and for various reasons, including the increased expense of insuring a pregnant woman on a show, I quickly became an "actress non grata."

"Congratulations! Have your baby, and let us know when you're back out there," was the gist of every conversation about my work that I had.

As excited as I was to be able to conceive and, I hoped, carry a healthy baby, I was also deeply disappointed by the work piece. I didn't feel comfortable crying to Tod about it—it was his baby, too—and I was the one who lobbied to get pregnant quickly. Feeling heavily conflicted and just plain heavy, I shuffled in to Dr. Gregory T. Wuliger's office at the Saban Community Clinic. I had twelve free sessions with him at the clinic and then worked with him steadily for the next seven years. He was compassionate, insightful, and forty dollars an hour.

Most cities and towns, particularly ones with colleges, universities, or therapy training centers, offer effective talk therapy on a sliding scale based on your household income. Will you be working with Freud or one of his relatives? No. But you can make progress in your relationship by learning effective communication skills guided by a professional for a dedicated hour. The only stipulation being that you both have to be willing to show up, sober, and tell the truth. (Going to therapy after a few drinks can lead to alcohol-infused histrionics. I have experimented with this exact exercise, so you don't have to. You're welcome.)

Once in a great while, even just getting humble enough as a couple to be willing to ask for help with your marriage can have positive results. One wife had such an eye-opening phone experience just trying to get placed with a therapist in her insurance plan that she and her husband never actually had to meet with a counselor.

KEITH AND JULIET
Perspective in a Phone Call

With very few exceptions, the long-term happy couples I met with sought out professional help. Keith and Juliet, both screenwriters who left the West Coast for upstate New York, where they both teach what they learned in Hollywood to college students, have been married for twenty-five years. They found that just one phone call to the Writers Guild health plan for a referral gave them the support they needed. They couldn't wait to tell me the hysterically funny story of the most troubled time in their marriage.

"We were really struggling," Juliet started.

"Oh, you're going to tell it?" Keith asked.

"Yes, I'm telling this one. You can tell a different story."

Three sentences and I felt I knew a lot about their marriage.

Juliet continued, "So I called the Writers Guild for free therapy and the woman on the phone said, 'Well, we need to know more about you before we assign you someone,' so I said, 'I work with my husband,' and then she just started laughing and laughing and laughing. That did it."

That did what, I thought? Someone laughing at my problems with Tod wouldn't do it for me. What's up with that? I didn't say that out loud. After all, I'm a professional. But I did ask Juliet to explain this telephonic laser on her marriage that caused their spontaneous healing.

"It was the perspective it gave me," she said. "The fact that my plight made them laugh so uproariously told me that obviously nothing we were going through was so special or insurmountable or dire. I told Keith, and we realized that what we needed to do was put some boundaries around how we worked together. So we did."

After this, Julliette and Keith set a boundary for themselves that they rely on to protect their marriage: "Don't talk about what goes on in the office once the office door is closed for the day."

Being the daughter of people who worked twenty-four/seven and talked about their work over breakfast, lunch, and dinner, I liked this idea very much. However, Phyllis Moen, a sociology professor at the University of Minnesota, who has spent tens of years studying couples who work together, disagrees. Moen contends that establishing boundaries for couples that work together is no longer relevant. Apparently, part of what makes working couples competitive in business is their constant access to each other.

"These days, everyone experiences blurring of boundaries because of new technologies," she has stated. Moen encourages couples to feel free to interrupt each other at any time, "Otherwise, pressures at work get translated to stress at home, and no one understands why." She says when issues pop up, whether work-related or home-related, jump right on them so you can get back to doing what you want to be doing.[4]

At the risk of sounding outdated, I'm still a proponent of putting some boundaries around business matters, to the best of your ability, to allow for some space to enjoy each other as non-workers, too. If it's a life-changing deal, like a Silicon Valley financier calling with an offer to buy your app in the middle of dinner, then take the call. Obviously if it's a time-sensitive communication that could pay off big and give you and your family a better life, then by all means go ahead and drive each other nuts until the deal closes. Otherwise, take a break.

The divergence of opinion around the setting of work-life boundaries is yet another example of how you as a unique couple must pay attention to each other and figure out exactly what works for you and then stick to it with confidence. No study, TV personality, girlfriend, boyfriend, parent, in-law, person at the check-out line, or book—including this one—knows specifically what is best for your marriage. We can only offer suggestions and guidance.

GOING TO THERAPY LIKE YOU GO TO THE GYM

Most people do not experience the nearly instantaneous healing that Juliet and Keith had as the result of one miraculous phone call. In fact, some couples wouldn't even want instant healing. Judy Cohen and

David Katz, children's book publishers who have been married thirty-four years, loved seeing their therapist. David had mixed feelings about marrying a woman sixteen years older than him who had been married twice before, and so they started therapy very early in their relationship. They remained committed to this same therapist for twenty-seven years, seeing her weekly for twenty-two of those years and then sporadically after that. According to Judy, this relationship maintenance was no big deal at all: "For us going to therapy is like going to the gym." You do it on a regular basis to stay in shape, emotionally." People who believe in couples' therapy-as-gym for your marriage make this analogy because, like working out regularly, going to a marriage counselor is something they go to consistently, whether they feel like it or not. Like going to the gym to stay fit and feel vital, they see a weekly therapy appointment as a way to stay on course with their intention to maintain a healthy, strong relationship.

Which was exactly the point of view that Laura A. Wasser, a leading divorce lawyer and the author of *It Doesn't Have to Be That Way*, had when she talked to me about couples going to counseling to preserve their marriage.[5] Wasser's father is also a divorce lawyer, and she herself is a child of divorce, so she knows intimately what breaks up couples. Mostly, it's a breakdown of communication, which she believes can be avoided by setting an appointment with a couples counselor every week. "Get in a room together and air your grievances," Wasser advises. "Otherwise you run the risk of having an infected and infested situation full of resentment. You need a safe haven for communication, and a weekly therapy appointment can provide this. It's a place to figure out a way to fix problems and let the air out of tires."

Even if you don't set a weekly appointment, there is great value in talking through a disagreement with a neutral third party. David Basche put it to me this way: "Sometimes if we're at an impasse, rather than walking away and thinking something bad is gonna happen with the marriage, we can say, 'You know what? We can agree to disagree, but we need help with this. Let's have a session.' There's no shame in it, no needing to be right or wrong, just a commitment to solving whatever it is for the greater good of the marriage." Having a therapist also keeps disagreements from escalating to the point where someone does irreparable damage by saying words they can't take back.

Sometimes you start couples therapy and one partner realizes that he or she must do individual work—as one highly therapized wife told me, "I realized I could leave my marriage and look for something better, but I'd be taking me along, so I'd better at least make sure I get to the bottom of my issues before I got to husband number two, or three, or *four*, and realized the only thing consistent about all of them was me!"

At this point we've talked extensively about therapy in all its incarnations, but what if it's still not your thing? You still have options for helping your marriage stay healthy and happy.

A TWELVE STEP COMMUNITY FOR MARRIED PEOPLE

When comedians find themselves feeling ungrounded and in need of support but don't want to pay a coach or take a class, often they look for a "comedy buddy": someone who gets you out when you don't feel like it and with whom you test new material, share war stories, and offer and receive encouragement.

The equivalent of the comedy buddy for couples is a group called Recovering Couples Anonymous, or RCA. Like all Twelve Step groups it is based on the Twelve Steps and Twelve Traditions of Alcoholics Anonymous. RCA was brought to my attention by a writing student of mine, whom I'll call Eve, who has been married for over thirty-five years.

"If we hadn't found this group there is no question we'd be divorced," Eve told me plainly over tea. She learned about RCA after she and her husband had joined other Twelve Step programs to deal with individual addiction problems, which had been plaguing them for decades. "I learned about RCA a few weeks later," Eve said, "and we were both willing to try it because we were both so filled with anger towards each other and despair."

RCA calls itself "a fellowship of recovering couples." Its home page continues:

> We suffer from many different addictions, and we share our experience, strength and hope with one another that we may solve our common problems and help other recovering couples restore their relationships.
>
> The only requirement for membership is a desire to remain committed to each other and to develop new intimacy. Our primary purpose is to stay committed in loving and intimate relationships and to help other couples achieve freedom from addicted and destructive relationships.[6]

RCA provides a list of "tools of recovery" at its website, which reads like the greatest hits of what to do to communicate better as a couple.[7] Many of these suggestions have been touched on in this book. As with all Twelve Step programs, you attend meetings with other people, in this case couples, and get a sponsor. Your sponsor is another couple who is more experienced in the program, with whom you speak regularly and honestly. The sponsor couple are in your life to support you in your goal to be happily married. No one pays anyone for this service. RCA seems like a great way to find a supportive couple (or several) with like-minded goals who also have wisdom to share. (RCA considers the wisdom sharing they can offer not as a substitute for professional counseling but as a valuable complement to it.)[8]

As with all Twelve Step recovery programs, there is a spiritual element in joining RCA. The significant difference between RCA and all the other Twelve Step programs is that you enter into it with a partner, and it is a joint commitment to turn your marriage over to God. The program also welcomes agnostics and atheists, so it's still an option for you even if you don't have particular religious beliefs. But it is essential that you and your partner admit powerlessness and acknowledge that as a couple you cannot go it alone, that you must call upon a higher power. I did find that a noticeable percentage of the happy couples I met shared some kind of spiritual life, if not outright religious beliefs.

MARITAL SUPPORT IN YOUR CHURCH OR TEMPLE

I am not a religious person, and I didn't become affiliated with a religious community until I had children, so I didn't really think about the possibility of going to see a religious leader for marital counseling. But speaking to long-term couples made me realize that I am late to the party on this because many people take advantage of this option.

The funny and encouraging story Chase told me about consulting her Japanese Buddhist sensei when she was concerned that Mark had stopped chanting revealed that she had no problem approaching this woman for marital counseling. For the record, they also saw a therapist for over six years to help them get through some marital growing pains and they both say they would go again if they felt the need.

I am convinced that Chase was far from alone in her instinct to turn to a spiritual leader when her marriage was in crisis. Although there is nothing in the scripture that says, "And then Cain and his wife met with the local rabbi to talk about why she never knows when he is going to be home for dinner," for as long as religious communities have existed, people have consulted with the leaders of their faith for guidance when they were unhappy in their marriage.

Even today, most people make a covenant before God when they marry. Even the non-religious—even atheists—usually make vows to each other to love, honor, respect, cherish, and whatever other verbs they throw in there that are sacred to that couple and their relationship. It makes sense, then, to turn to religious and spiritual leaders for guidance when it feels like these vows are coming undone.

Kathy Keller, who coauthored the best-selling book *The Meaning of Marriage* with her husband, Pastor Tim Keller, has strong feelings about the vows that couples take on their wedding. I put in a call to her to find out more.

KATHY KELLER
Marriage Is the Path to Growth

In the three hours I spent talking to Keller it became clear that she and her husband, Tim, practice what they preach. They have counseled many troubled couples since he founded the Redeemer Presbyterian Church in New York City in 1989. Over the twenty-five years that he has been a pastor, and the thirty-eight years they have been married, their position on divorce has not softened. They straight up do not believe in the failure of marriage. What they do believe, fiercely, is that humans are flawed, and working at your marriage is one of the few hopes you have of becoming less so.

For clarification, the Kellers define themselves as Christian Apologists. They reject the label "evangelical" because of its fundamentalist implication, although they do believe in the importance of being born again. Concerning marriage, in our conversation Kathy focused again on the importance of serving each other, being compassionate toward each other, and making sure you don't "become roommates"—sharing a living space but without sharing sexual intimacy.

Her ideas were uncomplicated and forthright:

- About a couple's dynamic: "If you want to know where the problems are going to show up in your future, imagine your mother married to his father." Take a minute and do this. It's eerily illuminating.
- On the delights of imperfection: "We are all flawed sinners, not perfect people. Anyone who says 'I don't need to be changed' isn't living in reality."
- Go to therapy before there are conflicts or rifts: All couples at the Kellers' Redeemer Church in New York City are encouraged to engage in two months of counseling at the church before getting married.

In their book, Tim Keller brings up a point we talked about earlier, managing expectations. His personal view is that our expectations are less of each other and more of marriage itself. Over the years he has often heard, "This should be easier, it shouldn't be this hard if we're really soul mates." He has little patience for this kind of thinking, wondering why people who want to achieve greatness in marriage are put off by the hard work. As he has said, "Would someone who wants to play professional baseball say, 'It shouldn't be so hard to hit a fastball'?" The Kellers believe one of the real challenges with marriage today is the outsized expectations that spouses have of each other.

In times of struggle, Tim and Kathy help couples tease out these unrealistic expectations, get a reality check, and remind them of the Christian values of love and service.

My discussion with Kathy about Christianity gave me a lot to think about in terms of creating a successful marriage. Because a husband and wife enter into a marriage as Christians, humble and knowing that they are flawed, and also knowing that neither one has all the answers, imagine how much more open each would be to listening to the other and changing? Add to this the goals of serving your fellow humans and being compassionate, and it all seems like a fantastic starting place for marriage. You don't have to be a Christian to take some of these ideas to heart.

As attractive as the Christian perspective on marriage was to me, it's unlikely that Tod and I will be converting to Christianity anytime soon. We're Jewish, and since our children started preschool, we have belonged to a temple in Los Angeles. Since it had never occurred to me, before I started working on this book, that one of the jobs of religious leaders was to provide individual counseling to congregants, the idea of sitting down with Rabbi John L. Rosove, the senior rabbi at Temple Israel of Hollywood, to talk about my marriage had, naturally, never entered my mind.

Having heard a strong Christian point of view, I was interested in what counsel Judaism offers to struggling couples. A congregational rabbi for over twenty-five years, Rosove, too, has a long history of working with couples.

Temple Israel is a reform Jewish synagogue. The reform movement of Judaism grew out of a desire to embrace new thinking and contemporary culture in nineteenth-century Germany while not discarding all Judaism's traditions. It differentiated itself from orthodox Judaism. Practically speaking this means that men and women worship together, they do not observe kosher dietary laws, there are female rabbis, and their focus is principally on social justice.

Rabbi Rosove is not a remote interpreter of God's word. He is both engaged with his community and engaging in his ideas about contemporary Judaism. Fortunately for me, he had many engrossing opinions to share about the nature and care of long-term marriage. Rosove stressed unity as a couple, leaning on the support of a community, and not hurting each other unnecessarily. He led off with his thoughts about the value of a shared history for a couple.

"The longer people are together, the past is prologue. If they have faith that they are in the valley of their relationship, and they've been there before and they've come out of it, and they've done it enough times, that is a sign that they will come out of it again." Rosove believes strongly in the need for community. Particularly during such challenging times, "People shouldn't suffer in isolation."

He explained in detail how the community can serve a couple in trouble. "Sometimes they can't get out of the valley alone. They need a therapist; they need a community, or some dear friends or a rabbi or someone to remind them of that. They came together for certain reasons, hopefully they were healthy reasons, that they liked each other, they respected each other, they had passion together, and they believed in each other, they trust each other. If those things are all there, there's plenty of hope. Everybody gets into valleys. The best marriages go into the dumps sometimes and sometimes you just have to wait it out."

Rabbi Rosove gave me a list of reasons why people struggle in a marriage. Sitting across from him on his well-worn couch, I couldn't help but feel like each of the problems he mentioned had been brought in by a couple who sat across from him in my exact seat.

"It may be based on one or both partners," Rosove said. "What he or she is doing and where they are in their lives. It could be professional, could be menopausal, could be financial, could be, 'Is this all there is to my professional world and I'm not going to go any higher?'

Could be when kids leave the home, or after the death of a parent, it could be something that changes the life of one of them or both of them and they are in some kind of ether. It's at that point"—he sat forward in his chair—"that they have to remember that it is likely that they have been there before, and that they will come out of this. Nothing is fatal except for death itself."

And then he added, "But you have to do things that are not stupid, either." I was intrigued. "Sometimes not telling the other person something is a good thing," Rabbi Rosove continued. "I don't believe that every thought in your head should be expressed to your partner. Sometimes your thoughts can be very hurtful if expressed out loud in words." I knew this personally from the "brutally honest" lesson that Tod and I had learned.

"Forgiveness is very important, too," he continued. "Some people are better at forgiving than others. Forgiving is really about letting go, it's not about forgetting. It's just saying, 'All right, it's done, it's over, I'm going forward, I'm not going to dwell on the past, just don't do it again.' Sometimes the breach is so bad that's it's almost impossible to recover from—I'm thinking of infidelity, probably the worst breach you can do. And if you do it, if you slip, keep it to yourself."

Didn't see that coming.

"If it's an affair, then you're in trouble. But if it's a one-time thing, you're on a business trip and you're away and you get drunk, and you do something stupid, just keep it to yourself. Go to a therapist. Go to someone who won't reveal. Work it out yourself. Better not to tell. What for? If it's a one-shot thing, and you don't do it serially."

"Huh," I said, nodding, not sure how I felt about this stance. If a tree drops its pants in the forest and no one knows about it, does it matter? Not that I disagreed necessarily, it was just surprising to hear this position from a person who marries people and witnesses them taking vows of honesty and (presumably) fidelity.

In recalling this part of our conversation later, I remembered an experience I'd had with Rabbi Rosove a few years before. All the parents of the preschool were asked to attend a mandatory study group of sorts, essentially to meet him and each other without the toddlers around. We sat in a big circle with him as he read a section of the Hebrew Bible. I arrived late, so I don't recall which section it was, but I know he somehow managed to work in the topic of fidelity. He made direct eye contact with as many of us as he could and said, "I want to be very clear about this. I don't believe a couple ever recovers from infidelity. They don't, no matter what you hear."

At the time I was struck by how bold a statement this was make to a group of young, exhausted, and probably sex-starved parents. It felt like a warning: "Just in case you're thinking about it, and you probably will, don't do it. It will crush your marriage."

The more nuanced take on infidelity that I heard in the privacy of his office, although surprising, was not inconsistent with this passionate belief. We were having a frank conversation about long-term marriage, and he was speaking to me about the realities of the biggest threats to their success. It would be an oversimplification in this context to say, "Don't do it." The fact is, it happens. His experience informed his instruction that people weigh carefully if an indiscretion is worth sharing, because it definitely will cause major, if not irreparable, damage.

As we were finishing up Rabbi Rosove added, "And sometimes people should be divorced. Judaism does not condemn divorce. The problem is that sometimes people come to me for permission. I can't give you permission. Only you can do that."

The rabbi's reassurance that regardless of gender, race, religion, or creed, all marriages go through bad times was comforting. And I love the idea that the more you get through as a couple, the more confidence you have that you'll survive the latest rift. I heard this from couples, too. His assertion that in long-term marriage, forgiving isn't about forgetting, but about choosing to let go of the anger, or bitterness, or hurt also stayed with me. You can't force yourself to forget something. Until we're old, and then we forget everything. So there's that to look forward to—maybe that's why couples who make it into their eighties seem the happiest!

As for Rabbi Rosove's position on infidelity, I still don't know where I come down on this. There is something to be said for not destroying a marriage by sharing information that was, essentially, a meaningless encounter. I'd probably die of guilt, or get an ulcer or lockjaw or some flesh-eating disease that attacks my face by hiding this from Tod. Since he expressed his zero-tolerance for infidelity before we married, I haven't given thought to whether I would want to know if Tod cheated on me. If he ever did, I believe eventually I would find out and I'm certain the reveal would hurt more than the transgression itself. Learning he had sex with someone else would cut deep, but the fact that he lied to me, and the maintenance of the lie for however long it was kept up, that would kill me.

But as usual, it's a personal choice. If for you, keeping a happy marriage means sparing your spouse unnecessary pain and doing work on your own addressing your wandering eye (and hands and probably a few other body parts), then that is what is best for you. But one thing is for sure: if you never have sex with anyone other than your spouse, you never have to debate whether to tell or not.

As to Rabbi Rosove's last point, regarding the truth that some people genuinely benefit from divorce, he was not the first professional I met with who has come to this conclusion in their career. Many therapists and clergy have felt that some couples were coming to them for permission to end their misery. As you can imagine, none of them is comfortable being put in this position.

Having gotten a solid dose of religious perspectives on marriage, I was ready to speak with one more nondenominational counselor. Through Geri Hurley I found Dr. David Pretzel, who has been a licensed marriage counselor since 1968.

Geri had mentioned him in our first meeting: "Once I was so angry with Maury and I had to see a therapist about it. He asked how we got along. I said, 'I don't know how we get along, but I'm going to get a divorce.' And he said, 'Oh, you are? So you no longer laugh together?' And I looked at him and I said, 'He's the funniest person I know.' And he says, 'You're not ready for a divorce yet.'" I had written his name down, knowing I would track down this therapist to find out why he held humor in marriage in as high regard as I do.

I met Pretzel in his office in Pasadena. At over six feet tall, lean, with neatly groomed white hair, he looked more Jimmy Stewart than Carl Jung. Knowing how valuable (expensive!) his time was, I leapt right in and asked Pretzel about the comment he'd made to Geri. He explained:

> I look for humor in a couple as part of a whole relationship. Love, understanding, compassion. What I mean by humor is the ability not to take myself too seriously, the individual journey that plays into the relationship. A lot of marital arguments are not about what they are arguing about, it's about other stuff, like control. One way to get past these stupid arguments is to see how ridiculous I'm being, not how ridiculous you're being. Part of my definition of humor is the ability to laugh at oneself, because if I'm laughing about the other person, there's probably some hostility there. For instance, sarcasm is not humor; it's an expression of hostility. That's not being funny. If I'm being sarcastic, I'm really not talking about what needs to be talked about—I'm trivializing it or doing something else with it. This is a very bad and destructive habit.

Pretzel's distinction between types of humor in marriage was consistent with what therapist Jan Jorden also touched upon, and because of how important it is, it bears repeating. The hostility behind sarcasm, and a spouse's eagerness to make fun of the other person, is a sure sign of hostility.

Pretzel also noted how valuable humor is for changing perspective on a situation. Remember the healing power of Juliet's phone call with the Writers Guild insurance people. Hearing someone laugh about her desperate plight of trying to write and live with her writer husband had that exact effect and helped shift her perspective, which allowed her to lighten up about it.

Say you have done everything you can to stay in the game, whether it's being a comic or remaining married. You've done everything you can to help yourself and yet the facts just keep staring you in the face;

it's never going to be a fit. I felt exactly this way about stand-up the morning of 9/11, waking up in South Dakota in the middle of a college tour, unable to get home. After spending ten years being a committed comic—performing, teaching, and traveling—I had a moment of clarity driving through cornfields trying to get to an airport from which I could catch a flight west. Given the realities of what it means to be a successful working comic, forever on the road, it wasn't right for me. It goes without saying that the prospect of ending a marriage is a lot more devastating, but where there is overlap is in the humility, acceptance, and action I needed to move on.

All of the many therapists I spoke with acknowledged that there is deep sadness in the room when the coin finally drops that two people would be better off living apart. Whatever the specifics to the unique couple, when you are ready to admit you did your best but it's just not going to work, it then becomes time to think about the cleanest way to end your marriage. According to the divorce lawyer Laura L. Wasser, a couple should take steps to end a bad marriage sooner rather than later. "Once you are clear that it's not going to work, get out of the relationship before you hate each other. That way you have a better chance of a calm life. Especially when there are children involved. It protects the possibility that you will enjoy someone as a coparent." People often ask, "When do you know if it's time to split?" She doesn't know of a specific sign, but she did say that the ones who are "still passionate, still throwing things at each other and screaming, these people are often not done. When spouses are civil and detached, it's clear that a reconciliation is not going to happen."

I didn't anticipate her saying this, but Wasser also believes 100 percent in the need for a sense of humor even in the dissolution of a marriage, particularly when there are children involved. In fact, if she's not feeling any levity in the room, she'll actually ask some questions to try to reawaken it. Wasser will often encourage a couple to "hark back to one thing that was funny, something funny that you had together so you can remember how to enjoy each other as people." Her motivation for doing this is that "you are going to be a family even in divorce, so you have to learn how to smile around each other."

I liked Wasser's memory-jogging exercise for couples heading into divorce so much, it made me think about using this technique in less dire circumstances. After you've had a solid "adult time-out" and a chance to calm down, take a moment to remember something funny that the other person did or said to lighten the mood before you get back to resolving the bigger issue.

For couples who are still too passionate about each other to walk away entirely, sometimes a separation is in order—not just the adult time-out for an hour that Latimer uses, but a genuine physical separation for months or even longer. This can be what you need to remember and appreciate what you had with the person before it all unraveled.

Get out of a bad marriage definitely. But there is something to be said for the feeling of accomplishment if you stay in it. The saddest thing for me is seeing a kid at graduation where the poor kid has to negotiate all the sets of parents, I'm with my Dad and his new girlfriend and my mom and her husband and we're going out to dinner, but they don't like each other . . . I want to hold hands with Liz at the graduation. "You see, you see what we did?" We're gonna hold hands at graduation and we're gonna hold hands when he moves right back into the house.

—LEW SCHNEIDER

Zeke and Sarah (not their real names) are my favorite example of a couple who did exactly this after reaching out for a lot of help during their seventeen-year marriage. This couple fought tooth and nail to stay husband and wife. They also fought a mountain of white powder, many dozens of vials of pills, and hundreds of bottles, and spent nearly a year apart before coming together again to create the happy marriage they share today. At their worst they never imagined their current life, which includes two young children, four dogs, satisfying work, and a lot of laughter. They are without question the most kick-ass example of what it means to pull out all the stops to save your marriage. Or what can happen when you surrender to its being over and, having nothing to lose, finally start speaking honestly and from the heart.

ZEKE AND SARAH

From Here to Sobriety

Zeke and Sarah met through mutual friends twenty years ago; they have been married for seventeen. I was very interested to interview them after reading a story Zeke wrote in which he said that in the seventeen years he and Sarah had been married they'd seen eleven therapists. I asked if I could meet with them to hear the details.

Sitting in their living room with the ticking of dog paws in the background, the sound of little-girl giggles coming from another room, I found it hard to believe these two were ever the down and dirty addicts they describe.

"I remember the first time I ever laid eyes on him," Sarah recalled. "We were at a friend's house and the woman who introduced us called out his name and I remember turning around and seeing the side of his face, with his little round glasses. That was the party where I got really drunk and showed everybody my tattoo. His girlfriend hated me."

"Yeah, I remember that night," Zeke said. "I must have thought, 'Hey, there's a girl who drinks more than me, she'll make me look good!'" Sarah almost spewed Diet Coke out of her nose laughing at this.

Anxious to follow up on Zeke's confession about the eleven therapists they had seen, I asked how that all started. Sarah explained that after they had moved in together they were having some issues—"nothing big"—but Zeke suggested they should see someone

"I'd been going to therapists since I was, like, two," he joked.

According to Sarah, the challenge at the time, before the drugs and alcohol got out of hand, was, "When I came home, I'd been at work, I'd been on the phone all day, and Zeke wanted to connect and I really didn't."

"In retrospect now, I see it's really all about the Twelve Traditions of Marriage," Zeke interjected. I hadn't heard of these, so I asked him to say more about this.

"The Twelve Traditions of Marriage are based on the program of Alcoholics Anonymous" he told me. "According to Tradition Twelve, 'The main principle in a relationship is selflessness. Our greatest gift is to be of help to one another and we can't do that if we are selfish.'"

Much like the Christian idea of service and the Jewish idea of unity, I can see how this approach to marriage would also be very helpful. Unfortunately for them, Zeke didn't know anything about this way of thinking for the first eight years they were together. That was the period when they met their plethora of therapists, some helpful, some not. After burning through a few, Zeke found one he liked very much. "Dr. Brown turned out to be an incredible advocate—for my point of view. Finally, someone who'd speak 'truth to power' in my relationship! However, this truth eluded Sarah. Word to the wise: if your marital therapist starts sounding like your personal attorney, bail immediately. Which is what we did one day, spontaneously, midsession. Sarah was ecstatic. I'd finally stood up for *her*, which won me big brownie points."

"Yeah, but it didn't last," she said. So they found someone else, a UCLA specialist who loved to pontificate. "I couldn't take that guy," Sarah said.

Then they saw people individually, and even tried putting all four people in the room together. "But I was so hostile about how much this double date was costing it was not helpful," said Zeke.

During this same period their drug and alcohol abuse was spinning out of control. Finally Zeke got sober, but Sarah didn't. She moved out and went to live in a friend's apartment, and hit bottom. Ultimately she too decided to get sober. She had Zeke drive her to a sober living facility, on the site of a mental hospital.

Zeke would visit Sarah for family day, full of resentment.

"They had an Al-Anon meeting for the families and AA for me, but I was on phenobarbital, which they gave people back then, and I was so high I could barely hold my head up. "Zeke was mad."

After this, she moved back home. But she wasn't sure she wanted to be married anymore, so she asked Zeke to leave. "When couples sober up they rarely stay together. You really have to learn to be in a whole other relationship," she said.

Zeke clarified. "My sponsor told me to move out, that I needed to support Sarah's sobriety. So I moved in with my mom for almost a year. Not fun. Then over Labor Day, when Sarah went back east to visit her parents, I took back the reins—by moving back in. I was only supposed to take care of the dogs for the weekend. But when she returned, I gave her an ultimatum: 'Guess what? I'm not leaving. So, we can either reconcile or get a divorce. It's up to you.' She loved that."

"Yep," Sarah said, quietly.

"Fortunately, she agreed to try to reconcile," Zeke said. Which is what led them to their fourteenth and final therapist, Dr. Royal. "After the first session," said Zeke, "she told us to bring a list of our respective 'needs' next week." He elaborated:

"Needs?" I had never considered them. I had always operated intuitively, flinging myself into relationships, acting and re-acting, vainly analyzing it all at each turn. Needs implied awareness. Accountability. It implied that I actually knew what they were, and would be capable of articulating them, like a sane, mature "adult." At any rate, one of us showed up without a list. So that exercise was tabled. We chewed on more pressing issues. There had been a lot of damage that year we'd been apart. Trust had been abused. Resentment lingered. But we hung in there, saving up all the crap for our weekly meeting with Dr. Royal, continuing to live together. Our marriage circled the drain. We had different visions for our future, and we refused to compromise. It was irreconcilable. Our only option was divorce. I remember the sense of

244 Take My Spouse, Please

calm I had, knowing that the decision hadn't been made lightly, but only after years of grinding work.

Then the session was over. We left her office, having to deal with the logistics. I got in my car. Sarah got into hers. She called me on the cell phone. With nothing left to fear or protect, we began talking openly about our deepest, darkest internal truths. We shared our perception of events that had driven us apart. Over and over again, we discovered that we'd had very different interpretations of them, and had made assumptions about the other's feelings and motives. Now, laying bare the truth, we saw how mistaken we both had been. This foreign entity, forgiveness, entered our hearts. I didn't realize it at the time, but at that moment, our marriage experienced a profound spiritual transformation. Surrendering to its total failure, we found freedom. We finally got around to talking about our needs. Not what I think hers are, but what they actually are. We don't have to take care of each other's needs all the time—being aware of them, and having each other's back are what's important. And, oh, yeah, I had to stop being a selfish putz. It's only taken fifteen years.

I was grateful for Zeke's joke as an opportunity to blink back what I was pretty sure was a tear.

Then he added one more thought. "Marriage is a fascinating paradox. One of those shrinks said that the best marriages are the ones where nothing is resolved—that way the line of communication is always open."

"I completely agree," Sarah said. "In a marriage, you have to approach someone with an open mind and genuine curiosity, rather than having a formulated opinion of them and expecting a specific response and the condemnation that can come with that. That's what can keep a marriage healthy, is being open to surprise."

An open mind, curiosity, being open to surprise, this all sounded very familiar! I thought of Mark, the chanting teacher and his breakthrough of finally letting go of his idea of what his marriage should be, and Michele, the French mother of seven and her advice to always be discovering each other, and of course, Paul Dooley's words, "The element of surprise, that's practically the definition of comedy!" and all the happiness experts who agreed on how important this was for keeping long-term marriages happy.

I'm not sure exactly what gave Zeke and Sarah their perseverance, but my suspicion is that it had something to do with faith. Bear with me—I am not talking about God or Jesus here, although we have heard compelling reasons why a religious approach to marriage can be helpful, and the Buddhist one, too. But the faith that I am talking about here, the faith that keeps these marriages together, is a faith I heard described by Scott J. Tonigan, a researcher at the University of New Mexico, who is quoted in Charles Duhigg's brilliant book, *The Power of Habit: Why We Do What We Do in Life and Business.* Tonigan told Duhigg of a recent discovery he and his peers had made regarding why some people stay sober and others don't. "Belief seems critical. You don't have to believe in God, but you do need the capacity to believe that things will get better."[9]

The capacity to believe that things will get better.

As married people who want to stay married we need to read that phrase again, all by itself. Because after spending two years looking at long-term marriages up close and personal, trying to get whatever clues I can for how they stay intact and find humor through the most daunting challenges, *this* half-sentence is the keystone.

All long-term couples—gay or straight, Hollywood icons or schoolteachers—through thick and thin and back to thick again, have been able to maintain the belief that no matter what, their marriages will get better.

Unsurprisingly, this trust underpins every tool I teach. It is also the same faith that every comic and every artist must also have to persevere. The only thing that will take a career, a person, or a couple down for the count is losing the faith that things can get better.

There is a window of opportunity when you've stopped enjoying each other, in between "I'm not happy" and "I need to get out of this." You owe it to your marriage (and your spouse) to take advantage of this window and do whatever you can to recapture the joy that made you want to commit to each other in the first place. Wherever you are on the happiness spectrum now, nurture the faith that it will get better and don't be afraid to get the help you need to find your way back to laughter.

TIPS ON GETTING HELP

- Know that you and your spouse deserve to have a happy marriage. As corny as it may sound, say it out loud ten times: "I deserve to have a happy marriage." Then make a list of what is not working and figure out some resources for help.

- Don't be afraid to get help from trained professionals: a therapist, a religious leader, a Twelve Step program, and books that such experts have published (see the "Resources" section in the back).

- Consider seeing a therapist regularly, the way some people go to the gym. This a great way to protect your marriage from the buildup of anger and resentment.

- Get real about the expectations you have for your spouse and your marriage. Let go of perfect; we're all flawed. That means you, too. Let this humility keep you open to growth and change in your marriage. Challenge yourself to accept and appreciate your spouse and see how you can make his or her life better.

- Practice forgiveness. This does not mean forgetting. It means making a conscious choice to let go whatever anger and resentment has caused a rift. Be mindful of what you share with your spouse. Do not be unnecessarily hurtful.

- Work on having a sense of humor about yourself. Find ways to lighten up about your expectations of yourself and your marriage.

- When you get to a place where you truly know in your heart, after using whatever means available to you for help, that the marriage is not going to work, take steps to end it before things get ugly.

- Keep the faith that no matter where you are, the marriage can and will get better.

Epilogue

Someone pour me a drink! What a ride this book turned out to be. We went from talking about showing up for each other, to kicking up your sex life a notch, to how to use good timing to work for you, to making nice married friends and then getting some help when you need it. If you're reflecting on all this a little perplexed, wondering what happened to the comedy book you bought, the fun romp where you learn to lighten up a little with your spouse, read some gossip about other couples married longer than you, and possibly learn some witty comebacks to make your better half laugh, how the heck did it get so intense? Believe me, I get it. You may be feeling like you bit off more than you wanted to chew here. To this I say, welcome to long-term marriage. I am as surprised as you are, so please let me begin this wrap-up by saying, Thank you.

Thank you for getting to the end with me. My next immediate thought is that long-term marriage, even when you're looking at people who laugh a lot, is not a frivolous endeavor. There's a reason they call marriage an institution. When marriages are real and long, this shit is deep. Let's face it, the word "institution" doesn't exactly give anyone the giggles.

So it makes me proud that against these odds, with the help of some generous, candid, and entertaining couples, we have been able to see that despite the weight and complexity of a long marriage, there are, in fact, many laughs to be shared.

The most valuable knowledge of my life has come to me in the same way as the lessons I learned writing this book. They also started off as a lark, a funny idea or impulse, and then, without my permission, became something much more. I have learned everything that has made a difference in my life by tricking myself into thinking it was going to be fun, or at least funny. Even becoming a mother happened this way. All I did was have sex and eat a lot and I got these little humans to live with who changed me forever.

Now it has happened again. I thought applying the rules of comedy to long-term marriage was a fun idea. We'd hear some inspiring stories, learn some helpful, handy tools to laugh a little bit more, get some sound-bite advice from professionals, and all have a good laugh about the idiosyncrasies of couples in long-term marriages. All of which we did.

What I didn't anticipate was how moved I would be by every couple I spoke with and that I would fall in love with them and wish I could move in and engage in a weird threesome where all I did was follow them around taking notes. I somehow didn't foresee the amount of work it takes for a couple to keep laughing together. Not "hard labor" work, but commitment, honesty, loyalty, and communication—also not surprisingly, all characteristics of comedians working at the top of their game. By the time I realized the depth of what I had gotten myself into with this book, I was already too far along to throw it under the bed and hide. For this I am grateful.

Laughter has been the way in and the way through for the most important lessons of my life. Now I can add healing my marriage to this list. I had a suspicion that, for the long haul, laughing together was key. This instinct has been confirmed. What I didn't appreciate was how much courage this takes to create and maintain. The courage to tell each other the truth, to allow a glimmer of "I need you" to pierce through the armor of "I'm fine" once in a while, and to dance around the kitchen wearing only a dish towel if the spirit moves you. This is the kind of risk taking is necessary for the truly "hardest thing to do," joyfully sustaining the most significant relationship in our lives. If I ever doubted it, I never will again. It is clearer to me now than eighty-proof vodka that in figuring out how to keep laughing together as couples, we are destined to love bigger, longer, and deeper.

Notes

Chapter 1. Show Up

1. When God first calls to Abraham, Abraham responds "Hineni," meaning "I am here" (Genesis 22:1). Moses responds to the voice from the burning bush with the same word, "Hineni" (Exodus 3:4). Whenever it is uttered, it is a call to action. All the Jewish commentaries I read on this word, written by everyone from rabbis to bloggers, stressed that Hineni means not just "Here I am" but also "I am ready."

Chapter 2. Listen

1. In addition to developing the well-known and respected approach to couples therapy called Imago (www.imagorelationships.org), Harville Hendrix also wrote the best seller *Getting the Love You Want: A Guide for Couples* (New York: Henry Holt, 2007).

Chapter 3. Give the People What They Want

1. Daniel Bergner, "Unexcited? There May Be a Pill for That," *The New York Times Magazine*, May 22, 2013, p. 26.

2. Sonja Lyubomirsky quoted in Lynn Gigy and Joan B. Kelly, "Reasons for Divorce: Perspectives of Divorcing Men and Women," *Journal of Divorce and Remarriage* 18 (1992): 169–87.

3. Helen Fisher, *Why We Love: The Nature and Chemistry of Romantic Love* (reprint, New York: Holt Paperbacks, 1994).

4. Helen Fisher, quoted in Linda Carroll, "Dull Days Wreck a Marriage Faster Than Fighting," May 21, 2009 (www.nbcnews.com/id/30808963/ns/health-behavior/t/dull-days-wreck-marriage-faster-fighting/#.U-o_mEg2mR4).

5. Names have been changed to protect this couple's privacy.

6. Rachel Sussman, *The Breakup Bible: The Smart Woman's Guide to Healing from a Breakup or Divorce* (New York: Three Rivers Press, 2011).

7. Rachel Sussman, "Do Open Marriages Work?," *Huffington Post*, January 24, 2012 (www.huffingtonpost.com/rachel-a-sussman-lcsw/do-open-marriages-work_b_1222016.html).

8. David G. Blanchflower and Andrew J. Oswald, "Money, Sex and Happiness: An Empirical Study," November 2004, *Scandinavian Journal of Economics* 106, no. 3 (2004): 393–415. I don't know why the Scandinavians felt compelled to study Americans instead of their own people, but I thank them for this. And for Wasa Crispbread.

9. Bergner, "Unexcited?"

10. Robert Provine, "The Science of Laughter," *Psychology Today* (online edition), November 1, 2000 (www.psychologytoday.com/articles/200011/the-science-laughter).

11. Dr. K's Videos can be viewed at the Laughter Yoga website (www.laughteryoga.org/english/gallery/videos/99).

12. "David Letterman—Ray Romano on Sex vs. Laughter," *The Late Show with David Letterman*, CBS, October 14, 2013.

13. Robert Biswas-Diener and Todd B. Kashdan, "What Happy People Do Differently," *Psychology Today* (online edition), July 2, 2013.

14. Steve Skrovan, phone interview, March 2014.

Chapter 4. Know Your Audience

1. Vassilis Saroglou, Christelle Lacour, and Marie-Eve Demeure, "Bad Humor, Bad Marriage: Humor Styles in Divorced and Married Couples," *Europe's Journal of Psychology* 6, no. 3 (2010): 94–121.
2. Carol Bainbridge, "Introvert," About Parenting (website) (http://giftedkids.about.com/od/glossary/g/introvert.htm).

Chapter 5. Pay Attention to Timing

1. Johanna Stein, *How Not to Calm a Child on a Plane: And Other Lessons in Parenting from a Highly Questionable Source* (Boston: Da Capo Lifelong Books, 2014).

Chapter 6. Keep Surprising Them

1. Sonja Lyubomirsky, quoted in Jane E. Brody, "That Loving Feeling Takes a Lot of Work," *Well* (blog), January 14, 2013 (http://well.blogs.nytimes.com/2013/01/14/that-loving-feeling-takes-a-lot-of-work/).

Chapter 8. Find Ways to Relax

1. "Jerry Seinfeld Talks Transcendental Meditation at David Lynch Foundation Gala," David Lynch Foundation (www.youtube.com/watch?v=uh7Yru3cHoA).
2. The chant was made famous in the 1993 movie about Tina Turner, *What's Love Got to Do With It.* You can learn more about the chant at www.nichirenbuddhism.net.
3. David Schnarch, *Passionate Marriage: Keeping Love and Intimacy Alive in Committed Relationships* (reprint, New York: Norton, 2009), pp. 160–63.
4. Annette Goodheart, *Laughter Therapy: How to Laugh about*

Everything in Your Life That Isn't Really Funny (Santa Barbara: Less Stress Press, 1994), pp. 74–75.

5. Ibid.

6. Ibid., p. 23.

7. Norman Cousins, *Anatomy of an Illness: As Perceived by the Patient* (reprint, New York: Norton, 2005).

8. Scott Weems, *Ha! The Science of When We Laugh and Why* (New York: Basic Books, 2014), xiv.

9. Scott Weems, www.psychologytoday.com/blog/what-s-sofunny/201408 /does-humor-make-you-smarter.

10. Weems, *Ha!*, *p.*73.

Chapter 9. Watch Your Wardrobe

1. If physical appearance is something neither of you values, then thanks for reading this chapter anyway, and as long as you're showering, you're probably all good.

Chapter 10. Stay Current

1. John Gottman and Nan Silver, *The Seven Principles for Making Marriage Work: A Practical Guide from the Country's Foremost Relationship Expert* (New York: Random House/Harmony, 2000).

2. "Oldest Living Couple on Earth Gives Great Relationship Advice," May 3, 2014 (www.yourblackworld.net/2012/02/featured-blogger-soldest-living-couple-on-earth-gives-great-relationship-advice/).

3. *LA 411*, now *Variety 411*, is the most comprehensive directory for TV and film production.

Chapter 11. Stick with the Winners

1. Clive Thompson, "Are Your Friends Making You Fat?," *New York Times*, September 10, 2009, article discussing the results of a study conducted by Nicholas Christakis and James Fowler, "The Spread of Obesity in a Large Social Network over 32 Years," *New England*

Journal of Medicine 357, no. 4 (July 2007): 370–79 (http://fowler
.ucsd.edu/spread_of_obesity.pdf).

2. Ibid.

Chapter 12. Have Patience

1. Mazursky quoted in, "Carly Brien and Alejandro de Castro: As-
sured That It's Just Meant to Be," *New York Times* Weddings/Cel-
ebrations, October 14, 2013.

2. Waller's findings reported and paraphrased in Sylvia Niehuis,
Linda Skogrand, and Ted L. Huston, "When Marriages Die: Pre-
marital and Early Marriage Precursors to Divorce," *The Forum for
Family and Consumer Issues* (online journal), n.d. (http://ncsu.edu
/ffci/publications/2006/v11-n1-2006-june/fa-1-marriages-die.php).

3. Katherine Jacobs Bao and Sonja Lyubomirsky, "Making It Last:
Combating Hedonic Adaptation in Romantic Relationships,"
Journal of Positive Psychology 8 (2013): 196–206.

4. Ted L. Huston, Sylvia Niehuis, and S. E. Smith, "The Early Marital Roots of Conjugal Distress and Divorce," *Current Directions in
Psychological Science* 10 (2001): 116–19, cited in Katherine
Jacobs Bao and Sonja Lyubomirsky, "Making It Last: Combating
Hedonic Adaptation in Romantic Relationships," *Journal of Positive Psychology,* in press. (http://sonjalyubomirsky.com/files/2012
/09/Bao-Lyubomirsky-in-press.pdf).

Chapter 13. Get Help to Get Better

1. Carol Leifer, *How to Succeed in Business without Really Crying*
(Philadelphia: Quirk Books, 2014), p. 104.

2. Louis C. K., www.popsugar.com/love/Louis-CK-Quotes-About-
Marriage-Divorce-31909829.

3. John Bingham, "Happier Relationships for Couples without Children," *The Telegraph*, January 12, 2014.

4. Phyllis Moen, quoted and paraphrased by Bruce Feiler, "Together,
at Home and at Work," *New York Times*, November 15, 2013.

5. Laura A. Wasser, *It Doesn't Have to Be That Way: How to Divorce without Destroying Your Family or Bankrupting Yourself* (New York: St. Martin's Press, 2013).

6. RCA website (www.recovering-couples.org).

7. "RCA Tools of Recovery," RCA website (www.recovering-couples.org/couples-resources/tools-of-rca).

8. See "Letter to Professionals," RCA website (www.recovering-couples.org/for-professionals/professional-letter).

9. Scott J. Tonigan, quoted in Charles Duhigg, *The Power of Habit: Why We Do What We Do in Life and Business* (New York: Random House, 2012), p. 85.

Resources

There's no way to cover every resource available to all couples here, but I wanted to list some key ones based on the topics discussed in this book: helpful websites for finding a therapist, comedy clubs for when you are looking to laugh outside your home, and a handpicked reading list.

Obviously I believe books are valuable tools for keeping a marriage healthy. You can absorb a lot of helpful information from reading them. But just reading relationship books will not be enough to create real change. In the same way that reading diet books doesn't make you skinny, just reading relationship books will not give you the marital equivalent of six-pack abs. You also have to take whatever actions these experts prescribe. Ideally, you and your spouse would set up regular sessions to work through their exercises. And because going it alone as a couple when you both want change can be challenging, a few websites to help you find a therapist are right at the top.

Where to Go for Help

American Association of Marriage and Family Therapy
www.therapistlocator.net

California Association of Marriage and Family Therapy
www.counselingcalifornia.com

National Domestic Violence Hotline
(800) 799-SAFE (7233)
www.thehotline.org

Recovery Couples Anonymous
www.recovering-couples.org/couples-resources/tools-of-rca

Where to Go for Laughter

The Comic Strip
1568 2nd Ave.
New York, NY 10028
(212) 861-9386
www.comicstriplive.com

The Improv
8162 Melrose Ave.
Los Angeles, CA 90048
(323) 651-2583
www.hollywood.improv.com

Dr. Madan Kataria, "Dr. K"
"Guru of Giggling"
www.laughteryoga.org/english/diary

The Laugh Factory
8001 Sunset Blvd
Los Angeles, CA 90046
(323) 656-1336
www.laughfactory.com

Recommended Reading

Cousins, Norman. *Anatomy of an Illness: As Perceived by the Patient.* New York: Norton, 2005.

Goodheart, Annette. *Laughter Therapy: How to Laugh about Everything in Your Life That Isn't Really Funny.* Santa Barbara: Less Stress Press, 1994.

Fisher, Helen. *Why We Love: The Nature and Chemistry of Romantic Love.* New York: Holt Paperbacks, 1994.

Gottman, John and Nan Silver. *The Seven Principles for Making Marriage Work: A Practical Guide from the Country's Foremost Relationship Expert.* New York: Random House/Harmony, 2000.

Hendrix, Harville. *Getting the Love You Want: A Guide for Couples.* New York: Henry Holt, 2007.

Keller, Tim with Kathy Keller. *The Meaning of Marriage: Facing the Complexities of Commitment with the Wisdom of God.* New York: Dutton Publishing, 2011.

Love, Patricia and Steven Stosny. *How to Improve Your Marriage without Talking about It.* New York: Broadway Books, 2008.

Orbuch, Terri K. *5 Simple Steps to Take Your Marriage from Good to Great.* New York: Random House/Delacorte, 2009.

Perret, Gene. *Comedy Writing Step by Step.* Los Angeles: Samuel French Trade, 1990.

Schnarch, David. *Passionate Marriage: Keeping Love and Intimacy Alive in Committed Relationships.* New York: Norton, 2009.

Vorhaus, John. *The Comic Toolbox: How To Be Funny Even If You're Not.* Los Angeles: Silman-James Press, 1994.

Wasser, Laura A. *It Doesn't Have to Be That Way: How to Divorce without Destroying Your Family or Bankrupting Yourself.* New York: St. Martin's Press, 2013.

Weems, Scott. *Ha! The Science of When We Laugh and Why.* New York: Basic Books, 2014.

About the Author

DANI KLEIN MODISETT has been working in the comedy world for the past twenty years as both a writer and performer. She created and produced several live shows, most notably "Afterbirth . . . Stories You Won't Read in a Parenting Magazine," which ran for ten years in Los Angeles and several major U.S. cities.

©Allison Schallert

Dani has also written and produced a variety of online video content, including a series for Deepak Chopra, and a short video also titled "Take My Spouse, Please," which can be found online at *The New York Times.*

Dani is the editor of the anthology *Afterbirth: Stories You Won't Read in a Parenting Magazine* (St. Martin's, 2009). Dani's writing has been featured in the *New York Times,* the *Los Angeles Times, Parents Magazine, LA Parent Magazine,* and the *Huffington Post.* She is a regular contributor to Mom.me, where she has an ongoing column called "Mistake of the Week."

Dani lives in Los Angeles with her husband, Tod, and her two sons, Gabriel and Gideon. Read more about her at www.daniklein.com.